{ *Bytes and Backbeats*

TRACKING POP

SERIES EDITORS: LORI BURNS, JOHN COVACH, AND ALBIN ZAK

In one form or another, the influence of popular music has permeated cultural activities and perception on a global scale. Interdisciplinary in nature, Tracking Pop is intended as a wide-ranging exploration of pop music and its cultural situation. In addition to providing resources for students and scholars working in the field of popular culture, the books in this series will appeal to general readers and music lovers, for whom pop has provided the soundtrack of their lives.

Listening to Popular Music: Or, How I Learned to Stop Worrying and Love Led Zeppelin
by Theodore Gracyk

Sounding Out Pop: Analytical Essays in Popular Music
edited by Mark Spicer and John Covach

I Don't Sound Like Nobody: Remaking Music in 1950s America
by Albin J. Zak III

Soul Music: Tracking the Spiritual Roots of Pop from Plato to Motown
by Joel Rudinow

Are We Not New Wave? Modern Pop at the Turn of the 1980s
by Theo Cateforis

Bytes and Backbeats: Repurposing Music in the Digital Age
by Steve Savage

Bytes and Backbeats

Repurposing Music in the Digital Age

STEVE SAVAGE

THE UNIVERSITY OF MICHIGAN PRESS / ANN ARBOR

Published in the United States of America by
The University of Michigan Press
Manufactured in the United States of America
⊗ Printed on acid-free paper

2014   2013   2012   4   3   2

A CIP catalog record for this book is available from the British Library.

Library of Congress Cataloging-in-Publication Data

Savage, Steve, 1948–
    Bytes and backbeats : repurposing music in the digital age / Steve
Savage.
        p. cm. — (Tracking pop)
    Includes bibliographical references and index.
    ISBN 978-0-472-11785-7 (cloth : alk. paper) —
    ISBN 978-0-472-02773-6 (e-book)
    1. Popular music—Production and direction.   2. Sound recordings—
Production and direction. I. Title.
ML3470.S32 2011
781.6409'051—dc22   2011007217

FOR TAMARA
Together we explored the world while I explored this world.

Preface

Several of the gracious readers of this book in its various drafts suggested that I should include some biographical information to help orient the reader to this work. I suppose all authors have a story about what brought them to their book, but perhaps in this case it is particularly relevant. My story begins with a career as a drummer during which time I played in numerous unsuccessful rock bands, learned some jazz without ever coming close to mastering it, studied and performed African music with a master drummer from Ghana, and spent a couple of years actually making a living as a musician playing in a dance band. I found playing four hours of cover songs five nights a week rather trying and abandoned that, and after a short but glorious stint in a punk band, I and my career transitioned into production and recording.

I discovered that the other side of the glass—the control room side rather than the recording room side—fit me better, and my career slowly built around recording. I had a 12-track studio in my garage (a short-lived Akai home-recording format) and recorded demos for rock bands for dirt cheap. One of those bands put its resources together to go into a professional studio to record a single and asked me to be the engineer/producer. I got my first taste of making commercial recordings and I was hooked. From there I recorded a variety of fledgling "new wave" artists' singles and albums in the heady early 1980s and cut my teeth on 24-track analog recording. After a stint as house producer for a small indie label—where I built and learned to operate a lovely little state-of-the-art studio—I became a full-time independent record producer and engineer.

One tends to get work in areas where one has some successes, so it was through my work with the very talented songwriter Bonnie Hayes that I have ended up working on many singer/songwriter music projects, and after three Grammy-nominated CDs with the master blues artist Robert Cray, I have had the pleasure of working on many blues records. I have also recorded jazz, R & B, rap, hip-hop, country, opera, music for musicals, and children's records. I have been the engineer and/or producer on over 100 commercial releases and have served as the primary recording engineer and mixer on eight Grammy-nominated CDs including records for Robert Cray, John Hammond Jr., Elvin Bishop, and the Gospel Hummingbirds. I have also taught recording at the college level one night a week for the past twelve years.

There was a recent survey conducted by the Recording Academy (the Grammy folks—an organization that I have been very active in) and sent to all the members of the Producers and Engineers wing of the Academy. Among the questions asked were these:

> In your opinion, do the tasks performed by the producer, recording engineer, sound editor, DAW [digital audio workstation] operator and mixer each involve specialized skill sets and sensitivities that are differentiable from one another?
>
> Do you specialize mainly in one of these tasks, or are you aware of audio production professionals in your technical/creative community who specialize mainly in one these tasks?
>
> On sound recordings you were recently involved with, was each one of the 3 tasks of producing, engineering and editing performed by separate individuals, or were all 3 tasks performed by a single person?

I never saw the results of this survey, but I know what the answers were for most of us that do this work professionally. While these functions are defined separately on paper, they are not clearly differentiated in practice. We may specialize (I've done more mixing than anything else in the past several years), but we are almost all capable of, and called upon to take on, all of these roles as a routine part of our work. And in most recordings the three tasks mentioned in the last question are performed by the same individual, but in partnership with a variety of other people, including the musicians. These are the reasons that I and others are transitioning to the term *recordist* for people who work as active participants in the making of recordings. Functions such as engineer, producer, DAW operator, mixer, editor, and so on blur into one job held by the person taking primary responsibility for the recording at any given moment (and who this person or persons are may be as fluid as the jobs themselves). An even grayer area concerns the term *musician,* as the roles and functions of music making have been so altered by the contemporary recording environment. It is often impossible to really differentiate between who is responsible for the music and who is responsible for the recording. An exploration of the intersection of the recordist and the music maker occupies the lion's share of the work that follows.

The evolution of the book you are reading follows from the preceding career. Having become obsessed with music, I did not finish college coming out of high school. About a dozen years ago I decided to return to school, just because I always enjoyed the classroom. At the urging of a friend I stayed focused on getting a degree rather than simply taking classes, and after finishing my BA in Philosophy and Religion, and wanting more, my advisor recommended the Department of Humanities at San Francisco State University. There, through the good graces of Professor Cristina Ruotolo, I encountered a chapter from Michael Chanan's book *Repeated Takes* and was surprised to discover a segment of academia that was considering the cultural implications of the work (recording) that I had been doing professionally for many years. This connected my return to school to my professional work in an unexpected way, and once again, I was hooked. Since then I have explored this field in some depth, having the good fortune of studying with the musicologist Nicholas Cook, whose work I admire (and who I reference fairly extensively in the following). Other colleagues that have provided welcomed and much-valued support and guidance include Philip Auslander, Serge Lacasse, Mark Katz, Mary Francis, Henry Stobart, Julie Brown, and Nikki Dibben, and it was especially satisfying to connect with Michael Chanan, whose earlier work had set me upon this journey.

Throughout this more recent academic work I have maintained my active career as a practitioner, and despite growing commitments as an educator I continue to work primarily as a recordist. Although I admire the writing of many musicologists and cultural commentators, it is my work as a recordist, as much as or more than my research, that guides my writing. I have been profoundly affected by the fluid nature of the creative process and the way that I must embrace and foster the unpredictable to be an effective recordist. The notion of fluidity, expressed especially in the forms of collaboration and community in the recording studio, has migrated from my work to my research.

I hope that my thousands of hours of studio work inform my analytical work in a way that fosters a deeper understanding and appreciation for the process of making contemporary recordings. As the recordist you are there for the hundreds of hours required to make many popular music recordings. If you're not there the whole time, then when something extraordinary happens you're very likely to miss it. Those extraordinary moments—along with the hours of concentrated work, of sound under the microscope, of repetition and revision—bind the process together in the same ways that have always made music central to the human experience. Music remains central to my experience, and my work continues to feed my profound love of music whether in the studio, in the classroom, or as an author.

Acknowledgments

The involvement of those individuals that have had the most direct impact on this work is acknowledged as part of the narrative in the preceding preface. I am also grateful to the University of Michigan Press, and especially Chris Hebert and Albin Zak for their support in bringing this book into the Tracking Pop series. Beyond that I wish to simply express my gratitude to all of those who have participated with me in my musical life. I am blessed to have stimulating collaborators in the world of music production, wonderful colleagues in the academic world, and a family anchored by the love and support of my wife Tamara and our daughters, Sophia and Thalia. To all of you I offer my deepest gratitude for participating with me in all the ways that have nourished this book.

As is perhaps inevitable in a work such as this, I know that I will be continually encountering earlier sources that are relevant to the work here and new sources that both reinforce and expand various of the ideas that I present. To the extent that the work is deficient in acknowledging relevant sources I can only offer my regrets that they were not referenced as they might have been. At the same time I certainly welcome all additions to the literature. It is especially satisfying to continue meeting and developing relationships with the increasing number of colleagues who straddle the lines with me between researcher and practitioner in the field of popular music.

An earlier version of much of the material in chapter 5 originally appeared in the *Journal of Popular Music Studies,* Blackwell Press, volume 18, issue 3 (December 2006): 332–40.

Contents

Audio Clips

Clip numbers referenced in the text are available for streaming at my website: www.stevesavage.net.

Clip 1   The Jenny Thing song "When You Hold Her"—mixed but not "fixed."
Clip 2   The Jenny Thing song "When You Hold Her"—mixed and "fixed."
Clip 3   Isolated example of a Freddie Hughes "lipsmack."
Clip 4   The same lipsmack in its musical context.
Clip 5   The same passage with the lipsmack removed.
Clip 6   A passage from Bob Dylan's "Sad-eyed Lady of the Lowlands" with a "popped 'p.'"
Clip 7   A passage from Bob Dylan's "Sad-eyed Lady of the Lowlands" with the "popped 'p'" removed.
Clip 8   A passage from Green Day's "American Idiot" with slurred "esses."
Clip 9   A passage from Stevie Wonder's "Signed, Sealed, Delivered, I'm Yours" with pronounced breaths.
Clip 10   A passage from Tori Amos's "Cruel" with heavy compression and pronounced breaths.
Clip 11   A jazz "improvisation" played by Dana Atherton, Dan Feiszli, and Jason Lewis. Recorded and constructed by Steve Savage.
Clip 12   My constructed version of the African folklore piece "Milee Yookoee."

Clips 1 and 2, The Jenny Thing, "When You Hold Her" 1994, used by permission of KSS Records. All other tracks are short clips used under Fair Use or Fair Dealing, improvised segments of recordings or musical constructions based on works in the public domain.

{ Introduction
  Reproduction and New Paradigms

The Construction of Music Via Repurposed Audio

Music today is being created, performed, and listened to in ways that are profoundly different from music practices prior to the migration to digital audio. The traditional timeline from the composer through the performer to the consumer has been radically altered under new working paradigms, providing significant new opportunities for musical participation and community. Technology and personal agency interact to undermine the conventionally polarized view of musical functions and experience. The creation and exchange of contemporary music extends far beyond neat categories such as composer, songwriter, musician, performer, consumer, or audience. Much of popular music is constructed from a variety of sources using vastly expanded creative tools. The role of the recordist as collaborator and creative participant has been dramatically increased. The consumer of music has extraordinary new alternatives for acquiring, sharing, and responding to music. Contemporary music is new in part because it can be constructed in utterly new ways.

I frequently use the term *construction* in this book to distinguish contemporary methods of popular music creation from the compositional models of the past. The term *composition* itself suggests a kind of musical construction—music is inevitably a product of the designing and piecing together of multiple elements—but the long history of composition ties it to conventional musical procedures. Compositions are traditionally constructed from a series of motifs or melodies; realized through arrangements of voices and/or instruments in unison, harmony, or counterpoint; and learned via oral/aural tradition, played from notation, or improvised. Contemporary practice takes us much further along the road of constructed music, a road that is built from a broad new assortment of composition techniques made available by computing power and drawing musical building materials from a wide range of sources. This book tells the story of some of these techniques and places them in a broader cultural and musical context.

My motivation for adopting the term *construction* is to break out of thinking of music creation in terms of conventional composition/performance routines and to identify how it has been transformed by this new array of techniques. I do not intend this reference to constrain the understanding of music creation to a structural model, rather to expand it to include all the tools of the imagination, of design, and of technology. The techniques developed as a part of the digital control of contemporary audio production are paradigmatic because their technological scope has so deeply broadened the process of music creation and reception, and greatly expanded the network of people that may be intimately involved in the composition (read construction) of the final music recording.

As construction is one defining metaphor for these new archetypes, so the notion of *repurposing*[1] encompasses the ways that the age of digital record production has spawned these new techniques of music creation. I adopt the idea of repurposing as central to understanding how every aspect of musical activity has been transformed. This transformation is both tangible in its new approaches to music making and conceptual in compelling new ways of thinking about music. The evolution of audio recording technology has moved both the practice and the critical debate beyond questions concerned primarily with the status of reproduction. The focus turns now to issues surrounding the manipulation and transformation of audio reproductions—in a word the *repurposing* of musical performance as audio recording.

In a sense, recordings themselves represent a repurposing of live performance, but contemporary practices have made the term more distinctively appropriate for referencing the multitude of ways that audio may be used to construct recordings. Webster's informs us that the prefix *re-* suggests the use of something again as well the use of something anew.[2] Repurposing audio may accomplish both by creating new music from elements that had been used previously (*used again*) and/or by transforming elements so as to adapt their use as desired (*made anew*).[3] The notion of repurposing is suggestive of the rampant explosion in the manipulation of sounds to create musical performances. These sounds may originate from any source, including original recordings, samples, sound effects, historic recordings, and so on. Contemporary recording practice frequently puts audio to new or renewed purpose before it finds its ultimate place in the final recording. Recordists cut, copy, and paste; they fix, they enhance, they thicken, they borrow, and they downright reinvent original performances in order to create a final recording. It is often the case that the final recording sounds relatively "normal"—like a rock-and-roll band playing a song for example—but in most cases the process of creation has reached far beyond the simple recording of the musicians playing their part.

Repurposing welcomes the new paradigm of music construction without prejudice. Repurposing acknowledges the ways that reproduction has evolved as both copy and original simultaneously. Repurposing focuses the attention on musical construction as a new beginning with a new purpose, rather than on original sources or meanings. One of the seminal projects in the kind of new construction made possible by computer-based digital audio manipulations was the 1989 CD *Plunderphonics* from the producer John Oswald. *Plunderphonics* took audio from previously released material, some well known and some obscure, and recrafted it into wholly original recordings. At the same time the rap and hip-hop genres had begun using samples of previous recordings in such a widespread fashion as to be redefining the nature of music creation. In both cases the media responses often focused on the source material and issues surrounding copyright violations, rather than on the newly created music, independent of its sources.

There has been a delicate, and sometimes uneasy, balance between the sources used in construction of new music and the music itself. In the case of *Plunderphonics* Oswald purposely called attention to the connection to the historical recordings. In most of the more contemporary use of repurposed audio the source material is primarily a tool rather than a reference. The implications of the word *plunderphonics,* the negative connotations of the word *plunder* and the apparent pride in a kind of violation of historical recordings, are at odds with the evolution of repurposed audio's overwhelming presence in popular music construction. While issues surrounding copyright remain significant (and are considered at some length in chapter 9), it is not appropriate for there to be any absolute value judgment associated with the broad practice of using repurposed audio in new music creation. New practices are redefining music creation in ways that profoundly affect our notions of authorship, improvisation, collaboration, and musical timeline. Identifying these developments in the context of repurposing helps us redefine the *understanding* of music recording at the same time that the *practice* of music recording is itself being redefined.

Presentation, Performance, and Participation

This study of contemporary music is organized around presentation in Part I, performance in Part II, and participation in Part III. The continuum from creator(s) to listener(s) encompasses composition, performance, improvisation, and audience with new musical practices transforming each element, while the traditional distinctions between elements are increasingly blurred. The notion of repurposing focuses the attention on the fundamental ways that these age-old musical activities have been made new.

In the following chapters presentation is framed as "art or artifice," performance as "artist or artisan," and participation as "integration or (dis)integration." Each pairing is seen as a flawed dichotomy in judging contemporary music practice. For example, cultural and historical contingencies must be considered central to value systems that attempt to classify musical creation as either "art" or "artifice." I argue that the tension within presentation between a naturalizing "art" and a self-conscious "artifice" reflects and feeds into our evolving notions of creativity, authenticity, and community. It is reductive to relegate technologically driven effects to artifice. Ultimately it is listeners who must decide whether they approve or reject the results of contemporary practices, and they will do so on their own terms and with their own set of evolved cultural contingencies outside any preconceived notions of art or artifice.[4]

Similar conflicts arise in attempting to elevate performers to the status of artists or relegate them to the role of artisans. The historical forces that have reserved the label of artist for the composer in opposition to the interpretative artisanship of the performer lose meaning when the roles become blurred by contemporary production practices such as those detailed in this book. And the bias toward traditional music participation, whether it is the formal participation by role such as composer, arranger, performer, audience, or the models from other times or cultures, ignores the manner in which new music practice integrates itself into contemporary culture. From the transnational communities of interest on the Internet to the explosive capabilities of home recording, new integrative practices continue music's power to bring people, communities, and cultures together. The new models of musical presentation, performance, and participation break down the strict hierarchical dichotomies, revealing much more complex relationships within musical practice.

Within the new paradigms of music presentation questions arise about how much performances should be altered. What are we to make of the effect and impact of such alterations? What are the deeper implications when we supposedly "fix" a musical performance? New models have surfaced whereby composition is a *result* of the process of recording and editing rather than a precursor to it. In many instances the creation of contemporary recordings partially or completely replaces the model of the original, preexisting composition—and the process is now often collaborative rather than isolated to the individual composer. These creative opportunities are heightened by the technologies that support quick and intuitive responses to music manipulation. The capabilities of computer-controlled digital audio are an integral part of musical presentation. Composition and performance are constantly in play,[5] along with the sonic qualities that embodied traditional recording concerns, long past any project's initial recording sessions.

The widespread manipulations that create the new paradigms of musical presentation fuel debates surrounding the question of musical authenticity. I argue that there can be no notion of authenticity that is not historically and culturally contingent. The hidden messages behind deterministic claims to authenticity are primarily driven by nostalgia. This is clearly seen in considering prerecording technologies such as the acoustic piano. A combination of nostalgia and the profound historical and cultural connections to the instrument seem to grant it a separate ontological status from a synthesizer, but this cannot be the case in any absolute sense. Ultimately time may well grant the synthesizer the same nostalgic and cultural status as a piano. This process has already started in regards to some legacy synthesizers such as the Moog. Similarly, I argue that Barthes's famous "grain of the voice" must be extended beyond live performance to include elements that reside in the presentation of vocal recordings, despite his protestations to the contrary. Embracing the breadth of the collaborative model in popular music also serves to undermine nostalgic concepts of musical significance. All of these observations break down traditional ideas about authenticity, genius, and the hierarchy of aesthetics characterized by a division between art and artifice.

Attempts to characterize the composer as artist and the performer as artisan also quickly collapse under the new musical paradigms. I argue that intervention through technology joins improvisation in blurring traditional categorizations such as composer and performer. Digital technologies emerge as partners in the large-scale shifts in the way compositions and performances are created in popular music. Some of the recording experiences that I describe here provide evidence of how both recording and studio manipulation may embody spontaneous musical creation, despite their roles in the mediation of performance. The fluidity of the working environment further obscures any imagined line between the work of an artist and the applied craft of an artisan. I also challenge the view that portrays the fleeting musical performance as being in conflict with the permanence of audio recordings. Rather, creative modes of record production have come to expand upon and support live performance—an intertwining rather than an opposition.

While collaborative opportunities have expanded, contemporary recording technologies have undermined the traditional reliance on collaboration among live musicians in music performance. The potential for isolating performers in both time and space has yielded wholly new capabilities for recordists to alter performances. Collaboration now occurs on many levels, often starting in the interaction between musicians, but typically progressing on to broader interaction in the editing process. Final performance decision-making may occur in collaboration between musicians and recordists or even unilaterally by the recordist. Producers have traditionally made decisions about which recorded performance to use, or about which elements to use in the case of editing together of multiple performances, but today's decisions about performance may include the radical reordering of musical phrases as well as the creation of entirely new musical ideas through manipulation of the rhythm, duration, and pitch of notes played. This requires a combination of musical and technical skills that may be embodied in many different collaborative groupings, blurring the lines between performance and composition.

Such practices have not only challenged the hegemony of the solo composer, they have altered the very nature of musical composition. The flexibility of computer-based music construction yields not only an array of new choices for the composer/constructionist but elongates the process such that the ability to make compositional revisions is available from the beginning of the recording all the way up to the final mix. One striking development from this flexibility has been the evolution of a much more random quality to the progression of musical ideas in popular music, undermining traditional song forms and musical phrasings. This is fostered by the combining of compositional, unintentional, and improvisational elements made possible by current editing techniques. Even more radical are the "mash-ups" created by combining elements from various and often-unlikely sources. Musical composition of this sort had never been even remotely possible prior to computer-based digital audio editing.

New models of participation also feed these new creative models of music production and reception. Expanded networks are an essential part of the creative process of recording, and reciprocity is central to understanding the network of forces at work in popular music. The flow of music from writer to player to recording to listener has become a process of networking and reciprocal relationships. Although the new paradigms of participation may produce cultural aesthetics that are considered casualties of contemporary practices (too many cooks, lowest common denominator, etc.), I emphasize the ways that the new capabilities of music creation lend themselves to positive new forms of music, musical process, and community. Music has always been intertwined with social participation, but the models are changing in dramatic ways. One such example is the implicit communities that have developed in the age of easy transnational communication via the Internet. I argue for the continuing centrality of musical community despite the ways that these communities may defy conventional social structures.

Cultural models for music participation differ around the world and over each cultural history. Each music culture provides unique social models, but they may also help us to uncover the ways in which musical participation is a universal human experience. Some lament the way that computer manipulations allow for creation of music through "knowing" rather than "doing"—that is, if we know what music we want to create, the computer gives us the capability to construct that music, even though we aren't able to perform it in the traditional sense on a musical instrument. I contend that the basic relationship between tools and creativity remains the same, whether it is an African playing a djembe or an American making music on his computer (or vice versa). And there is a certain democratizing effect to the ability to create through knowing—it makes musical activities including composing, arranging, and performing available to a much wider range of people by radically changing the necessary skill set. This does not alter the demands that music making requires in the form of skills, only the nature of those skills. It does not make creating music any easier—rudimental skill still creates rudimental music, and extraordinary music still demands extraordinary skill levels.

The ability to create so many different kinds of music through knowing has also had a tremendous influence on the current hybridization of different musical cultures and genres. Sample-based musical construction has allowed the integration of musical styles in broader and more accessible forms than ever before. While this is still widely debated in regards to merit, I argue that it should be viewed as a form of social exchange that acts as a constructivist force—it feeds musical participation and provides valuable social and cultural meaning. Thus, I argue for a reexamination of so-called musical appropriation. The issues surrounding hybridization are complex, and later in the book I examine both positive and negative effects, but I embrace hybridization and I argue against the use of the word *appropriation,* which is highly charged with negative, reductive connotations. I propose the term *repurpose* as an appropriate reference to the historical and cultural status of musical expressions that may feed or inspire new musical creations. Repurposing embraces the *new* creation as primary, without ignoring the references to origination. The idea that we might "appropriate" music from other cultures is both inaccurate in implication and inappropriate as a term for describing musical hybridization.

The dynamic between creating and consuming music is also being transformed. New forms of musical participation and new communities of music makers are evolving from new technologies. The mp3 format that spawned music downloading; the iPod and other new playback technologies; social networking sites such as Facebook and MySpace that are heavily oriented toward musical tastes; Pandora, Amazon, and other sites that provide personal and collaborative filtering of music preferences; and easily accessed programs like GarageBand and Audacity that provide full-scale recording and composition capabilities are all driving new relationships to music that extend beyond the traditionally passive role of the music consumer. It may be too early to know how far the new creative capabilities will reach into the general population—the extent to which music software in the computer and the interactive models of Web 2.0 are descendants of the piano in the nineteenth-century parlor—but there are indications of movement in this direction and beyond. In any event, the expanded capabilities that run from access to huge libraries of music on the Internet, to the flexibility of playlists on the iPod, to the recording and composition tools that arrive free with the program GarageBand on every Macintosh computer suggest the breadth of possibilities for the future of music.

While it is the intention of this book to represent a balanced analysis of contemporary music creation, it unabashedly embraces technology as an integral and increasingly powerful partner in music making. When taken in conjunction with the kind of audio manipulation I chronicle here in the various studio and application studies, music making in the digital environment represents not just a change in degree, but a fundamental change in "kind"—a change that strikes at the very heart of music creation. It is a change that requires many new and different skills and sensibilities, where the only fundamental link to traditional music creation lies in the essential need for music makers to use their ears to create musically appealing pieces if they are to attract an audience.

The Breakdown of Traditional Musical Paradigms

In an interview from an unknown source (but probably from the mid-1970s) the producer, ambient music composer, and recording theoretician Brian Eno outlined the future of the intersection of recording studio technology with music composition and performance:

> "If you had a sign above every studio door saying 'This Studio is a Musical Instrument' it would make such a different approach to recording" he asserts as if unaware that he'd dropped something of a bombshell. "You see my interest for quite a while has been in using the studio not as a machine that you feed input into and have it transferred onto a piece of tape. It's a means not simply of re-creating but of actually changing a sound. Sometimes it is even a source of that sound."[6]

The interviewer describes the opening sentence as a "bombshell," and perhaps it is for the time—but this integration of recording with composition and performance has become the standard for contemporary music. As recently as 1996 pivotal figures in popular musicology such as Simon Frith were still commenting on the "confusion between musician and technician, between aesthetic and engineering sound decisions."[7] This reference to confusion is no longer applicable. There is a complete integration of recording technology with compositional and performance practices in most recordings of popular music. Most musicians are technicians or at least interface easily and naturally with technicians. And engineering sound decisions are considered an integral part of the more traditional compositional and arrangement decisions that form musical performances.

As Eno suggests, for some of the foremost creators of popular music recordings new production practices had already begun to reshape their working models by the mid-1970s. While technology is the "centerpiece" of this transformation, it is more specifically the use of contemporary production techniques, including sampling, that are primarily responsible for the more thorough breakdown of the traditional forms of musical activities.[8] Digital audio and the power of the personal computer have pressed Eno's observation into the mainstream of virtually all popular music production. Timothy Warner observes that "digital technology . . . has fundamentally altered the ways in which musical gestures are created, manipulated and interact with one another."[9] Warner's comment identifies the element that is at the heart of these changes—it is the digital environment that has driven the current transformation of music creation.

The extent to which technology is at the center of these changes in music practices suggests changes in the mandate for musicologists. Borrowing from practices in ethnomusicology is helpful in this process. Nicholas Cook observes that ethnomusicologists tend to see the "study of *all* music in terms of its social and cultural context, embracing production, reception and signification,"[10] and I argue the same for the study of music technology and its intersection with music practice. Musicology must encompass contemporary technologies of recording such as the new paradigm of music construction. Whereas the focus of musicology has tended to be on the finished product (either score or recording), there are calls for a shift toward the study of musical activities that are socially embedded processes.[11] Studies such as mine reveal these processes as not simply socially embedded but also technologically embedded, with production techniques inseparable from music composition and performance.

While musical sounds are still at the heart of a musical culture, we must now allow for the sonic imaginings that have been made possible by digital audio technology. Whereas musical creation has been focused on the musical note, that essential focus has changed in the environment of re-purposed audio. Musical creation no longer necessarily emanates from the musical note. The mechanisms that have been employed to arrive at a complete work—from traditional forms of composition and arrangement—have been altered down to the root level. Musical sounds are often imagined and reimagined as sounds that have been repurposed, and they may be sourced from a variety of materials including not only notes but original recordings, loop libraries, sound effect libraries, samples from original or historical recordings, and so on.

As the intentional objects of musical sound have been transformed, so *access* to those objects has crossed many of the previous boundaries between the creator of music and the listener. Most listeners understand how samples work and know that music is constructed in pieces and from performances dislocated in space and time. Many have access to music construction techniques on their computer. In the contemporary environment the listeners have a better understanding of the objects of music creation than they ever had of notes. This familiarity with the process of music making brings the creator of music and the listener closer together in shared activities that begin to blur the distinction between the two. While recording has physically distanced the performer and the listener, and it is true that the performer in the studio does not usually have the benefit of immediate feedback from a live audience, the digital age has strengthened this connection in other ways. The ability for the listener to respond to the performer is heightened in the age of individual song downloads, online forums, blogs, and even TV talent shows that are driven by audience feedback tallied via Internet voting. Even more collaborative feedback is sometimes given when artists provide the materials for the public to remake videos or remix songs and when artists participate in extensive website interactions with fans.

In regards to music reception Michael Chanan observes that listeners who have even amateur-level musical skills "listen differently from those who don't, even if they are indifferent or bad performers."[12] Chanan also notes that, whereas Roland Barthes has suggested that these skills have disappeared, they are actually always present, just changing with "different historical and class aspects."[13] Contemporary amateur music skills are such that they may involve neither indifferent nor bad performers, but musicians who do no performing at all in the traditional sense of playing a musical instrument. Cook argues that musical culture requires cognitive capabilities whereby people must gain certain understandings in order to create, perform, and receive "acceptable" music within their culture: "If this is the case, then ear training forms the basic means by which the identity of a music culture is maintained."[14] I agree that ear training is at the center of a culture's music identity, but I also argue that the nature of that ear training has changed radically under the new musical paradigm. New forms of music creation and performance require ear training for a whole new set of musical practices. *In today's musical culture ear training and musical skills include capturing, compiling, and "fixing" audio as essential to the process of music construction.*

The manner in which many listeners, including nonmusicians, adapt the constructive model of music creation to music reception alters their experience of music as well. Listeners develop their musical ear by constructing and sharing playlists from their entire music library. Listeners have tremendously expanded opportunities to audition music before they buy, and to buy music on a song-by-song basis. In this work I supply particular narratives that provide further opportunities for ongoing ear training and for developing an understanding that heightens the experience of listening.

As the practice of music transforms, the histories of musical practice are also being undone. The idea that a piece of music was written or played by a particular person at a particular time has been a less reliable notion for some time as production techniques have evolved in complexity. But the editing and manipulative techniques of contemporary popular music construction obscure clear distinctions between most all musical functions. The number of people involved and their ability to alter performance, the extended timeline of the process, the complex nature of the large files that comprise the master recordings all combine to ensure that much of the true genesis of the musical creation will be obscured over time. Who was responsible for what element of the final recording? Which elements are actually heard as they were performed and which have been moved, reconstructed, or altered and by whom? What was the source audio for some of the elements in the final recording? On the one hand this speaks to the value of ethnographies and recording histories, but these can only scratch the surface of musical events.

The recordist occupies the central role in the making of popular music and is the best candidate for illuminating the process. Because the task is impossibly large, we will never be able to trace the histories of most recordings, but through the eyes and ears of the recordist we can have a much better understanding of their creation. Recording functions have traditionally been divided between the recording engineer and the record producer, though those responsibilities have become increasingly fluid over time. As I mentioned in the preface, a recent survey from the Recording Academy divided recording functions into five categories: the producer, recording engineer, sound editor, DAW (digital audio workstation) operator, and mixer. It was assumed that the same person might take on more than one of these roles but they might be shared by as many as five people or more over the course of a project. The musicians are also more than just initiators of sound in the fluid production of popular music, often adopting one or more of the recordist's functions. It is from the point of view of the complete battery of recordists that the broadest understanding of the making of popular recordings might be obtained.

The Evolution of Recording Technology

Audio recording changed the basic relationships between music and culture that had evolved with the oral and notational forms of musical record-keeping. Scores had separated music and performance, but only for those who could read them. Recordings allowed the general public's reception of music to be dislocated from its performance, and over time recordings came to occupy the lion's share of musical sound occurrences in the world. This change affected the entire music continuum from composer to consumer. Digital audio has further disrupted this continuum. Popular music is often made from a convoluted process that extends far beyond the simple timeline traced by the 4 minutes song. Recordists are now responsible for much of the actual content of the music we hear, though they are not usually listed as performers. And music consumers get their music from a dizzying array of delivery and reception technologies: from CDs to mp3s, from ambient music to iPods, and from the Internet to wireless handheld Blackberries and iPhones.

There are enormous socially embedded forces participating in the technological evolution that feeds the current state of music production. New technologies don't simply appear as some inevitable progression of scientific research. Current audio recording technology emerges in the interaction between cultural desires and innovation. Invention is limited to scientific capability but directed by creative aspirations. Steve Jones notes that "without technology, popular music would not exist in its present form."[15] We must add to this the inverse proposition that without popular music we would not have the existing audio technology. Although the musicians and technologies feed off each other, it is human desires that are the primary motivators of the technological developments. Developers are constantly surveying their users for input on how to improve their particular products and what new products to develop. The latest devices are, first and foremost, the manifestations of the wishes and dreams of the music community—though the technologies may channel these desires, and the devices may themselves inspire new and original musical expressions in their specific application. Songwriters will sometimes compose entire songs inspired by a sound they happened onto while auditioning sound patches on their synthesizer.[16] As Chanan observes: "The truth is that the changes that have revolutionized musical perception and practice over the past hundred years are part of a protracted dialogue between music and science, technology and the sonic imagination."[17] This balance between device and desire, between technology and agency, is explored more thoroughly in chapter 3.

In popular music the ultimate conflation of desire and technology is the recording studio itself. Early recordings were made primarily on location or in rooms full of the necessary recording equipment. The separation between the studio room used for the musicians (the recording space) and the room used for making the recording (the control room) came from the desire to isolate the noise made by the equipment as well as to separate the monitoring of the recording from the actual production of the sound. This corresponds to the separation between musical activity and production activity. As the desire and ability to manipulate both sound and recording grew, the focus of activity has shifted from the recording space to the control room where the performances are manipulated through the use of production technologies that yield the final recording.

The Evolution of Commentary on Recording Technology

In 1936 Walter Benjamin's essay "The Work of Art in the Age of Mechanical Reproduction" was published. Since that time his essay has served as a focal point in the ongoing discussion regarding the meaning of reproduction of artworks, including recorded music. However, well before the appearance of Benjamin's analysis, issues regarding mechanical reproduction of art had been addressed in significant forums. Early skirmishes over the meaning of reproduced art occurred just after the beginning of the twentieth century.[18] Nonetheless it is Benjamin that sets the groundwork for the larger cultural debate by establishing an essential difference between the original work of art and its reproduction: "Even the most perfect reproduction of a work of art is lacking in one element: its presence in time and space, its unique existence at the place where it happens to be."[19] In probably the most frequently quoted passage from the essay he taints reproduction when he asserts that if one incorporates this unique presence in the term *aura,* then "that which withers in the age of mechanical reproduction is the aura of the work of art."[20] And lest there be any doubt about value, Benjamin declares that as a result of mechanical reproduction of an original work of art "the quality of its presence is always depreciated."[21] For

Benjamin this value is contained in the historical and traditional features in original works of art, and he identifies these as elements of authenticity. He maintains that the authority of original art objects is jeopardized by reproduction and that the result is a decay of "aura" in society as a whole. This follows from the contention that "the unique value of the 'authentic' work of art has its basis in ritual, the location of its original use value."[22]

At this point Benjamin surprises. What has seemed a clear bias toward the negative impact of mechanical reproduction shifts on this issue of ritual. For Benjamin, what begins as ritual steeped in magic, and becomes religion, is the enslaver of art. The tone shifts abruptly and he reveals two radical and important concepts: "for the first time in world history, mechanical reproduction emancipates the work of art from its parasitical dependence on ritual. To an ever increasing degree the work of art reproduced becomes the work of art designed for reproducibility."[23] Benjamin has identified what he considers to be a very positive effect of mechanical reproduction—the democratization of art—at the same time acknowledging the dynamic between original and copy that creates a kind of reciprocity. At the apogee of these ideas lies photography,[24] a relatively new art form where there is no original in the traditional sense. Instead of ritual, artistic production becomes based on what Benjamin identifies as a political dynamic: the political influence on aesthetic expression wrests art from religion by focusing the production of art on a desired outcome, without resorting to moral justification. Beyond the copy's obvious debt to the original, the copy is seen to have a profound effect *on* the original.[25]

These ideas are essential to understanding the continuing relationship of technology to the mechanical reproduction of music. Does "aura" exist in the performance alone or is it bestowed by cultural attitudes? Does each new advance in technology bring the equivalent claim of degradation that Benjamin identifies at this watershed moment in the analysis of mechanical reproduction? The phonograph record epitomizes the degraded copy in Benjamin's model, yet fast-forward to the present and the contemporary fetishizing of vinyl records suggests a strong aura. And in the wake of such attitudes digital audio is seen by some as having diminished the LP record experience, but how will CDs be perceived seventy years from now? Benjamin's ultimate ability to recognize the reciprocity between original and copy begins to break down his own reductive attitude that claims a diminished presence to any mechanical reproduction of art. And in what should be a predictable outcome of technological advance, the copy challenges the original and finds ways that may surpass the capabilities of the so-called original object of art. The fruits of technology find their own source of originality and aura whether it's the Beatles' "A Day in the Life" or DJ Danger Mouse's *The Grey Album* (which combines the vocals from Jay-Z's *The Black Album* with reprocessed tracks from the Beatles' *White Album*).

In the last twenty-five years a variety of writings have expanded and commented on Benjamin's essay in ways directly related to music recording. Michael Chanan's work in the 1990s deals directly with the impact of contemporary audio production techniques and with issues raised by Benjamin. Chanan portrays the dislocation inherent in mechanical reproduction as a change in the musical community as well as in the scope of the musical work. Both are dispersed—in his words "atomized"—and Chanan considers this "both a symptom and one of the causes of the condition of postmodernism [whereby] reproduction pushes music into the realm of noise pollution."[26] Chanan further identifies the postmodern condition with a "fluid heterogeneous mix of styles."[27] It is my contention, throughout the following chapters, that there are many positive developments contained in the postmodern expression of musical community and in the mixing of musical styles that lie within what Chanan refers to generally as *musica practica*—"the practical aspects of music making."[28] Just as postmodernism itself has evolved from a primarily dark view of the cultural condition as fragmented and alienating, to a culture that has embraced fragmentation as stimulating and animated with possibilities; so many makers of music have embraced its ubiquitous presence and hybridized identity as positive elements of contemporary aesthetics.

For all of Benjamin's interest in the loss of aura that results from mechanical reproduction, he still suggests the transformative potential of new technologies by referencing Paul Valéry's *Aesthetics:* "We must expect great innovations to transform the entire technique of the arts, thereby affecting artistic invention itself and perhaps even bringing about an amazing change in our very notion of art."[29] Such transformative changes characterize the new paradigm of music construction described here. However, whereas recording may have changed the nature of music's presence in the world, contemporary recording techniques have fundamentally changed the way music is created. The extended timeline of music production and the process of editing and repurposing allow for a process that repeatedly shifts back and forth between creation and performance. Musical creativity is witnessing its own transformation, fueled by the evolving technology.

Jonathan Sterne challenges many of the assumptions that have followed in the wake of the Benjamin essay. Sterne argues that the emphasis on "face to face communication and bodily presences [making them] the yardstick by which to measure all communicative activity"[30] taints sound reproduction before it's even truly considered "by virtue of its 'decontextualizing' sound from its 'proper' interpersonal context."[31] Much of my work here describes the conditions in which live interaction is receding in the wake of the postmodern condition of fragmentation and dislocation that pervades modes of communication, allowing for the embrace of that condition as well as acknowledging what might be considered the negative effects. There are innumerable examples in contemporary life where both the decontextualized modes of interpersonal and musical communication are preferred. From the legacy telephone that was reborn in the cell phone, to email, to Facebook, to YouTube, to video Skype, the prevalence of alternative modes of communication dwarfs the face-to-face paradigm. Similarly, the CD, the mp3, the download, the iPod, satellite radio, the webcast, and so on have broadened the reach of reproduced sound and further eclipsed the primacy of live music performance. In fact, live music performance is itself often reinforced by sound amplification, augmented with samples accompanying performance, and even visually enhanced via large-screen projection. Live music performance is often judged in comparison to recorded performance, and not always favorably. It seems that "So much better than the recording" is no more likely a judgment than "Couldn't stand up to the recorded version." And ultimately these various modes of communication and reception are subject to a constantly shifting perception of value. It is by breaking out of the culture of nostalgia that these modes typically progress from disdain to reluctant acceptance to embrace.

It is nostalgia masquerading as value that drives the initial rejection of new modes of communication. This is not to say that technologies are completely benign, subject only to the irrational preferences born of nostalgia, but it is the sense that something (or many things) has been sacrificed that frequently dominates the reception of new technologies. The interventionist capabilities of new audio technology that are detailed in the following pages violate the primacy of authorship that prevailed in the music hierarchy from Beethoven through Dylan. Yet these same capabilities have generated new forms of creative expression; new opportunities for creative collaboration; new pieces of art that excite and stimulate, challenge, and provoke new generations. Of course, the progression that leads to the eventual embrace of new modes of experience may also morph into the new nostalgia. One day the iPod may inspire something like the affection some people currently have for vinyl records.

The history of recording is a history of creative collaboration, of a network of participants that share in the responsibilities that ultimately produce recorded works of music. This is a history of collaboration between
people and machines as well.[32] The difference in the contemporary landscape, however, is not just one of scale. Contemporary capabilities, such as
the ones I present in the following chapters, are indicative of levels of involvement and influence that incorporate whole new working methodolo-
gies. The compositional timeline constantly shifts as it proceeds through
networks of writing, recording, repurposing, editing, processing, and mixing. Music is made new through these expanded networks of process that
have been transformed by the application of digital technology.

The breakdown of traditional modes of communication, the exploitation of repurposing, and the deliberate confusing of the distinction between original and copy have also been witnessed in media other than music. Commentaries on the relationship of the copy to the original may take
a more literal kind of interpretation in the visual arts. For example, the pop
artist Roy Lichtenstein's large-scale reproductions of comic book images
emphasized the highly reductive nature of that form. They were, in part, a
comment on the sense that the public seemed to process these comic images as "real" while the artist's work revealed how little resemblance they
bear to the objects they represent. At the same time Lichtenstein was ex-
ploding the notions of the "high" and "low" status of visual communication and artistic expression. Lichtenstein's work anticipates certain kinds of
electronic synthesis that reduce musical sounds in ways that reveal similar
postmodern aesthetic experiences. His creation of original works based on
ubiquitous, mass-produced images also suggests contemporary musical
constructions that use well-known recordings through sampling. Many
other contemporary artists, including the bulk of the work categorized as
"pop art," share qualities with current music practices that blur the lines
between original and copy, often employing various technologies such as
photocopying or video in the process.

Photography is at the center of Benjamin's essay, and ultimately it is
photography that yields some of the most dramatic developments in the
art of reproduction. Susan Sontag comments that "photographs have become so much the leading visual experience that we now have works of art
which are produced in order to be photographed."[33] Artists such as
Christo, Robert Smithson, and Andy Goldsworthy create original works
meant to disintegrate or to be dismantled, leaving only a photographic
record. Yet Sontag maintains: "The photograph is not, even ostensibly,

meant to lead us back to an original experience."[34] Benjamin recognized that photography presented early examples of the elevation of reproduction in contemporary culture. Photography remains the touchstone in the breakdown of the original/copy dichotomy.

To some extent this book represents the ongoing encounter with Benjamin and his successors. The methodology, as befitting the point of view, borrows from a wide variety of disciplines. I challenge many traditional attitudes about the creation and reception of music through a combination of designed recording projects, ethnographic studies of contemporary music practice, and critical analysis. An integral part of the work is three original audio projects using newly imagined techniques of computer-based recording. These application studies draw from rock and roll, jazz, and African folklore music respectively. These original studies pinpoint areas of contemporary practice that are particularly significant in the cultural evolution of the musical experience. Parts I, II, and III also include a studio study that highlights the experiences of music practices in the field, from the professional recording studio to the weekend warriors making music in their bedrooms. These application and studio studies provide context for the final chapter in each part, which considers broader social and cultural conditions of contemporary music.

part one { Repurposing Presentation

Introduction to Part I

Part I examines the way that the presentation of recorded music has been altered by music production within the computerized environment of the DAW. I describe the implementation of a variety of these new capabilities in the postrecording process (work on the recording done after the actual recording is made). Through the description and analysis of an application study and a studio study I examine the meaning and impact of these technologies. Both studies examine the level of polish being employed in current popular music recordings. Use of these techniques has generated a reaction against excessive refining within a genre that has traditionally valued a certain rough and raw musical aesthetic. I explore the impact of the aesthetic judgments that have come into play since computer-based audio has opened the door to these levels of musical "fixing" and performance "cleansing," noting some of the creative rewards along with the more frequently articulated shortcomings of these practices.

With the ability to correct both rhythm and pitch, current pop music recordings have acquired a new level of musical accuracy as defined in terms of metronomic timing and regulated intonation. The application study (chapter 1) describes the process of this musical "fixing" of one particular pop song. The elaborate procedure is detailed and sets up an examination of the way these manipulations have affected musical construction and collaboration. Notions of cultural value are weighed against this kind of manipulation of musical performance. This expanded process of mixing and manipulation of musical elements, these new paradigms of presentation, are considered within the context of more traditional musical activities such as composition and arranging.

I argue that *despite* the wholesale changes in production capabilities there is not a *fundamental* change in the relationship between technology and music making. Technological mediation has achieved new heights in regards to degree, but it is not changed in kind—technology has always mediated music creation and reception. Yet the new technologies that allow the relatively easy "fixing" of human performance and "humanizing" of electronically constructed performances challenge long-standing practices and prejudices. And it is in part *because* of revolutionary technologies that popular music enjoys a kind of creative renewal.

The studio study (chapter 2) explores other new elements of music construction generated by DAW-based technology. I examine the intersection of the technical part of the recording process with some of the sounds that singers make outside of the essential verbal elements that create the words they sing. I consider the significance of this interaction for the listener— what might be said about how the recording process affects the experience of these nonverbal sounds and in turn how this perception might affect the experience of the music. The analysis centers on an expanded understanding of Roland Barthes's notion of the "grain" of the voice; I extend Barthes's approach to music aesthetics to include the way aesthetics are now intertwined with technology. In doing so I also appeal to Barthes (in absentia, of course) to accept the "grain" of the voice that I find to be an inextricable part of the contemporary recording process.

Music recording has always and primarily been a particular presentation of original, live musical performances. As apparent from the application and studio studies here, it is the extent of access to and manipulation of all manner of source material that has been expanded in such dramatic fashion through the use of various tools in the digital audio domain. As a result, the process involved that generates the final musical recording is increasingly obscured. As some of these practices are examined in these studies, the new capabilities created by the technologies encounter traditional ideas about the writers and performers of music, and ultimately the way "their" music is presented. The blurring of roles, and in the process the breakdown of the dichotomy between art and artifice, is the inevitable outcome of this encounter.

In the final chapter of Part I, I look more generally into the theoretical sides of the correlation between music, recording, and the human experience. I begin by examining the debate regarding technological determinism—the extent to which technology drives culture versus culture driving technology. This introduces further explorations of art, artifice, authenticity, and reciprocity and how they all figure into a necessary reconsideration of the place of recording in the contemporary music experience. The results illustrate the limiting nature of hierarchical judgments about how music is presented. There is no better indication of this than the fact that lower fidelity mp3s are preferred by many to CDs, and the history of audio technologies is riddled with similar examples—cassettes versus LPs, and so on. Many consumers have long preferred recorded music to live performance. Factors governing the presentation of music, its meaning, and its reception reflect constantly shifting historical and cultural conditions.

one

$\left\{\begin{array}{l} \\ \\ \end{array}\right.$ Application Study
Rock Band

"In Tune and in Time"

One of the first responsibilities that a producer of popular music takes on is the requirement that the final product delivered to the record company be "in tune and in time." That is to say, the musical performances are to realize a certain standard of technical proficiency in pitch and rhythm. The legacy of this central role for a producer may be found in the many rough performances that were a part of the early history of rock and roll. Along with a heavy reliance on attitude came some rather oblique relationships to musicianship on the part of some of the musicians. Thus, especially in the "band era" of the 1960s and 1970s, came the need for some QC (quality control) and the centrality of the producer's role as the arbiter of traditional musical standards. The long-dreamed-of tools for relatively easy pitch and rhythm "fixing" have now arrived along with the DAW. In regards to the direction of technological influence ("top-down" versus "bottom-up"), the realization of this desire suggests that the pitch and rhythm tools of computer-based audio may be seen as a striking example of agency driving technology (we needed to fix stuff, and now we can). However, as we shall see through this volume, there are always elements working in both directions. Perhaps some of what is generally considered to be excessive "fixing" of rhythm and pitch may be considered to be examples of technology driving agency (we can fix stuff, so we do). In any case, the ease and degree of control over pitch and rhythm have dramatically changed, so the new paradigm of music construction is in full bloom when it comes to realizing the producer's dictum that performances must be "in tune and in time."

Prior to the current computer technology the producer had relatively few options in the control of intonation and rhythmic accuracy in musical performances. The primary tool was, after a studio take that wasn't up to the desired standard, to get on the "talk-back"[1] to the performing musician and say something like: "That was great, but can you do it one more time for me: It was a little pitchy" (meaning either too sharp or flat for use) or "It felt a little awkward" (meaning not good enough rhythmically for use). Here the final recorded performances were created through selective repetition. Bits of performances would be captured to allow a complete, musically acceptable performance to be pieced together. If the musician was very capable, then little or no such repetition would be necessary, but in the case of the relatively inexperienced rock-and-roll band member, this could be a long and tedious process. Over time certain techniques and technologies developed that could be applied after the performance, and these aided this process in small ways—tape editing, "flying in,"[2] and later judicious use of a harmonizer[3] could correct problems in certain instances—but these options were time-consuming and only successful in a very limited number of circumstances. For the most part getting the required performance out of the musician, sometimes one arduous bit at a time, was the only viable option.

To explore the changes in the application of control over tuning and timing I undertook a project involving a song that I had recorded in 1994 for the band "The Jenny Thing." I had made the original recording using the dominant professional recording technology at the time, which was a 24-track analog tape recorder. This meant I had twenty-four individual tracks for recording on which to build the music for each song. The original sessions were carried out in the typical studio production style of the time. We recorded the initial "basic" tracks of drums, bass, guitar, and vocal together, but all of the performances other than the drum track were considered "scratch" tracks—that is, they were played as guide tracks to be later "scratched" or discarded in favor of new takes of these performances. All of the instruments, as well as each element of the drum set, were recorded on their own individual tracks. All of the instruments and the lead vocal were isolated from each other so that there wasn't "bleed" from one sound into the recording of the other, facilitating the replacement of parts later. Additional parts such as lead guitar tracks, harmony vocals, and percussion tracks were added later. By recording each part at different times I was able to focus the attention and the process of revision on the execution of each individual performance until it was considered acceptable. This was a relatively low-budget record, so the standard for "acceptable" had to take into consideration the capabilities of the musician along with the overall time that the budget allowed for the entire recording and mixing process. This remains the dominant procedure in pop music today, though the weight of performance control has shifted from being almost completely a part of the original recording to a balance between recording and the kind of postrecording manipulation that I was now going to apply to this production. My goal in this study is to apply to this older recording the process of rhythm and pitch "fixing" currently used in pop production, allowing me to compare the original master as it was released on record to what would probably comprise the master recording if this song were produced using contemporary technology.

My first task was to transfer from the analog tape to digital audio in the DAW. For the software needed to control the digital audio stored on the computer's hard drive I used today's dominant professional recording software, Avid's Pro Tools.[4] While making the transfer and listening to the original audio I noted a slight tempo fluctuation during the song's introduction. I remembered being continually aggravated by this when I produced the original track. This was a case where I had deemed the inconsistency to be slight enough to be acceptable, though it was significant enough to have bothered me throughout the process. I smiled to myself knowing that now I would be able to "fix" this slight problem, and then thought of the countless number of examples of such occurrences in other recordings made before the current capabilities were available. How many slight problems in recorded performances have haunted musicians and producers before there was a means of correcting them as a part of the production process? But before I explore the meaning of such musical "fixing," I provide a narrative of the process I undertook in applying contemporary production practices to this particular piece of music.

First, a caveat: I use the terms *fix, correct, consistent,* and the like as technical terms, while recognizing that these also carry significant implications about the value of the alterations being made. The reality is much more complex, for value in musical performance is most often ascribed to deviations from the standard to which we are "fixing." The implied values of such words as *fixing* are not necessarily a reflection of how one might value the actual effect of this process. In fact they may be completely at odds with such implications (supposedly "fixed" performances may be considered inferior to the original). I will be addressing questions of value in this more general sense later in this chapter, but for the moment I ask the reader to temporarily indulge the use of the language for the sake of the narrative.

Fixing in Pro Tools

As with most popular music, this song was recorded to a click track generated by a metronome. That is to say, the drummer listened to a click when laying his initial track while the other musicians played to the (click-informed) drummer's performance. Using contemporary production techniques where we would be recording directly into the computer, with the click generated by the computer, the bar and beat information would already be an integral part of the recording and established before any music was played. With this historical recording I had an individual audio track with the click from the metronome recorded separately, but this was not integrated into the computer clocking function—Pro Tools wasn't able to give a readout of the metronomic bar and beat information. In fact, because it was recorded using analog gear, the original metronomic timing was not perfect. Slight variations in the creation of the click by any analog clocking device (metronome), combined with minute variations in speed from an analog tape recorder, mean that it is not possible to simply assign the correct bpm (beats per minute) reading to the audio now in Pro Tools and have the music line up correctly with the bar and beat information. Fortunately there are tools to assist us in adjusting for these inconsistencies so that we can work within the traditional music organization of bars and beats along with the clocking precision of a computer.

In the Pro Tools program there is a plug-in[5] tool called Beat Detective. As the name suggests, this tool investigates rhythmic qualities of audio data. It distinguishes beat information by identifying transients (high-frequency leading sound elements) that are likely candidates for marking the beginning of each beat. In this case, because I had the click track recorded on a separate audio track, it was an easy matter for Beat Detective to create a tempo map from the position of each click and thus organize the file into bars and beats. To do this Beat Detective assigns an exact tempo for each beat, to within three decimal points of bpms, thus yielding a bar and beat map that remains consistent with the original click. Beat Detective does not alter the placement of the beats, but it identifies and organizes them in a way that makes them conform to a bar and beat structure. By doing this I had a tempo map that represented the "ideal time" when the performances were made. This was the "correct" beat structure that the drummer was conforming to when laying the initial drum track.

I then used another feature of Beat Detective to slice all of the various drum tracks into separate regions,[6] setting a variety of parameters to help it make "intelligent" decisions about how to read the transients and divide the performance into various beat-related elements. As is typical in contemporary drum set recording, there were individual tracks for bass drum, snare drum, tom-toms, and hi-hat cymbals, as well as separate stereo recordings of overhead microphones to capture the cymbals, and room mics to capture the overall sound of the drums in the room. Beat Detective processed each track separately. Using Beat Detective on overhead and room tracks is difficult because of the complexity of the information. As sophisticated as Beat Detective is, it has trouble determining beat divisions when the audio consists of all of the drum instruments mixed together.

Once Beat Detective had created individual regions from each track of the drum performance, I used the "quantize" function to correct the timing of the drum performance. Quantizing takes the beginning of each separated region of audio and moves it along the musical timeline to the beginning of the nearest user-defined beat subdivision (in this case the smallest subdivision was eighth-note triplets, as this song used a "shuffle" or triplet subdivision of the beat). Quantizing each track individually yielded the most accurate results, but it also meant that where there were inconsistencies in the quantizing process between individual tracks I would have to make manual changes for the parts to conform to each other. While this process created a much more accurate version of the original drum performance in terms of note placement relative to the "ideal" of metronomic time, there was still considerable variation in the volume and timbre of each individual sound, as well as internal variations within the larger segments that were quantized into position. Thus the resulting performance was not the same as a performance coming from a drum machine, where every note may be metronomically placed and there is generally little or no variation in dynamics or timbre.[7] Quantizing these tracks took about two hours, but this is remarkably efficient considering the literally thousands of edits, adjustments of beat placements and extension of regions to close gaps, creation of crossfades in order to smooth transitions, and about twenty manual adjustments at places where the automated process produced slightly anomalous results.

In working with the drum track I made several other typical alterations to the files in order to create cleaner and more consistent performances. There were a few weak or bad-sounding bass drum or snare drum hits that had come from inconsistent striking of the drum, and I replaced those with better-sounding hits using a basic cut-and-paste function. There is also a tool in Pro Tools called Strip Silence that allows one to create silence below a user-definable amplitude threshold. In this way it is possible to quickly eliminate leakage sound from adjacent instruments, and for drums this can create a much cleaner overall sound. For example, the tom-tom tracks had substantial off-axis[8] leakage from the snare drum, bass drum, and hi-hat. By stripping away all parts of the audio file other than the actual tom-tom hits I could remove the clouding effect of this leaked audio. Strip Silence provides a very efficient means of eliminating these off-axis sounds.

After "fixing" the drum part I proceeded to work on the timing of the bass guitar part. With the first two-thirds of the performance I was able to capture and separate regions into beat-oriented sections using Beat Detective. I then quantized to eighth-note triplets and smoothed the transitions using the automated fill and crossfade function. This extends audio regions where necessary to fill in the gaps created by moving the regions to their corrected beat placement. It then creates a short crossfade between adjacent audio regions to create smooth transitions. In a few places I used the copy-and-paste function to replace a poorly played part with the same part from a different section of the song. The last one-third of the bass part is continuous legato triplets with little dynamics and enough sustain to make it impossible for the computer to discern the break points needed to create the individual beats. This portion of the music consisted of a repeated two-bar pattern, so I found the best iteration, massaged it into shape, making slight adjustments to both rhythm and dynamics, and then pasted that "fixed" two-bar phrase throughout. I had to requantize each two-bar section to the appropriate downbeat because of the slight tempo fluctuations of the click. There was one musical variation at one transition point (the same pattern played up an octave) and I left that from the original performance. Then I used the automated smoothing function to close gaps and create crossfades on this final section. The result of this work was a more rhythmically stable bass track that sounded more accurately played to the drum track.

The Wonderful World of Auto-Tune

Having started to work with audio that contained pitch information—in this case the bass guitar track—it was now time to employ some pitch correction. The most frequently used tool for pitch correction in the digital domain is a plug-in called Auto-Tune. Auto-Tune and its various successors employ pitch detection algorithms that are capable of reading very small variations in pitch in real time (single-voice only, it cannot read multiple notes played at the same time). Once the software has determined the continuous pitch information for a segment of audio, it creates a graphic representation of that pitch on a grid where the vertical axis is pitch and the horizontal axis is time. The user can then redraw the pitch representation on the graph to alter the pitch. When the original audio is played back through the plug-in, it adjusts the pitch to the redrawn graphic information. In this way variations in pitch deemed incorrect can be "corrected" in exactly the way the user desires. This may be gentle correction to move pitch variations closer to the actual note, or aggressive changes that lock the pitch to the desired note. There is also an automatic mode that corrects pitch in real time as the audio is fed through the plug-in. In this mode the audio is gently moved toward whatever note the original audio is closest to, though you can dictate which notes are "valid" by indicating scale function or even by designating your own custom scale.[9]

I tried the Auto-Tune's auto-mode on the bass guitar and found that it nudged the pitch into a slightly more stable-sounding place. After all, the bass guitar is a fretted instrument so most of the pitch information was pretty accurate in the first place. However, variations in each string's tuning, and pitch shifting caused when the string is stretched slightly by the pressure of the finger on the string against the fretboard were reduced by the application of Auto-Tune.

I then moved onto the lead vocal, where Auto-Tune is frequently used for pitch correction. Many rock singers have a less than exacting ability to execute accurate intonation. The relative merits of variations from the ideal pitch may be argued, but for this exercise, and for most of the vocals heard in rock production today, Auto-Tune is used to "improve" the accuracy of a singer's pitch. In this instance I used the graphical mode, which allows for more aggressive retuning of each vocal line than the automatic mode. Although I sometimes used a straight line in the graphic window to "flatten" the pitch to the exact note, the program has settings for how quickly and completely it "corrects" the singer's performance in line with the graphical model that the user has created. For this project I have the parameters set to the fast side of the "retune" continuum and the choosy side of the "tracking" continuum, so corrections are made pretty quickly to conform quite accurately to the graphic representation. Thus, even though

I may graphically indicate a flat line for the pitch on the note desired, there will still be some pitch variation in the final audio as the program does not track the note immediately or retune it completely. "Correcting" the vocal pitch performance took about two hours. Although the pitch accuracy of the original vocal was quite good, the vocal intonation sounds more stable after this process.

Although I do not feel the need to adjust the timing of any of the vocal lines, this is something that is also done in contemporary production. Vocal lines (or words) may be moved slightly to "improve" their rhythmical accuracy. They may even be moved by beats or bars to fit into the overall composition in a different way, creating a different vocal arrangement. Certain functions, such as vamps at the end of songs where there might be a long passage of vocal ad-libbing, are often the result of extensive editing. In the past we might painstakingly construct an "ad-lib" section by recording one "riff" at a time, with the singer performing and reperforming certain phrases as we worked through the section of the song—*composition through recording*. Now we are more likely to record several versions of the vocal vamp and then construct the ad-lib sequence through the editing process—*composition through editing*. In one recent project of mine an entire ending ad-lib section was created by repurposing pieces sung at completely different locations in the arrangement and using them for a newly constructed vocal ad-lib ending.

Finally I work on the guitar tracks. Because these are primarily chordal parts it is not possible to use Auto-Tune on them. It is also difficult for Beat Detective to determine beat information because the transients at the beginning of beats are not necessarily that pronounced. However, because of the repetitive nature of these parts, it is often possible to find iterations of particular phrases that are played particularly well and to use these in places where the same phrases are not as well executed. I do this with the guitar tracks, eliminating any rough spots and generally creating more accurate performances. I am done "fixing": total time, about twelve hours.

I then mix the song—balancing levels between instruments and voice and optimizing the sound relative to frequencies, dynamics, and ambiences according to my personal aesthetic. I run one version using the original "unfixed" audio and one version using the "fixed" tracks (audio clips 1 and 2). It is not my intention to make a formalized survey of responses, but I did take an informal reading by playing the two mixes for some of my recording classes. I find that in general students are not able to identify what separates the two recordings. In fact they often misidentify the differences between the two versions as changes in arrangement or instrumentation that did not occur. This, for one thing, suggests that people listen very differently when they are asked to listen.[10] For the most part I do get responses that identify the "fixed" mix as being "clearer," more "polished," more "stable," and more "professional," but I also get some responses that identify the "unfixed" mix as "cleaner" or that otherwise apparently reverse the nature of the two versions. I do not pursue listening tests, as my interest is in the implications of the process rather than in gathering statistical data from such tests.

Meaning in Manipulation

The process described above—from "fixing" to mixing—raises many questions regarding the cultural, social, and philosophical position of contemporary music creation. Before considering each of these areas in the following sections, I want to consider the root idea of audio manipulation, its epistemology. In doing so I will address some basic objections that arise in relation to the kind of manipulation of audio here described. Have we become so removed from the original music as to have lost the essence of its meaning? Do critiques of recordings in regards to performance technique (Barthes) or musical expression (Robert Philip) or rhythmic subtlety (David Epstein) miss the point by failing to identify or acknowledge the new forms of musical creativity that have emerged within the contemporary technological context?[11]

There is first the musical act, and this is profoundly human. In some form human agency is required in order to produce what it is that we call music. All music is once removed from the act that created it. That is to say that music is already a secondary product; it is, in Anthony Gritten's words, the "trace left by an act."[12] Musical instruments themselves are technological objects that are inserted between the musical act and the music. Equally, vocal technique is necessary for vocal expression to become singing. Music is not a natural phenomenon but is necessarily a product of human activity. Musical construction begins before there is music. It begins in the musical act, but the constructive nature of music is then an inherent part of its very call from act into existence. Thus construction, most often through a musical instrument, means that *technological mediation is part of the entire history of musical creation.*

Technology is, of course, essential to the act of recording. The advent of recording created a universe of music that was necessarily mediated through complex technology. While recording did not actually alter the fundamental dependence of music on technology, the kind of nostalgic values that Adorno and Benjamin express seem to draw on a distinction between "natural" and "technologically mediated" music. If there is to be such a distinction, it is more accurately understood as between "natural-ized" and "mechanized" technology. That is to say that earlier, prerecord-ing music technology was viewed as natural because the technological as-pects had already been deeply integrated into the cultural process. Audio recording technology inserts itself into the musical process between the music creation and the music preservation. It is the technology that is needed to produce the audio preservation of music, just as flutes, pianos, and the like were the needed technology to produce the sound of music. However, it is not the case that live performance remains the arena of mu-sic unaffected by the technology of audio recording. In fact technological effects on so-called live performance have made it more of a relative to recordings than a stranger.[13]

Technology not directly connected to the musical act manipulates and mediates virtually all music in contemporary culture—both live and recorded. The musical object is already a product of technology, its "trace" left not only by the act but by the mediation of technology as well. The ap-plication project I have described represents a dramatic shift in the *way* technology mediates our relationship to music creation. It is indicative of new kinds of music creations. As production increasingly takes on the qualities of both performance *and* composition, all of these activities blur in the final recorded presentation. Contemporary production techniques greatly expand the manner in which people may be involved in musical construction, and in doing so redefine the very nature of what it means to be a musician. Théberge notes that "an understanding of the basic tech-nologies, routines and practices of studio recording has gradually become an essential part of every musician's store of knowledge and skill."[14] How-ever, technological expertise does not obviate the need for some of the tra-ditional relationships of people to music creation. When Cook says that the creative imagination in music production requires "some degree of specifically musical training,"[15] he may not have been anticipating the kind of production I am employing here, yet musical training is required to effectively edit and manipulate music even in highly automated cir-cumstances. Has the technology trumped musical knowledge? Certainly it has not completely done so, as basic principles of music remain relevant to application of the creative imagination in these circumstances as well. The more developed the practitioner's musical ear, the more sophisticated the relationship to the editing and "fixing" process.[16] The manner in which such sophistication may be acquired, however, may be far from those recognized in the traditional music classroom.[17]

As to musical content, the same kinds of considerations apply. Frederic Jameson indicates that music follows the Sapir-Whorf hypothesis, which posits new thought as the result of expanded language capabilities, and this suggests how "music of a given period is able to express new kinds of content."[18] We may extrapolate the same for technological applications to music, allowing them to express new kinds of content as well. The vocabulary of music is as much wrapped up in digital technology now as it was in previous times with new instruments or new cross-cultural influences. And these new kinds of musical content are not to be understood as cold, objective applications based on some kind of mathematical treatment. As Arnold Pacey argues, technology participates on all levels: "No aspect of human life, be it music, medicine, or technology, can be adequately discussed if we are always restricted to a scientific mode of discourse."[19] So even the most audacious forms of contemporary manipulation of audio data are not to be completely divorced from the technology of musical instruments or of live sound production. That is to say that Gritten's "traces of the act" may be understood in technological terms—as a part of the postrecording process whereby music is the result—in the same way that he describes them in the terms of live musical production.

New technologies continue to participate in music's ability to express new kinds of content. The fact that there is no music without technology (instruments) or technique (voice) undermines the conservative forces that have sought to minimize the qualities of musicianship and the creative forces of composition that are dependent on the technologies of recording. It is nostalgia disguised as the "natural" that fuels the conventional critiques of contemporary music and its practices. The new techniques and expressions of musical creativity are today becoming naturalized in contemporary culture. It is in this context that I begin a more detailed look into the application project described above.

Variations and "Fixing"

The bulk of the work on the pop song as described above was done to "improve" on the extent of deviations from "perfect" rhythm and pitch in the original performances. In contrast it is common to make claims for inconsistencies of musical performance as being essential to the emotional content of the performance. These inconsistencies may be random (as reflected in the randomization functions of some musical software), or an intentional and consistent kind of note placement that is systematically applied by a musician as a part of an overall performance structure. This systematic approach is most often associated with popular music forms and is thought of in terms of rhythmic "groove." Performance inconsistencies may also take the form of nuanced deviations from nominal (score-based) values; in this case the deviations are not consistently applied, rather they vary the expressive intention over different passages and sections of the music. This approach is widespread in Western art music. Although the two approaches may coexist, they are fundamentally different. They share a reliance on inconsistency for effect, but differ completely in how such deviations are applied. In either case, most observers acknowledge the value of inconsistencies as essential elements of musical performance. However, many also argue for the inability of a machine, or a human programmer, to reconstruct such inconsistencies in a way that matches the emotional impact of a singular human performance. Others are busy constructing automated feel factors, groove templates, and randomizing algorithms in order to emulate and control, and even it may be argued, improve upon the quality of deviation in a musical performance in order to provide a greater emotional impact. These programmable approaches may seek to emulate either the groove-based or the expressive-based approach to rhythmic variations. The objective of both forms of variation, and both modes of implementation (the human and the programmed), is a greater emotional impact.

In *Performing Rites,* Frith notes Charles Keil's model of participatory discrepancies: "A PD is 'a slight human inconsistency' in the way that a musician executes rhythm, pitch and timbre,"[20] and goes on to provide a good summary of various positions regarding PDs. As an example of a highly restrictive outlook on the application of PDs he references David Epstein's claim that session musicians can't play "naturally or 'musically'" to a click track.[21] Epstein suggests that the mechanized influence of the metronomic click track robs the potential for a truly "musical" performance. It is difficult to divorce Epstein's negative assertion from the fact that professionally his work has been as a conductor. He seems to be reflecting a very specific viewpoint regarding rhythmic practice that may be appropriate to his own work but is dislocated from many other approaches to performance. Just as the concert musician must balance his or her own expressive inclinations against the conductor's lead, so might a studio musician balance his or her expression against the click track. The studio musician might engage the click track as another musical part just as concert musicians collaborate with the conductor as their musical partner. It is true that the conductor's lead is personalized rather than mechanized, and it may be that strict adherence to metronomic time would rob most classical music performances of their musicality. But Epstein's comment is aimed at the studio musician who often performs to metronomic time. This practice is so widespread that Epstein appears to be condemning virtually all of contemporary popular music, and indeed one might better interpret his comment as a reflection of this broader judgment, rather than the more specific condemnation of the relationship of popular music to metronomic time. Musicians in popular music are frequently interacting with the equivalent of a click track (a strictly metronomic element) as an essential element in locating rhythmic interest. With the use of drum machines (and other sequenced parts) as part of finished recordings, this practice extends beyond the more hidden relationship of playing to click track. If we accept popular music as "natural" or "musical" at all, then we must accept the active relationship to metronomic time.

In contrast to the Epstein reference, Frith acknowledges Prögler's descriptions of how "digital instrument makers have sought to 'humanize' their programs, have become concerned with 'imperfections,' 'inaccuracies,' 'perturbations,' 'offsets,' 'adjustments,' 'shifts' and 'feel.'"[22] An early and comprehensive description of the kind of PD associated with Western art music performance is found in Leonard B. Meyer's 1956 work *Emotion and Meaning in Music*. Meyer argues that emotional responses to music may be analyzed through "a process in which the relationship of deviation and norms to affective aesthetic responses can be examined and discussed."[23] By describing and analyzing musical inconsistencies this work suggests ways that one may intervene in the application of PDs. However, having been written prior to our ability to manipulate the details of performances after they have been recorded, Meyer's work doesn't address the questions of rhythmic programming or "fixing." One of the early writings to address the possibility of creating emotional responses by rhythmic programming was Michael Stewart's 1987 article, "The Feel Factor." Stewart catalogs the effects of various departures from metronomic note placement in popular music. He suggests how a trained musician may create a more compelling performance when playing with intention against a click track, using the application of PDs to create specific effects such as "nervous" or "heavy." He uses this analysis as a basis for suggesting ways that programmers may re-create or alter performances to generate or heighten such emotional responses. Other important work in this area has been done by Ernest Cholakis in developing the technology for creating groove templates.[24] His work also suggests ways that programming may "improve" upon original performances by altering PDs in specific ways to produce predictable emotional responses.

I have had extensive conversations with studio drummers about their interaction with the click track. Many of them have become expert at adjusting their performances' relationship to metronomic time to suit the music or artist that is being recorded. Some artists prefer a drum track that pushes the beat, where the drums tend to land slightly ahead of the metronomic pulse (more exciting or more nervous, depending on one's point of view) and some artists prefer a drummer that lays the beat behind the click track (heavy or "grooving," though again, subject to some subjective interpretation). Although much of the work analyzing PDs has been motivated by programming considerations, it has served to guide many musical performances as well. This is a typical example of technologies working on both sides of the spectrum—from the traditionally technological back to the more traditionally performative.

To extend this question further is to consider the many ways that location of rhythmic interest may vary. Changing aesthetics might find the focus of rhythmic interest on compositional complexity, on note placement, or on even less obvious elements such as harmonic rhythm. Relocation of the center of rhythmic attention is an inherent part of shifting musical interests in various cultures. The notion of "humanizing" rhythmic inconsistencies in mechanically generated performances may provide significant rhythmic interest in a localized cultural environment, as it seems to in contemporary popular music. At the same time, inconsistency may be "built into" the relations between levels in hierarchically "deep" music—such as in the relationship of performer to conductor in Western art music. Similarly the physical relationship of rhythm to the body may vary from culture to culture, and over time in any given culture, and this in turn may affect the location of rhythmic interest. These physical relationships may exist within the performers themselves, in collaboration with a conductor or in an exchange with dancers; and each may dictate a differing location of rhythmic interest.

But aesthetics are hardly the only consideration. For practitioners such as myself we must find a balance between the aesthetic and the practical.

The nature and degree of "fixing" are influenced by a variety of real-world considerations such as available time and budget, the wishes of the artist and others involved in the production, and one's own aesthetic regarding conforming to theoretical ideals of pitch and time. The fallacy that computers are time-savers is really exposed when it comes to "fixing" audio. The vastly expanded ability to correct small inconsistencies in pitch and timing is matched by the vastly expanded time it takes to make such corrections. We are almost always confronted with a situation where performances could be more completely "fixed," but where either budget or aesthetic judgment restricts further editing or processing. Although ideally the aesthetic and collaborative processes dictate the extent of "fixing," it is sometimes the purely practical time and money considerations that end up setting the limits on these activities.

How Do We Decide What Is "Right"?

The collaborative process has taken on entirely new dimensions as a result of the technological capabilities I have described here. The ability to "fix" affects the making of the initial recording as well as the process of editing and mixing. There is a standard Pro Tools joke that reflects the recording side of these new capabilities:

> A vocalist is recording his part for a song and singing rather poorly. When he finishes his "take," the producer gets on the talkback to the singer and says, "That sucked. Come on in."

The producer is suggesting that the vocal is complete and that the artist can come back into the control room, even though the producer has noted that the performance was not at all good. The assumption is that the quality of the performance doesn't matter because it's simply going to get corrected later anyway. Of course this is an exaggeration in order to create humor, but what is implied is now an everyday part of the recording process in many circumstances. Performers have heard how their performances can be corrected for pitch or rhythm and they, along with the other collaborators in the process, often take this into account in judging a performance. A singer or a producer may well say something like, "That take was great. One word was a little out of tune but we can just fix that." Thus "fixing" becomes a creative part of the recording process. There's a telling comparison with the much older studio saying, "We'll fix it in the mix," which was intended as satirical—an excuse used when a performer was unable to create a satisfactory performance and the producer was trying to avoid endlessly unsuccessful attempt to get it right—because the fact was that it really couldn't be "fixed in the mix." It is precisely that kind of "fixing" which is now a reality.

The same inclinations that lead to the desire to "fix" performances affect the control exerted over the initial performance. In either case it is some form of aesthetics that drives those decisions, although technology may dictate the means of implementation. The aesthetics come down to how those making the decisions hear things. Do we like the way it sounds or do we wish for it to sound differently? However, more than the simple aesthetics or personal taste may affect these decisions—they may be colored by the perceived demands of the marketplace or by the fear of how one's performance may be judged by one's colleagues. Ultimately it is a personal choice that is often made by the producer. The following rambling comment by prominent contemporary rock producer John Goodmanson indicates that the difficulty one may have in balancing personal aesthetics with success, and with the perceived demands of the marketplace, may affect the musical process in the studio:

> I wind up doing it instrument by instrument more now I think than I used to. I think that just has to do with how bands play together [since] I work with younger bands and now it's more major label stuff, so being closer to perfect is sort of more important than it used to be. Stuff that's more commercial, more like regular pop music, is definitely all about the energy, but then there's also a component of it where it needs to be pretty well locked, especially if you're shooting for FM radio. Really it comes down to what the players can pull off in the live take and what they can't pull off, then it gets rebuilt instrument by instrument.[25]

Such choices are also the product of cultural influences that are a reflection of the time. The cultural ear shifts, representing a new intersection of music and technology. A simple example is the use of drum machines in popular music. When first introduced in the 1970s drum machines were widely ridiculed as horribly stiff and unnatural sounding. They were considered useful for the songwriter in sketching ideas or making demos but hardly appropriate for final production. Nonetheless they started to be used in certain genres of music—especially disco, which initially adopted highly repetitive and "mechanized"-sounding drum performances—and became accepted in certain limited musical circles. Over time their use has grown exponentially, and we rarely hear about their stultifying effect on music or musical feel any more. People are still involved in programming music using the idea of participatory discrepancies (see Cholakis above), and the use of sampled drum loops that incorporate actual performances has become very common, but there is a lot of popular music that uses the "perfect" performance of a drum machine as its rhythmical basis. It is not just that the cultural ear has developed a high tolerance for the "stiff" performance of the metronomic drum machine: over time this tolerance has developed into a required and desired element for certain genres of popular music, such that much of disco, rap, or hip-hop would not sound stylistically correct without the drum machine's presence. This standard also affects the desire to fix human performances.

Just as early recordings seemed to make musicians want to play in a more technically correct manner, to adjust what sounded to them like errors in performance when they heard themselves played back via the recordings,[26] so contemporary musicians may wish to hear rhythmic performances that adhere more closely to the ideal of the drum machine or other quantized performances. More will be said on this later, but for now I observe that we have these new capabilities and we may choose to use them or not, to please our ear for whatever reasons. *The aesthetics of "fixing" is simply the aesthetics of hearing, of how we wish for things to sound.* But our ear is influenced by the capabilities of these technologies as well as by aesthetics. This is the essence of the "debate" between the effects of technology and the forces of cultural practice—technology and cultural practice are both continually feeding off of each other. And there is a synergy between the practitioner's ear and the public's ear as well. That is to say that production techniques (such as the use of drum machines) become acceptable and even expected by listeners, and this drives practitioners to conform to the expectations of previously produced music—drum machines might be necessary for a recording to really qualify as "disco," for example. And beyond this, applications in one genre cross over into others, so that technologies begin to appear in genres that might have previously rejected them as inappropriate—for example, drum machines in punk rock or synthesizers in folk music.

We could project into the future effects of such cultural imperatives but we don't necessarily have to: we can reference a popular science fiction book to do it for us. In Neal Stephenson's *Snow Crash* an aspiring rapper, Sushi K, confronts a crowd of teenage music fans: "He stares at the crowd, five thousand potential market shares, young people with funkiness on their minds. They've never heard any music before that wasn't perfect. It's either studio-perfect digital sound from their CD players or performance-perfect fuzz-grunge from the best people in the business."[27] Yet even "perfect" drum machine performances have very small fluctuations, as there is really no such thing as "perfect" clocking.[28] So, in spite of the futuristic reference, the continuum of deviation is inherent in all music—more or less "perfect" but never perfect. What has changed more dramatically than the level of adherence to the "perfect" performance is the people who now may contribute to that aspect of the performance. The performer used to be the primary arbiter of that continuum; the recordist is now a frequent contributor and often even the final arbiter in these aesthetic decisions.

The position of the performer's hegemony over PDs has changed in both popular music and Western art music. There is considerable overlap between the role of the producer in popular music and the conductor in concert music: the dynamic between the producer/conductor and the performing musicians is very similar in the sense that it may be highly interactive, but there is often the tension between the fact that authority is placed with the producer/conductor yet the actual production of sounds rests with the musician. The primary difference for the producer and the conductor is their relationship to musical time: for the most part the conductor exerts musical control prior to the performance—in rehearsal—and in real time as part of the performance of the music, while the popular music producer often exerts control after the fact as well. Similarly classical producers have found their own means of independent influence after the fact through the process of editing: sometimes multitudes of painstakingly chosen edits are used to construct a final recording. While this doesn't represent the same degree of intervention as when a popular music producer actually moves sounds around to alter the original performance, it is an evolution of the same impulse whereby people other than the original performer are making direct and significant alterations to the final recorded "performance."

Mixing and Mixing Metaphors

The final stage of this application project was the creation of the stereo mix. The considered mixing of audio elements has been practiced since the advent of recording, beginning with simple techniques such as the positioning of musicians relative to the primitive horns first used to capture sound. This process reached a whole new level of complexity and sophistication with the advent of multitrack recording. With these tape recorders (and now through the DAW) many disparate audio elements can be recorded at different times and even in different places, each synchronized to the same timeline. Along with having multiple audio elements comes the necessity of mixing these elements to create a final (generally stereo) audio program. For our purposes, without reviewing the entire history of mixing, it is valuable to note the major changes in mixing that have arrived with the use of the DAW.

Whereas pitch and time "fixing" have seen advancements that encompass wholly new capabilities, the art of mixing has been altered by more subtle improvements. The two primary advances in mixing technology of the past twenty years, automation and recall, have seen significant enhancements as a result of the DAW production techniques, but have not seen substantive changes in basic functionality. Mix automation is the ability to program (automate) changes in the relationship between elements dynamically, as movement over time. This means that volume relationships can be altered sequentially—for example, the vocal can be made louder in the chorus than in the verse—and this change in volume is stored in memory and reproduced automatically in reference to a consistent timeline. This kind of volume automation was first introduced on analog mixing consoles (using computer-assisted functionality) in the 1970s. Early systems were cumbersome and unreliable, but this process was refined and by the late 1980s very reliable systems were available for analog consoles.

Earlier techniques of mixing by altering the position of musicians relative to the horns or microphones, or using multiple microphones and altering their position to capture different instrumental balances, or even changing instrumentation for the sake of the clearer reproduction on primitive recording systems, had already established the precedent whereby recordists had significant influence over the final presentation of the musical performance.[29] Multitrack recording, combined with volume automation, allowed the recordists even greater control over the blend of elements in the final audio program. With sounds retaining their separate identity up until the final mix, and with dynamic automation of volume, producers have the kind of control over the final sound of the music, the relationship of the individual elements, that influences aspects of the arrangement and ultimately even the composition. Placement and balance of melodic, harmonic, and rhythmic elements can alter the listener's experience profoundly—as anyone who has heard certain contemporary remixes can attest.

DAWs greatly expand the implementation and functionality of automation, thereby further increasing control over the presentation of the final audio program. On the analog systems only volume (and muting, which is simply another means of volume control) was accessible through automation. When working entirely within the digital realm virtually every parameter of signal processing is available for automation. Panning effects, parameters of ambience effects (such as reverb), and subtle alterations in timbre (through equalization) can all be dynamically altered over the course of an audio program, and these changes can be memorized and automatically reproduced for each playback. Additionally the computer allows for a level of fine control over volume automation that was not possible when linked to an analog console. Through manipulation of graphic representations of volume (and every other parameter) against the waveform of the sound, the mixer can select the exact portion of the audio that s/he wishes to automate and control the variations to within one-tenth of a decibel. All of this is quickly and easily done with immediate playback of the results available to allow for an aural judgment of the effect. The enhanced ease and speed of automation technology assist in heightening intuitive responses to music construction. This in turn expands the creative capabilities of the recordist responsible for building the final mix.

This kind of intervention in the sound of the final audio represents a significant expansion in the capability of altering the arrangement (or orchestration) of music after it has been recorded. It is interesting to note that when complex mixing became a standard part of making audio recordings through the proliferation of multitrack recorders in the 1960s, it was often referred to as remixing. This was a reference to the idea that the original "mix" of the elements was the sound when they were played together (as though they had been played for a stage performance) and the studio process was a revision of this "live" mix by the musicians, a remix. Remix differentiated the aesthetic of reproduction from the aesthetic of live performance. As the process became ubiquitous (and the aesthetic less often based on live performance), the re- was dropped and the process was simply called *mixing*. Shortly thereafter the idea of remixing was reborn as new mixes that were different versions of the original mixed elements—most often for different intended audiences such as dance clubs. These remixes now frequently contain different elements than the original recordings, involving additional people in the compositional side of music creation.

The other advancement in mix technology involves the process of mix recall. Recall refers to the ability to re-create all of the settings involved in the mix process at a later time. Every knob, fader, and function (or their digital equivalent) must be remembered and reset in order to reproduce a particular audio mix. In the world of analog mixing boards and outboard processing gear this was accomplished through a combination of snapshot memory that allowed for a graphic recall of the mixing board's settings that could be then reset manually by the engineer, and extensive note taking and subsequent resetting of the parameters of the outboard gear—the additional processing gear used as an adjunct to the processing power of the mixing console. In the most disciplined studios this process took at least a half an hour and was about 90 percent reliable. When working entirely within the computer this process now takes less than a minute (the time it takes to open the file) and is 100 percent reliable.

Immediate, reliable recall allows for both a more extended and a more spontaneous relationship to the mixing process. Mixes can be listened to and critiqued over time and then easily and quickly changed without having to reset a mixing console. This increased functionality of automation and the ease of recall have created new opportunities that encourage the extension of the mixing process. It has made it easier for more people to be involved as mixes can be sent (via the Internet most frequently) to almost any location, feedback given via email, and then changes quickly made and resent for approval. It is now not uncommon for the mix process to be as lengthy as (or more lengthy than) the recording process.

Mixing is the one of the recordist's avenues to participating in the arranging and composing in a direct fashion as described above. It also provides opportunities for other creative collaborations that merge the musical and the technical. Typically in a mix session an artist may ask the recordist to make the audio sound more aggressive, or dreamier, or more magical or even more purple! The recordist has to interpret these metaphorical soundscapes and translate them into specific technical applications. Mixing is the most creative part of the technical aspects of making recordings because it requires interpretation and technical application within the context of what is often a very complex interrelationship between a wide variety of pitches, rhythms, dynamics, timbres, and ambiences. The tools available for manipulation of these elements have become enormously expanded within the realm of digital audio. "Fix it in the mix" is now so much of a reality as to have left the old satiric implication of this phrase meaningless.

From the Mixer to the Listener

Mixing is once removed from the recording process, which is once re-moved from the musical performance. It is a complex construction of sound and a convoluted process. Digital re-creations of acoustical spaces allow for simulations of ambiances not actually found in nature. Very ac-curate and discrete delayed versions of the sound source, reverbs with tails that end abruptly, and perfectly regular modulations represent unnatural acoustical phenomena that are frequently employed in mixes. Sonically the combinations of tonalities and ambiences often create acoustical impossi-bilities—sonic landscapes that could not actually exist in the physical world. The isolation of the instruments allows the mixer to place each sound in its own acoustical environment. No ensemble could possibly oc-cupy the number and variety of spaces created in many mixes. The mixing landscape is often a product of creative spatial imagination.[30]

The process is also unnatural in its dislocation from the music's tempo-ral timeline. Even prior to graphically based mix automation, the mixing engineer would frequently replay short sections of audio over and over—adjusting the mix until the engineer was satisfied with the small section. Now, adjustments are made off-line—that is, graphically against the rep-resentation of the waveform—and then listened to for effect. In either case, an outside listener at a mix session would hear bits of music played re-peatedly and sections of music played out of sequence for long periods of time before any kind of recognizable playback of the entire audio program might be heard. The music is "dressed up" for final presentation, one arti-cle of clothing and one accessory at a time, each design carefully tailored for fit and finish.

Interestingly this prompts a comparison between composing and mix-ing—the two far ends of the process that brings most music from initial creation to the form made available to the listener—as there is a disloca-tion for a composer between the process of creation and the final music as well. The composition process that is a primary means of bringing music into existence bears a close relationship to the process by which a mixer makes the final preparations for music to be heard. Because the composer is modeling when composing at the piano (or any instrument), "he hears the music as he imagines it in his 'inner ear.' "[31] If the composer tries to perform with too much emphasis on this part of the process—the inner ear—she may lose the audience who isn't hearing those connections. Sim-ilarly if a mixer focuses too much on the momentary relationships of sound, he may lose the flow of musical ideas and lose the listener. In either event, the actual compositional process (at the piano, say) and the mixing process are typically not very musical sounding when being done.

One might expect that both composing and mixing reflect a progression from the simple to the complex. Yet Beethoven often moved back and forth between simpler and more complex versions of his symphonies, finding what for him were the best choices by building from the bottom while at the same time he was editing from the top.[32] Similarly with mixing, the mixer frequently moves back and forth between focusing on an individual sound, and the building of the relationship between all the complex tonalities of an ensemble. The timbre, stereo positioning, and ambience of the flute (for example) may be set individually and then reset when placed in the context of the ensemble and then reset again when listened to in isolation at a later point. The composer imagines their creations with a kind of detail that most listeners are oblivious to, unless they study the music analytically. Like the composer, the mixer has a very intimate knowledge of the music, and the choices made in creating the mix are far beyond the understanding of the majority of listeners.

So in the end the "time-disordering operations found in a recording studio . . . become a means of exploring the temporal conditions of research and ethnographic representation,"[33] yet the same disordering operations are found in the compositional process. Thus the musicology of the creation of the contemporary recording has some direct parallels to the musicology of composition. Ultimately, as the processes of recording and composing become increasingly intertwined, we might also draw comparisons between DAWs and musical instruments, though the relationship to real-time performance is fundamentally different. But despite the dislocations of process in recording, it is the final ordering of music that may be its strongest attraction, its most basic correlation to the human condition: "What most authorities seem to agree is that music reflects in some way the order—the organization—that is necessary for the human nervous system to function."[34] And the use of a DAW is now frequently a major contributor to that ordering process.

two

{ ## Studio Study
Lipsmacks, Mouth Noises, and Heavy Breathing

Lipsmacks

This studio study continues the examination of how the presentation of popular music recordings is affected by the repurposing of audio after recording. Generally the practices described here represent a kind of "cleansing" of musical performances, as opposed to the "fixing" described in the previous application study. This study focuses on the nonverbal sounds that singers sometimes make as a part of the vocal production of singing. I have divided these vocal artifacts into three general categories: lipsmacks, mouth noises, and heavy breathing, though these are in no way intended as exhaustive.

I use the term *lipsmacks* to refer to a kind of nonverbal sound that sometimes occur between singer's words. A lipsmack is most commonly caused when a singer opens her mouth in preparation to sing. The separation of the two lips can cause an audible "smacking" or clicking type sound. This may be an occasional occurrence that passes relatively unnoticed, or it may be a common occurrence that can become a major distraction in a vocal performance. One artist that I have worked with, the blues singer Freddie Hughes,[1] is unable to stop himself from making frequent and loud lipsmacks between vocal lines. These sounds—distracting clicks that are not even identifiable as part of the vocal performance—have plagued his recordings. While they also occurred in live performance, extraneous sounds are much easier to ignore in a live setting where there are plenty of visual distractions. Prior to the advent of computer-based editing techniques, there were simply too many of these sounds, too closely placed to

Freddie's sung vocal, to remove them from the final recording. In the computer it's a relatively simple matter to remove the clicks and to create inaudible transitions around the places where the sound has been removed.

This simple action extends the sanction of the recording engineer beyond the kind of fixing discussed in chapter 1 and broadens my consideration of DAW-based alterations of musical performances. Given that nothing in a recording can be truly "original"—that is, identical to the source—what is essential to a singer's performance? Are all alterations beyond the most transparent translation of source to recording to be considered anathema? Here at the beginning I have provided one example of performance alteration that might be seen as generally positive and benign in terms of its effect on the substance of the performance. The ability to remove lipsmacks has certainly been a great relief to Freddie Hughes, as it has allowed him to make a record that didn't have a lot of distracting clicks and pops on it. The audio clips provide examples of Freddie's vocal before and after the clicks have been removed (audio clips 3, 4, 5).

Mouth Noises

By mouth noises I am referring to sounds that the mouth makes while singing certain words—artifacts of word production that are not a normal or necessary part of the word itself. Two common such artifacts are popped "p's" and excessive sibilance. Popped "p's" are created when the explosive kind of exhalation that might accompany a particularly expressive hard consonant is sung directly into a microphone ("p's" are the most common offenders, but any hard consonant might produce this effect). The effect of this exhalation is to vibrate the diaphragm of the microphone in a way that produces a relatively loud after-effect—a popped "p." As with a lipsmack, this may be perceived as a distracting, nonverbal artifact of the recording process. A popped "p" is in some sense "natural"—a result of a natural vocal occurrence—but it is so amplified and altered by its effect on the microphone as to make it "unnatural" to the ear and unique to recordings.

Thanks to the digital processing power of DAWs it is usually possible to eliminate the effect of the popped "p." This is done by isolating the popped "p" and filtering out most of the low frequencies. This generally removes the "pop"—the explosive sound that follows the initial articulation of the "p" sound—while retaining the high-frequency transients that make up the majority of the actual "p" sound. Bob Dylan's original recorded performance of "Sad-Eyed Lady of the Lowlands" contains many popped "p's" on lines such as "Where the sad-eyed prophets say that no man comes." The audio clips allow the listener to hear the original popped "p" and then the "cleaned-up" version (audio clips 6 and 7).

Is the application of this kind of editing clearly to be preferred? Is Dylan's performance more or less appealing with the popped "p's"? Does the vocal performance have more or less impact with the popped "p's"? If the popped "p's" had been removed before the record was released, would they have been missed by the listener? I will return to these questions, but first I will consider another of these types of recording artifacts.

Excessive sibilance is a part of vocal performance that may also be an artifact of recording. The enormous amount of high-frequency information in the sound of sung "esses" might be amplified by a variety of recording techniques. Compression, short delay, and high-frequency EQ[2] may all generate an unnatural level of the "s" sound in the recording of a vocal performance and may further slur and distort that "s" sound in the process. As with popped "p's" there are techniques for taming this excessive sibilance—primarily with a processing device called, appropriately enough, a "de-esser." De-essers automate a volume reduction in the sibilance, making the "esses" quieter and thus less intrusive and more in line with what their level might be in a live, acoustic performance. However, when the sibilance has undergone so much processing as to become smeared and distorted, it is not possible to "clean" it with a de-esser. The volume of the "s" may be reduced, but in these cases the recording process has changed the nature of the sound in a way that can't be undone without undoing the process, which may mean rerecording the performance. Only if the heightened "s" sound is created by processing done after the recording has been made, such as during the final mixing, would it be possible to undo this effect by a remix of the same performance in which the processing responsible for the excessive sibilance was removed.

Many modern recordings have instances of very exaggerated sibilance that could be avoided in this later mixing process. Why isn't it? Clearly some producers and artists enjoy the rather artificial effect of very pronounced sibilance. A good example is on the line "sound of hysteria" from a song by the band Green Day called "American Idiot." The strong sibilance on this line can be heard on the audio clip (audio clip 8). Perhaps the added and unnatural sibilance serves to underscore singer Billie Joe Armstrong's vitriolic sentiment and delivery. Incidentally, this degree of exaggerated sibilance would not have been possible in the age of the vinyl disc; high-frequency transients require very jagged grooves in vinyl in order to be reproduced, and if they are too prominent the needle is unable to track the grooves and the record will skip. In the age of vinyl recordings engineers had to monitor and reduce transient levels, especially sibilance, to avoid making LPs that skipped. The use of heightened sibilance as an effect is another example of how DAW production allows new forms of presentation.

In many instances the performer's relationship to the microphone—to the technology—has supplanted the primacy of his relationship to the audience, so that "while pop performers sing to an audience, real or imagined, they always sing first and foremost *to* the microphone. In return, the microphone reveals, in intimate detail, every nuance of the performer's vocal style."[3] As noted here, the microphone's interaction with the voice and the recording process may cause "unnatural" elements such as popped "p's" and excessively sibilant "esses." These sounds extend beyond the performer's vocal style in the traditional sense and may even be created without the performer being aware of them.

In regards to these kind of unnatural vocal sounds, how many people actually notice anything odd or distracting in Dylan's "p's" or Billie Joe's "esses?" Do Billie Joe's exaggerated "esses" and Dylan's explosive "p's" produce a positive or negative experience for the listener? Unlike with Freddie Hughes, where I think it's clearly an advantage to have rid ourselves of those distracting sounds, perhaps the sense of passion created by unnatural "p's" and "esses" is preferred by most listeners. There might be a heightened experience from the feeling that the listener is almost inside Dylan's mouth—and indeed it is the microphone being exceedingly close to the mouth when the recording is made that causes this effect. Are these unnaturally heightened vocal artifacts a kind of manufactured passion? Perhaps, but in all likelihood the listener simply accepts the sound of the recording without questioning whether or not it is "natural" or preferable. Whether to "clean up" the recording of these sounds or to leave them for their effect comes down to an *aesthetic* decision. For the practitioner it is an advantage to now have the tools available that allow this choice to be made based on aesthetics, rather than having been saddled with these artifacts of the recording process whether we like them or not.

Heavy Breathing

The most obvious and prevalent nonverbal sound produced by singers is the breaths between phrases. It is also here that recordists implement the most obvious and prevalent kind of manipulations of these sounds. The sense of exaggerated breathing in vocal performance may simply be part of an exaggerated performance (perhaps even a relative of the kind of heavy breathing that the phrase might first bring to mind). Vocalists may wish to emphasize the physical production of singing by dramatic emphasis of the breaths between phrases. However, there are technical aspects of recording that may also significantly affect the volume level of the singer's breaths. The most common of these is compression.

Compression reduces the overall dynamic range of a vocal performance and thereby increases the volume of quiet sounds relative to loud sounds. This means that the singer's breaths, normally quieter in volume than the actual singing, will be raised in volume and sound relatively louder. Compression is used in part to even out a vocalist's performance, to make it more consistent in level and thereby easier to follow both lyrics and vocal nuance. It is also used to add dramatic presence, to put the vocal more "in your face"—that is, by reducing the dynamic range the vocal presence is more constant and therefore feels closer. This is partially a product of close miking techniques, but it is magnified by the use of compression. The increase in volume of the breaths is part of the added presence and perhaps of the sense of drama. Is this affectation? The relative volume of the breaths is created artificially but the breaths themselves are critically real.

This phenomenon is not new to the digital age of recording and reproduction. The spectacular vocal performance on the 1970 recording of Stevie Wonder singing "Signed, Sealed, Delivered, I'm Yours" features very prominent between-line breathing that is clearly pumped up through compression (audio clip 9). However, contemporary recordings digitally created and reproduced may show even more obvious effects of compression. This is partially due to new tools of compression in the digital domain (especially a very powerful kind of compression called "brick-wall limiting")[4] and aided by the ability of CDs to reproduce denser audio than was possible on vinyl records. There are many examples of this kind of deep compression in contemporary popular music. While the effect may be heard on the entire recording it is most noticeable on the vocal—especially in the volume of the breaths. A clear example of this can be heard on the audio clip from the track "Cruel" by Tori Amos (audio clip 10).

The superior editing capabilities of computer-based audio recording have affected the status of singers' breaths. The removal or replacement of singers' breaths has become commonplace. This is a result of the kind of close scrutiny done to vocal performance—listened to and analyzed in isolation (a cappella)—combined with the simplicity of excising any element

cleanly and completely. Under these circumstances I often get singers asking me to remove certain breaths, or sometimes almost all of the breaths,
because they become self-conscious about how the breaths sound. If a particular passage sounds too empty without the offending breath I might
grab a shorter or quieter breath from a different part of the performance
and insert it. Frequently choices between breaths must be made as one edits together different takes of a vocal performance. In editing together two
lines that were not actually sung in sequence one has the choice of the
breath at the end of the first line or the breath at the beginning of the second. Manipulation or elimination of breaths has become very common in
contemporary production. A new piece of software called DeBreath has
been released that is directed solely at this process.[5] One might consider
some or all of this activity to be harmless, perhaps meaningless, or one
might consider the widespread removal of breaths to be a kind of steriliza-
tion of vocal performance. As such this activity would be in line with the
contemporary obsession with depilation, deodorants, and the like—even
something approaching a realization of the nineteenth-century fantasies of
autonomous, disembodied music. In any event, this is another example of
the more dramatic kinds of manipulation of performance made possible
by computer-based recording platforms.

What would seem clearly an advantage in removing distracting sounds
on the Freddie Hughes vocal, and a judgment call on Dylan and Green
Day, where artifacts of the recording process may or may not be perceived
as desirable, runs the gamut when it comes to breaths. From the removal
of breaths, to the replacement of an awkwardly sounding breath, to the alteration of the sound or level of breaths, one's judgment on the appropri-
ateness of such behavior may range from emphatically positive to ex-
tremely negative. Contemporary production opens many such complex
questions in regards to the relationship of original performance to final
recorded presentation. Some of the production techniques discussed here
may cause us to reevaluate these relationships, or at least to confront them
under new circumstances.

A Theoretical Basis

Roland Barthes is a valuable point of reference in attempting to draw
meaning from the manipulations of recorded audio that I've just described. In his seminal essay "The Grain of the Voice" (1977) Barthes attempts to describe what he considers the most important qualities of the

"sound" of the voice. He chooses to call these qualities "grain." Although Barthes speculates about whether he is the only one hearing this grain—he wonders whether he is hallucinating this quality that he is attempting to describe—what he does know is that if it exists, it is at the margin of our ability to describe it, and as such it is "able to bear traces of significance, to escape the tyranny of meaning."[6] This phrase "tyranny of meaning" evokes the ineffable element of the music experience. Barthes is acknowledging that while he may be attempting to describe the indescribable, he remains committed to the venture.

Barthes appeals to concerns beyond the phenomenon of vocal production (what he calls the "pheno-voice") to that place where the sound of the voice encounters language ("geno-voice"). If genotype is the genetic makeup of an organism, as opposed to its physical characteristics, then geno-voice is the underlying coding or "DNA" of vocal production. It is the essence of the voice that Barthes seeks to describe and comment on. Barthes identifies this critical subtext as residing in the kind of nonverbal aspects of vocal production that we've just been describing. What Barthes wants to hear from his singers is "the tongue, the glottis, the teeth, the mucous membranes, the nose."[7] For Barthes these are the elemental qualities of vocal production. Certainly the physicality of Dylan's "p's" and Billie Jo's "esses" participates in this subtext of vocal production. The fact that the recording process substantially alters these sounds (consciously or not)[8] opens questions of intentionality but doesn't alter their participation in Barthes's grain. And the issues that might surround their intentionality are as present for the choices made by the live performance in the studio as they are for the manipulations of the recording engineer either during or after the recorded performance. Popped "p's" and sibilant "esses" are not *just* artifacts of recording; they would not be created by the process if there weren't a certain kind of emphasis (or intentionality) on the part of the singer.

When it comes to breaths, however, Barthes isolates them as separate from the genotypical sounds made in the throat, the mouth, and the nose. He identifies breaths as part of the pheno-voice, part of vocal production, and makes it clear that the grain that he craves from singers is not just a bodily function but also physicality and sexuality. This distinction comes in the context of Barthes's discussion of two well-known concert music singers, Fischer-Dieskau and Panzera. In dismissing Fischer-Dieskau as without grain he notes that his singing is "beyond reproach . . . yet nothing seduces . . . (the diction is dramatic, the pauses, the checkings and releasings of breath, occur like shudders of passion) and hence never exceeds culture: here it is the soul which accompanies the song, not the body."[9] Whereas with Panzera, with whom Barthes perceives this elusive grain, "you never heard him *breathe* but only divide up the phrase."[10] Clearly it is not transcendence that Barthes seeks from his singers, but what is it about Panzera's unheard breath that yields this grain? I don't believe it is the actual breath that he's referring to but rather the reliance on breath for expression. He refers to the pedagogy that elevates singer's breaths to a "myth of respiration,"[11] and it is this interpretation of breaths that he wishes to deflate. He is reclaiming (at least) his own pleasure in listening to vocalists by privileging the more mundane realm of the physical and the visceral over the vaunted classical "breath."

It is difficult for me to relegate Stevie Wonder's breathing in "Signed, Sealed, Delivered, I'm Yours" to some glorified realm of spirituality or transcendence, despite Barthes's desire to dismiss singers' breaths as phenovoice. If any nonverbal sounds call up Barthes's geno-voice, this part of Wonder's performance would certainly qualify for me. Perhaps this difference from Barthes can be understood by accepting pop vocal performance as essentially different from classical. The distinction Barthes is making is in the perception of the listener, and breathing has not achieved this mythic status of supposed transcendence in pop vocal pedagogy (to the extent that such a thing exists). This might leave Wonder's breaths more free to participate in Barthes's grain, as they certainly do for me. A similar divergence from classical vocal performance is heard in the propensity toward vibratoless singing in pop music. This not only dramatically differentiates it from classical vocal style but also speaks to an aversion to the kind of pretension of interpretation that I think Barthes is hearing in classical vocalists' breathing.

Unfortunately, some of the computer-based work on nonverbal sounds tends to eliminate anything below the level of surface meaning—bits of both Barthes's pheno-voice and geno-voice are excised. The ease of computer-based editing, combined with vocalist's tendency toward self-consciousness and the recording culture's sometime obsession with a kind of perfection that promotes sterility, means that a significant number of popular recordings are "cleansed" of breaths and other artifacts either partially or completely. Yet there are also recording techniques that heighten many nonverbal sounds—the effects of compression, equalization, delay, and the like produce some of the artifacts such as the "p's" and "esses" described above. What is never really possible is a simple reproduction of what actually happened inside the singer's mouth. However, this conscious manipulation of vocal sounds that are produced at the visceral level takes us well beyond core issues of original versus copy or basic questions regarding the status of reproduction. The results are specific and unique to vocal recording and are also part of the evolution of the culture's acceptance of sounds that didn't previously exist. That is to say, the culture has come to accept the effects of heavy compression or equalization as "normal" within the context of recorded music. Our culture has absorbed these anomalies into its aural vocabulary.

Paradigms Unraveled

Barthes wants to "disengage this 'grain' from the acknowledged values of vocal music" and uses a "twofold opposition . . . theoretical, between the pheno-text and the geno-text, [and] paradigmatic, between two singers."[12] Further analysis may be balanced in this same twofold way, focusing on the practical examples above that I have observed in popular music recordings.

In his essay on musical collage, Nicholas Cook draws a link between Barthes's two essays "The Grain of the Voice" and "The Third Meaning" (which is about film analysis). Barthes calls his "third meaning" "the one 'too many,' the supplement that my intellection cannot succeed in absorbing, at once persistent and fleeting, smooth and elusive," and he labels this "*the obtuse meaning*."[13] For Barthes this is "outside (articulated) language while nevertheless within interlocution"—that is, part of the discussion but nonverbal—"a signifier without a signified, hence the difficulty in naming it."[14] Although he identifies this "obtuse meaning" within the context of his film analysis, he is clearly suggesting the same thing when describing the grain of the voice. Cook identifies this obtuse meaning as being repressed by the overt meaning—which is to say, in the context of the current discussion, that the message of the nonverbal sounds is missed as our attention is focused on the delivery of the verbal portion. What is missed in this process, according to Cook, is the "defamiliarization of the everyday; and its ineffability."[15] For Cook this resonates with other modern forms of creative expression such as surrealism. For me this calls to mind the "p's," "esses," and breaths under discussion. And though these sounds may be simply lost to listeners if they focus only on the words being sung, they may also be actually removed by the power of digital audio editing. Such removal may mean that even the *possibility* of tuning in to the ineffable is lost to the hegemony of the everyday (the lyrics alone).

Ultimately Barthes acknowledges that his idea of grain is a part of the ineffable quality of music, and, as much as he attempts to identify its qualities, music in general and grain in particular continue to resist any such identifications. Barthes opens his essay with a rhetorical question: "How, then, does language manage when it has to interpret music?" to which he answers: "Alas, it seems, very badly."[16] And to the extent that Barthes can locate grain, it is not connected primarily to linguistic expressiveness but in the close association of voice to physicality and secondarily to the intersection of the physical and the verbal. And again, the "p's," "esses," and breaths under discussion are certainly a step away from musical expression (Fisher-Dieskau) and toward the corporeal (Panzera).

In *Performing Rites* Simon Frith balances the destructive and constructive forces of the recording process in a manner that also privileges something that may be akin to Barthes's grain. In analyzing the interaction between the listener and the performer he notes, "The presence of *even* a recorded sound is the presence of the implied performer."[17] The use of "even" in this context belies the possibility of an enhanced presence of the recorded voice, and the subtext is the diminished capacity of recordings to call forth true "presence." Here again I think that we have to consider the ways that recordings might augment a singer's presence, without discounting the effect of the disembodied voice in recordings. Frith adds that the recorded performer's voice does have a strong physical presence for the listener: "the performer [is] called forth by the listener—and this is clearly a sensual/sexual presence, not just a meeting of minds."[18] And, although it is in the context of differing qualities of popular music genres (in this case the reference is to "pop"),[19] Frith acknowledges that recordings may surprise us with an added layer of intimacy: "It is as if the recording of music—its closeup effect—allows us to recreate, with even greater vividness, the 'art' and 'folk' experiences which the recording process itself destroys."[20] I especially like the use of "close-up effect" and "vividness" here to describe qualities of recordings (separate from the qualities of live performance) that might be closely linked to Barthes's vocal grain. They also describe qualities that are easily associated with the prominent "p's," "esses," and breaths that I have noted. Here Frith balances the unique powers of recording against the unique powers of live performance in a way that contradicts his previous use of "even" as a qualifier of recorded performances' ability to create presence.

Personal Hallucinations

Early in Barthes's "The Grain of the Voice" essay he asks, "Are we con-demned to the adjective? Are we reduced to the dilemma of either the predicable or ineffable?"[21] His answer is no—instead it is "better to change the musical object itself, as it presents itself to discourse, better to alter its level of perception or intellection, to displace the fringe of contact between music and language."[22] And Barthes proceeds to do just that, not only to challenge the language that is used to describe the experience of a singer's voice but to challenge what is valued in "the musical object itself" to suit his own experience (and love) of music. His analysis, however, fails to rec-ognize (or perhaps accept) the various ways the application of recording techniques may be participating in his relationship to this experience.

Here I have argued that the conscious manipulation of vocal sounds by the recording process participates in Barthes's notion of grain. I have shown that Barthes's idea of grain may be heard to reside *both* in the singer and in the recording of the singer. As the experience of grain is an individ-ual response, this is a personal vision—but it is reinforced by the culture's acceptance of sounds that have become so altered or exaggerated as to be considered new phenomena—a result of the digital age of recording and reproduction. Slowly but inexorably they have become a part of our aural vocabulary. As these sounds, especially nonverbal vocal sounds, take on new forms, they also have the potential to take on new meanings.

How did Barthes feel about the effects of recording? On the surface not very positively: "today, under the pressure of the mass long-playing record, there seems to be a flattening out of technique; which is paradoxical in that the various manners of playing are all flattened out into perfection: noth-ing is left but pheno-text."[23] But Barthes is only looking at the surface ef-fects of the recording process on some performers. Were he to have allowed his own radicalizing viewpoint that created the idea of the "grain of the voice" to be focused on some of these artifacts of vocal recordings that I have described, he might have come to a broader appreciation for the recording process. Perhaps this would have happened had he turned his at-tention to certain popular singing traditions, as opposed to Fischer-Dieskau and Panzera. This would have forced him to encounter the effects of technology: "A whole tradition of popular singing, from crooning to bossa nova, is unimaginable without the microphone."[24]

If at the outset of the essay Barthes boldly launches the discourse out past the clearly predicable, in the midst of it he feels compelled to question his endeavor. Is he reading qualities into voices? Is he the only one perceiving these sounds? "Am I hearing voices within the voice? but isn't it the truth of the voice to be hallucinated?"[25] He certainly doesn't claim to have exhausted the significance of the phonetics that he is analyzing, and thus is perhaps opening the door for the arguments I am making. For Barthes, his work is most valuable in holding "in check the attempts at *expressive reduction* operated by a whole culture against the poem and its melody."[26] He is trying to inject the creative element into his own analysis of creative expression. One may be accused of hallucinating if one strays beyond that which is easily predicable, but Barthes insists on the value, indeed the necessity of this wandering, in the study of musical meaning. This is not simply a value judgment. To look at this physicality of the voice, this grain, yields individual evaluation, but it is not "subjective": it isn't the subject that is reinforced, rather the intention is to lose the subject. It's the value that is outside of culture and "hidden behind 'I like' or 'I don't like.'"[27]

From the very beginning of sound recording the technology has interacted with the vocal source to alter the nature of the voice itself. As detailed above, contemporary recording techniques may further alter certain aspects of vocal production—especially those sounds in the mouth and throat that are of particular interest to Barthes and his notion of grain. I am arguing that these nonverbal effects, these hyperreal sounds from the mouth, also have the potential to pull us back to Barthes's poem and melody. In the end is Dylan better understood with his popped "p's"—or is Green Day's message made stronger by Billie Joe's amplified "esses"? Do these obscure or enhance our experience of these singers? In the same nonsubjective way Barthes describes, these artifacts may heighten rather than flatten, favor geno-text over pheno-text, perhaps adding grain as a part of the processing of recorded audio—though of course I may be hallucinating this. Is this "true grain" or is this artificial "grain"? Without judgment I contend that at least I, for one, do hear grain as a part of the ways recording has altered these vocal performances.[28]

So the technologies of recording may feed Barthes's abstract notion of grain. The technologies that today allow active participation in the manipulation of audio provide opportunities to eliminate or enhance elements within the ineffable grain. On the one hand the ideal of "perfection" as generated through musical "cleansing" and "fixing" is set against the notion of Barthes's elemental, geno-typical grain of musical expression. This control of performance in the face of the unknown is characteristic of a culture that has been steeped in positivism and now rides the dual crest of technology and information. On the other hand the ineffable mysteries of musical expression may be expanded in the interaction with technology. Some of the "unnatural" sounds of recording may become contributors to the underlying geno-type of Barthes's grain. Ultimately, the cultural imperatives that are exemplified by the "fixing" and "cleansing" of musical performances weigh in on both sides of the scale that balances the art of Barthes's geno-type and the artifice of his pheno-type.

three

{ Art or Artifice?

The Pendulum from Determinism to Social Construction

Determinism is a feature in various social science theories. For example, there is genetic determinism like that represented by one side of the "nature versus nurture" debate, and there is linguistic determinism whereby much of our thinking is understood to be determined by specific aspects of our particular language. Technological determinism often appears as one element in considerations of contemporary music practice. Technological determinism is a reductionist doctrine that, in its most extreme form, holds that a society's technology governs its cultural values and social structure. Consequently social and cultural changes are seen as led by technology—to use an economic model, this would be the "technology-push" theory, as opposed to the "demand-pull" theory. Technological determinism lends itself to an interpretation that puts technological development largely outside of cultural or political influence.

Opposing technological determinism is the theory of the social construction of technology. This holds that cultural phenomena such as aesthetics, politics, and economics shape both the uses of technology and the path of technological innovation. This theory emanates from the constructivist school of the sociology of scientific knowledge and posits human agency as the primary shaper of technology. This agency operates on the individual level as well as on the broader plane whereby technologies are understood to contain social structures that shape the manner in which they are used. The various arguments I have made regarding the existence and evolution of audio reproduction as manifestations of cultural longing are examples of the social constructionist point of view.

The attempt to balance technological determinism with both cultural and individual agency has been an important element in musicology. While earlier critiques often featured deterministic cautionary tales—from the warnings of the mass-cultural theorists of the Frankfurt School to the famous dictate from Marshall McLuhan, "The medium is the message"—the prominent view in more recent commentary has been to favor the social elements in understanding the position of technology. In regards to music and technology important work aimed at balancing the opposing forces of deterministic theory has been done by Paul Théberge and Timothy Taylor.

I embrace the views that favor social construction of technology, while acknowledging certain deterministic characteristics that technologies carry somewhat independently. However, the situation in contemporary music renders much of this discussion moot. Contemporary audio construction in the digital realm is so complex that it masks many of the elements and processes that are a party to the final audio program, thereby making judgments about the balance of deterministic forces impossible. *As the technology becomes more complex the processes involved in music creation are increasingly lost in the music itself.* This complexity argues for the kind of application and studio studies I undertake in this work.[1] Earlier relationships between technology and music creation or performance could be pretty transparent—such as that described by a person composing or performing at the technological wonder called the piano. Earlier composition, performance, and consumption models of all kinds are more easily traceable to technological elements such as historical series of scores, specific musical instruments, and particular reproduction technologies.

Thomas Porcello recognizes that while at one time recordings represented the fixing (in the sense of permanency) of a performance that was originally understood to be inviolable, currently "Reworkings of all kinds are increasingly, of course, a staple practice of popular music production and consumptions, as well as a driving force behind audio technology design and development."[2] He then asks whether "the shift from analog to digital recording has hyperbolized a process that was already underway before its advent."[3] My simple answer, expanded over most of my work here and understood under the terminology of "repurposing," is an unequivocal *yes*.

Outside of academia the weighing of this tension between determinism and voluntarism (individual agency) continues to frequently lean more toward the pessimism of a deterministic viewpoint. *New Yorker* music critic

Alex Ross wrote a 2005 article for the magazine titled "The Recording Effect: How Technology Has Transformed the Sound of Music" and the title itself suggests a deterministic position, though in the article he presents a fairly balanced viewpoint between what he terms the "party of doom" and the "technological utopians." Ross's piece draws from recent academic works that promote the social constructionist point of view and place agency in the pivotal position of control, a view summarized by Ross: "The machine is a mirror of our needs and fears."[4] But Ross concludes his essay by suggesting that "The fact that the Beatles broke up three years after they disappeared into the studio, and the fact that Gould died in strange psychic shape at the age of fifty, may tell us all we need to know about the seductions and sorrows of the art of recording."[5] I wrote to Ross and complained of his rather pessimistic and deterministic concluding remarks. I suggested that on behalf of the countless musicians for whom the contemporary recording environment is a wonderland of musical opportunity I would have hoped for a different ending for his piece. He responded with an apology for his "doomy" final words:

> Sometimes the piece simply ends of its own accord, as if it has a mind of its own. Recording is a subject on which it is very easy to go round in endless circles and this is simply the particular point on which I chose to stop. Perhaps I was just in a bad mood that day! I hope I made it clear in the piece that there is really no hard answer to any of these questions.[6]

Examples of technological determinism are found in relation to all contemporary media. In a 2007 article, also in *The New Yorker,* the film critic David Denby expresses a deterministic attitude toward movie technology. In Denby's celebration of the movie theater the primary attributes of the experience emanate from the screen itself: "The movie theatre is a public space that encourages private pleasures: as we watch, everything we are— our senses, our past, our unconscious—reaches out to the screen. The experience is the opposite of escape; it is more like absolute engagement."[7] This judgment is based on a historical relationship to movie technology and the movie experience. It is a socially constructed form of nostalgia that reads as determinism. The hidden message in many expressions of technological determinism is nostalgia. Ultimately, even the most mildly stated views of technological determinism must be understood as historically contingent. It is social construction that forms much of the response to technological qualities even though there appear to be qualities of the technology that are independent. For example, listening to an iPod may be an isolating experience; however, the response to that "isolation" is socially and historically constructed (and users have found communal iPod strategies such as sharing earbuds and playlists). Had the digital experience, which Denby rails against, preceded the analog experience, what would the claims about the inherent qualities of various platforms be? Denby also bemoans the movie theater's diminishing presence in the culture and claims that "No exhibition method is innocent of aesthetic qualities. Platform agnosticism may flourish among kids, but platform neutrality doesn't exist."[8] It's true that technologies contain aesthetic elements—they are not neutral—but our response to them is not neutral either. It is, at least in part, socially constructed rather than embedded in the technology.

So is the contemporary kid really "platform agnostic"—or are they simply accepting the various platforms offered on a neutral basis? Will they ultimately develop the same kind of nostalgia for the dominant paradigm of their youth at some later point in their life? Will they bemoan whatever the platform used by their children? Perhaps they will even condemn it as isolating when set in contrast to their iPod experience, which they shared with their friends via docking stations, iTunes libraries, links on their MySpace page, and so forth. Certainly the technology influences the aesthetic experience—it is not agnostic in the absolute sense—but the meaning attached to the quality of experience is inseparable from the social construction.

The Network of Audio Presentation

Various deterministic arguments regarding specific recording technologies may be countered with a more complete understanding that emphasizes voluntarism and in the process suggests a network of reciprocity between technology and agency. In critiques of the early evolution of sound recording the simple manifestation of the complex relationships required for innovation and invention is credited with an outsized authority. Thus, what Sterne calls "impact narratives" such as "The telephone changed the way we do business" or "The phonograph changed the way we listen to music" belie a deeper relationship between technological advance and the larger cultural context that includes "material, economic, technical, ideational, practical, and environmental changes."[9] The deterministic and myopic impact narrative is characterized by an incomplete notion of causality. These machines represent the tangible manifestations of complex relationships, but they are the result of an intricate mixture of cultural, social, and physical activities. The technologies did not just develop willy-nilly, leaving various capabilities in their wake. They were in part the manifestation of human desire—wishes that innovation, invention, and the network of interaction translated into devices capable of the reproduction and manipulation of sound. All of this suggests the ways that *audio recording technology is intertwined with the creative activity that produces art,* though it might typically be classified as artifice or even as a kind of deception.

The effects of the cultural desire for sound reproduction are also apparent in the social organizations that were developed around the early technologies. As people strove to create more accurate reproduction they also altered the source material to make it more suitable for reproduction. One could argue that this began with the very first recording. Edison may have chosen "Mary Had A Little Lamb" because it would be easily recognizable through the noise and low fidelity of the reproduction. Contemporary singers are trained in microphone technique, and instrumentalists are trained to play less dynamically for studio recordings to help maintain consistent recording levels. Reciprocity is essential in the interaction between an original and its duplication—it is a two-way street.[10] The hierarchy of source and copy is mitigated by recognition of the reciprocity. This suggestion of hierarchy in source and copy is an outgrowth of the nineteenth-century concept of individual creativity, both ideas sourcing a monological concept of authority. Rather than as hierarchy, production and reproduction are better understood as mutuality—with a commonality of cultural interaction. Early recordings focused on distinct audio events such as speeches partly because of the simplicity of the audio source. Musical recordings were selected and even arranged with the same sonic simplicity in mind, in part responding to technological demands, such as the need to be able to position all of the musicians close to the recording horn. The recording studio is itself an artifact of the desire to create "originals" most suited to reproduction. These are the same motivations reflected in the desire to "fix" contemporary audio—to make it more "listenable" by contemporary standards. Whereas previous generations focused on alterations in fidelity and performance in order to create what were considered to be higher quality recordings, contemporary practice focuses on manipulating the already recorded sounds: "the drive to achieve 'fidelity' in recording involved a clash of cultures, and the combination of science and aesthetics pulled recording technology in different ways. In the end, the use of technology to preserve elite culture became less important than the technological manipulation of sound to produce popular culture."[11]

It is the recordist who is at the center of these sound manipulations that are essential to the production of popular music culture. Many, including Toynbee, seem to have focused on the negative influence of recordists as part of the networking of reproduction: "musicianship is at odds with the values of the engineer."[12] Jacques Attali bitterly attacks the networking process that he believes has made musicians complicit with the sound engineer's concern for "the clinical purity of the acoustics," turning it into a new aesthetics that robs music of its energy, making it into "information free of noise."[13] But both arguments fail to recognize the connection between the evolution of studio production and the creative process. The network of popular music creation blurs the roles of recordist, musician, and composer. The performer is becoming the technician and in doing so is becoming the composer and more specifically the recomposer. And though this may mean fixing and manipulating further toward so-called perfection, that in itself might be seen as a compositional aesthetic. Sometimes that compositional aesthetic incorporates plenty of noise—noisy old samples and loops of old performances and the like, placed together with "perfect" drum machine parts and pitch-fixed vocals. It is as brave a new world of composition as Attali hopes for later in his work, but not in opposition to the aesthetic of the sound engineer that he decries. Instead it comes through the evolution of the work of the recordist, through the integration of performance and composition with the technical aspects of creating sound.

In general terms, as Lysloff and Gay argue, "technologies become saturated with social meaning as they acquire a history of use."[14] When technologies are interfacing with the creative arts this social meaning may find itself in conflict with much more deeply embedded social conceptions. As Tim Warner notes, the networking of musical creation may stand at odds with deeply ingrained notions of the artist: "The transposition of the Romantic notion of the artist as inspired individual into popular culture is undermined by the reality of pop music production, which is almost invariably the result of teamwork."[15] The breakdown in these traditional musicological conceptions involves more than simply embracing the fact of the network of musical functions that began in popular music production but which now encompasses musical creation in all genres. And the networks of function encompass more than technological mediation, the whole notion of creativity *must* now expand to include group work. This lifts creativity to a truly collaborative status—beyond the hegemony of the individual and beyond the notion of intertextuality that acknowledges outside influences. At the same time, technology itself has created its own mythologies that color the evaluation of current musical practices.

Analog and Digital: Which Is More of a Copy?

Musicology struggles with notions that have become ingrained within thinking about the technologies of recording. The network that forms the social process of sound reproduction creates reciprocity between all the elements so that even the distinction between original and copy begins to dissolve.[16] These relationships continue to break down the dichotomy between art and artifice and, to some extent, they are reflected in the contemporary debate over analog and digital recordings.

Since the advent of the CD and its eclipsing of the LP and the cassette as the primary delivery medium for commercial music, professionals and consumers have debated the relative merits of the two technologies. From a convenience standpoint there is little doubt that the CD is vastly superior, and it is much more robust in terms of reliability as well. But what about sound quality? Which sounds better, digital or analog? Here, of course, subjective judgments abound and opinions vary widely. In the early days of the CD one often heard complaints that digital sounds "cold and brittle" whereas analog sounds "warm." On the other hand some argued that digital sounds "clear and accurate" whereas analog sounds "cloudy and noisy." Technically there is a difference and it may be audible, though there is so much variation between different digital or analog reproduction technologies that it may be very difficult to distinguish between the effect of those technologies and the quality of the sound of the digital and analog source material. Regardless, the differences in judgment regarding sound reproduction are so *historically contingent* and so culturally based that meaning cannot be reduced to technical terms.

There are those who have argued for an ontology that separates the status of recording elements and they have made value judgments regarding digital audio technology as a result. Rothenbuhler and Peters in "Defining Phonography" argue that analog recordings "contain traces of the music [and therefore] there is an unbroken chain from the sound in the living room to the original sound as recorded."[17] This results from the physical relationship between the analog production of sound by the performer and its analog recording. They argue that because digital recording is removed from the physical or vibrational quality of the source, it is ontologically more distant. This analysis points to facts regarding digital recording technology, but this is only one way of understanding sound—one that bypasses the many shifting cultural referents, and that is not sufficient to grant analog and digital recording an ontology of their own. One might come to an opposing viewpoint by arguing essentially the same point— that there are inherent positive or negative qualities in the technologies themselves.

Andrew Goodwin, in his essay "Sample and Hold: Pop Music in the Age of Digital Reproduction," does just that, and thereby makes the same error while arguing the opposing viewpoint. He claims "digital recording techniques now ensure that the electronic encoding and decoding that takes place in capturing and then reproducing sound is such that there is no discernible difference between the sound recorded in the studio and the signal reproduced on the consumer's CD system."[18] He believes that this represents something new: the mass production of the aura, which is an unexpected but nonetheless fatal blow that confirms Benjamin's supposed prediction of the death of aura. That is, the supposed "aura" of the original is further debased by "the fact that *everyone* may purchase an 'original.'"[19] By ignoring the social dynamics of the process, he credits an artifact in the evolution of fidelity with an essence that suggests an ontological status. Though this argument grants a quality to digital recording that is the opposite of the one ascribed by Rothenbuhler and Peters, it fails for the same reason. Sound reproduction can have no essence outside of its interaction with its culture and its time.

Goodwin extends the reach of digital audio reproduction all the way to the point of crediting it with "the capacity to break the barrier between the original and the copy."[20] Again, this is an ontological assertion that falters under both technical and cultural scrutiny. The network of reproduction provides a much more subtle and complex relationship between original and copy, but the distinction between the two can never be completely removed. Technologically speaking the allure of digital has already been proven to be at least flawed in terms of fidelity—see Rothenbuhler and Peters above. Culturally the network itself describes the separation between original and copy at the same time as it defines the interrelationships. The unique status of original and copy is assured, but so is their close association.

In *The Recording Angel* Evan Eisenberg notes that "perfect preservation is a matter not simply of technology, but of ontology as well."[21] Perhaps so, and perhaps because perfect preservation is not possible, we are forced to leave an essentializing ontology out of the picture. Instead an ontology that recognizes historical contingencies is the appropriate model for understanding the nature of recordings.

Meaning and Musical Accuracy

Musical meaning changes over time; it is historically contingent rather than universal. Just as musical meaning is not inherent, so the relationship of recording to what is reproduced is culturally connected, and cultural value may be located in the mediation itself. This ongoing interaction between music and culture applies to "fixing" as well as to more traditional kinds of musical construction. How we hear "fixed" audio is, at least in part, a response within a historical context. Certainly the sense of musical "stability" that results from harmonic relationships refined by Auto-Tune and the emotional impact of "perfect" drum parts are both moving targets. As musical "fixing" becomes more pervasive the notion of artifice become further entrenched in most contemporary expressions of the art of music.

As Tia DeNora points out (referencing Hennion), there is a basic problem if one is "finding in the 'music itself' the very things analysis has reflexively brought to bear on it"[22] because there is no such thing as "music itself." Analysis itself is creating content, and thus the "value, authenticity, meaning and effect"[23] are interesting, not as any kind of intrinsic quality, but in terms of how they are identified or referred to by others. This again speaks to the cultural connectedness and hence the historicity of musical meaning, to its existence as a human construction and not as a natural phenomenon. "Simply put, a sociology of musical effect cannot presume to know what music causes."[24] I would add the same caveat for the effects of musical "fixing." The pendulum has already swung widely in acceptance of the kind of fixing I detail in the previous production studies.

What then can be said about musical meaning? For Pacey nature itself may be better understood through music: "There is in nature an element of the spontaneous and the purposive such as we also experience in music."[25] He also uses the musical experience (in this case of Bach) as an analogy for the way we may participate in technological development: "in such music, then, experience of regular, predictable, caused events coexists with perceptions of spontaneous, exuberant change, and perhaps of purpose."[26] These sweeping generalizations may resonate on a human level while avoiding the kind of overreaching inherent in analysis that seeks to connect specific musical constructions with similar levels of human response.

Just as Pacey's experience reflects this broad interaction between technology and music, so is it mirrored in the experience of music reproduction and manipulation. Recording technologies affect our musical experience in ways that may not be separable from the music itself. In fact, some argue that creation of a sound landscape through manipulation of the sounds has overtaken attempts at accurate reproduction of musical performance such that "production values are at the core of the aesthetic."[27] By the same token, the application of sonic manipulation obscures the distinction between "natural" musical sounds (acoustic instruments) and their electronic counterparts as a result of all the processing. For example Théberge notes that "the difference between the sound of processed acoustic drums and their electronic counterparts can be quite negligible."[28] Thus *recordings symbolize rather than imitate performances,* while at the same time standing on their own as musical artifacts. Clearly these qualities of sound affect the experience, and like the specifics of the musical expression, they enhance but do not define the meaning.

As technology has advanced the recording process, and ultimately yielded the ability to manipulate audio to the extent described in the application study above, the relationship between technological effect and musical performance, between artifice and art, now becomes *hopelessly* blurred. The expectation is changed by the technology, which is in turn changed by the expectations (desires) of human agency, driving the creation of new technologies. Similarly the cycles of what is taken for DeNora's "value, authenticity, meaning and effect"[29] follow this shifting cultural relationship to the technology of "fixing." Adorno argues for the unintended effect of artificiality as a positive influence on the sense of humanity in a recording—as described by Slavoj Žižek:

> In "The Curves of the Needle," a short essay on the gramophone from 1928, Adorno notes the fundamental paradox of recording: the more the machine makes its presence known (through obtrusive noises, its clumsiness and interruptions), the stronger the experience of the actual presence of the singer—or, to put it the other way round, the more perfect the recording, the more faithfully the machine reproduces a human voice, the more humanity is removed, the stronger the effect that we are dealing with something "inauthentic."[30]

While Adorno may be seeking relief from what he considers an essential flaw in all recordings, pop music icon David Byrne acknowledges something related regarding contemporary music production: "There's nothing naturalistic about it. Hasn't been for years. In fact, sometimes there's an obvious pride in creating something that is profoundly un-naturalistic, completely artificial sounding."[31] The difference here is the assumed acceptance of the entire process of creative artifice. Per Adorno we are reassured by the obviousness of the artifice, whereas for the contemporary listener we are stimulated by it. "Fixing" provides a similar level of reassurance for the listener in acknowledging the humanity of the producer's influence. The awareness of "fixing" is a part of this valued construction of production. We are both *reassured* and *stimulated* by it.

Relativity and Authenticity

The historically contingent nature of music appreciation is made apparent through the lens provided by reproduction. It is clearly illustrated in one of the earliest recordings. A 1902 recording of the last known castrato—Alessandro Moreschi—provides ample evidence:

> That the practice and tone of Italian solo singing can have changed so dramatically in under a century, so that what was then considered breathtakingly beautiful, subtle and stylish, should to our ears sound like an appalling caterwauling, as if the act of castration were actually being performed during the recording session, is a sobering warning for all musicians currently engaged in the re-creation and study of "authentic" music performances.[32]

Cycles of acceptance and rejection, of praise and scorn, of respect and ridicule have been repeated many times in the short history of mechanical reproduction. John Philip Sousa and others who disdained recording altogether, only to release recordings within a few years of claiming them worthless, mark the constantly shifting relationship that Lawrence Levine chronicles in *Highbrow/Lowbrow*. A more contemporary cycle, driven by the effects of recordings themselves, was already noted in the progression from ridicule to widespread acceptance of the drum machine in popular music production.

Understanding the evaluation of music in this way suggests that the word *authentic* is a problematic musical qualifier. One of the dictionary definitions is "not imaginary, false or imitation."[33] This sense of the word is irreconcilable with the subtleties of historical influence that are apparent in the study of recordings. Authentic music must then be somehow free of imitation—but if musicology has done anything it has at least shown that such a state of "pure" music is impossible. The dictionary also provides these examples of usage for the word: "an authentic colonial home" and "an authentic reproduction of a colonial home."[34] Under these guidelines the word *authentic* may either contain or exclude the idea of imitation. In musical terms this may be thought of as either original (not imitative) or as a part of a musical tradition (a form of imitation). When used in order to pass judgment on musical expression, as the term *authenticity* often is, this could cause one to confuse the sense in which music may be both original and derivative at the same time. This may be most obvious in the repetition of the standard repertoire of concert music or in an artist's version of another writer's song, but music is *always* a blend of originality and imitation. Thus the term *authentic,* when used to describe musical performance or recording, must be used as a relative concept—more or less authentic, yes, but simply authentic, never. For example, a particular recent recording might be said to be a relatively more authentic evocation of, say, 1930s big band jazz, than some other recent recording. This kind of relative scaling and specific reference is necessary to sufficiently qualify the sense in which the word *authentic* is being used.

The power of the recording itself may be seen in a political context, and therefore moves musical performance beyond any notion of musical authenticity. As with the rapid acceptance of drum programming, the power of reproduction itself may create cycles of credibility. Jacques Attali traces this kind of power to the earliest of reproductions of the word:

> Recording has always been a means of social control, a stake in politics, regardless of the available technologies. Power is no longer content to enact its legitimacy; it records and reproduces the society it rules. Stockpiling memory, retaining history or time, distributing speech, and manipulating information has always been an attribute of civil and priestly power, beginning with the Tables of the Law. But before the industrial age, this attribute did not occupy center sage: Moses stuttered and it was Aaron who spoke. But there was already no mistaking: the reality of power belonged to he who was able to reproduce the divine word, not to he who gave it voice on a daily basis. Possessing the means of recording allows one to monitor noises, to maintain them, and to control repetition within a determined code. In the final analysis, it allows one to impose one's own noise and to silence others.[35]

Powerful, yes, and Attali suggests the powers of reproduction that apply far beyond the musical experience. Those experiences may be influenced by outside factors; they are forever being altered by technological, cultural, and historical variations in their presentation, but ultimately musical recordings yield nothing more profound than the individuality of the experience of musical performance. In the twenty-first century the meaning of musicianship is undergoing some fairly radical redefinitions as it is heavily filtered through its interaction with technology, but the inappropriateness of a historical claim to authenticity remains.[36]

It may be helpful to be reminded that even the experience of the auditory sensation is now recognized as hopelessly intermixed with sensations in general. Oliver Sacks tells us: "There is increasing evidence from neuroscience for the extraordinarily rich interconnectedness and interactions of the sensory areas of the brain, and the difficulty, therefore, of saying that anything is purely visual or purely auditory, or purely anything."[37] Similarly, we must put to rest any notion of musical authenticity that is in any way absolute or undiluted.

Auto-Tune Is a Musical Instrument

In the introduction to this book I reference Brian Eno's call to consider the studio as a musical instrument, and later, in a different context, I will note Paul Théberge's observation regarding the transformation of the turntable into a musical instrument. I imagine that the notion of what constitutes music creation has been challenged by the introduction of new musical instruments from prior to the time of written history. One might be surprised then by the cultural resistance to new musical means of expression, but this would be to underestimate the strength of cultural norms and the power of nostalgia. "The introduction of new technologies and instruments provides a way of probing and breaching the often taken for granted norms, values, and conventions of musical culture."[38] This observation from frequent writers about technology Pinch and Bijsterveld is followed by the observation that "the significance of any individual instrument has been dwarfed in the 20th century by the dramatic changes in the way that music is recorded, stored, and consumed."[39] I agree with both assertions, and the second statement should be extended to include the notion that what constitutes a musical instrument is intertwined with these dramatic changes to the way contemporary music is created.

Studio technologies and musical instruments are now linked together as never before, further expanding the notion of what constitutes music expression. This is one step beyond Eno's notion of the recording process as a partner in music creation and challenges the notion of music in ways well beyond the question of what constitutes a musical sound. Just as I have argued for the blurring of roles in the creating of music, we are now witnessing the blurring of functions between technologies intended as transparent tools of production and those intended as musical instruments. As new territories are explored, the tension between art and artifice often returns to center stage.

Ever since its introduction Auto-Tune has been controversial. I chronicled its use on a specific project in chapter 1 and noted its widespread application as a means of "fixing" the pitch of vocal performances. "Right now, if you listen to pop, everything is in perfect pitch, perfect time and perfect tune," says producer Rick Rubin. "That's how ubiquitous Auto-Tune is."[40] In a spate of recent high-profile magazine articles this legacy of Auto-Tune is recounted in a fashion of which the following is typical:

> Most of the time, Auto-Tune is used imperceptibly, to correct flat or sharp notes. The New York producer Tom Beaujour, who records rock bands that sound nothing like contemporary R. & B. or pop, says that it gets used, in one way or another, in almost every session that he works on. Often, it solves logistical problems: an artist has left the studio and has no opportunity to return just to re-sing one or two off notes.[41]

However, recent widespread news reporting about Auto-Tune has been primarily motivated by the success of the work done by the rapper T-Pain, who has used Auto-Tune in a very dramatically apparent way—as a musical instrument really, rather than as a tool to fix vocals.

Something similar to the effects being explored by T-Pain had been done previously (and famously) using Auto-Tune on a 1998 track from Cher ("Believe") but it had received such negative attention that there hadn't been much use of Auto-Tune as a compositional tool—an instrument of sorts—until the emergence of T-Pain in 2005. Since then many well-known artists have used Auto-Tune in this much more apparent fashion, recomposing their vocal performances in ways that would be impossible for a singer to do with the natural voice. The transition from transparent production tool to T-Pain's work is called "ironic" by a writer for the *Washington Post*,[42] but where is the irony? Is it ironic because the tool has been used in ways that it wasn't originally intended to be? Is it ironic because we expect behind-the-scenes studio manipulation but have more trouble accepting obvious sonic manipulations? It is surprising but the "meaning" of this use of Auto-Tune is intended. Rather than ironic this is typical of human agency doing the unexpected with technology. It is emblematic of the never-ending progression from the vilified to the integrated in new forms of musical expression. The variety of views expressed in the magazine articles indicate that we are somewhere in the midst of this process now—still maligned in some corners but increasingly accepted by artists and audiences. This represents a recent progression that is similar to the one I chronicled elsewhere in this book in regards to drum machines and iPods. Each of these narratives constitutes some of the probing and breaching of musical conventions suggested by Pinch and Bijsterveld.

As also noted previously, the popular press tends toward the deterministic even as cultural critics have migrated heavily toward the cultural construction of technological effect. Some of the commentary on T-Pain's use of Auto-Tune attempts to have it both ways at once, disparaging the process as gimmick while in the same breath granting it creative significance: "Auto-Tune is the rare gimmick that can lead to innovation."[43] Yet that same writer, in *Time* magazine, hits a firmly deterministic and pessimistic note about the effect of the originally intended and widespread use of Auto-Tune: "It's hits that matter, and the average person listening to just one pop song on the radio will have a hard time hearing Auto-Tune's impact; it's effectively deceptive. But when track after track has perfect pitch, the songs are harder to differentiate from one another— which explains why pop is in a pretty serious lull at the moment."[44]

This is quite a leap of deterministic thinking—damning the entire state of pop music on the basis of a very specific technological effect. But it isn't just the critics who are jumping on the anti-Auto-Tune bandwagon. At the Fifty-first Grammy Awards the band Death Cab for Cutie wore blue ribbons on their sleeves to protest the use of Auto-Tune.[45] This would seem to me to be rather self-serving and narrow-minded thinking. Perhaps the band would like all audiences to yield to their "alternative" and "authentic" sound, but is the perceived failure of contemporary pop to be distinctive or innovative or "authentic" to be laid at the feet of Auto-Tune? Or for that matter is there any justification in seeing it as a particularly contemporary issue, rather than a part of the endless cycle of pop music's thesis and antithesis, innovation and recapitulation? As I indicated in describing the use of Auto-Tune in chapter 1, there are clear examples where Auto-Tune may allow an artist to salvage an extraordinary performance (though of course the definition of "salvage" may be at issue). Many artists and recordists consider Auto-Tune to be an essential part of the creative process. And

these questions only speak to issues regarding Auto-Tune when used in ac-
cordance with its initial intention. What about T-Pain and Auto-Tune as
musical instrument?

Vocal effects created by external technologies have been around for
quite awhile, from the Voice box (used famously by Peter Frampton to
make his guitar sound like a voice) to the Vocorder (used by many elec-
tronica artists as well as Pink Floyd, Prince, Madonna, etc., and employing
similar technology to Auto-Tune). So why is the current use of Auto-Tune
receiving so much attention? The writer from the *Washington Post* con-
trasted responses to T-Pain's success with recomposed vocals via Auto-Tune
in this way: "some purists saw [it] as yet another sign of the digital-music
apocalypse. The alternate view: Making your singing voice sound like a
Speak & Spell that's been submerged in a bathtub is no different from a
guitarist using a wah-wah pedal to tweak the timbre of an instrumental
line or a whammy bar to bend the pitch of a note."[46]

The *New Yorker* critic Sasha Frere-Jones speaks directly in favor of this
alternate view. He minimizes the significance of what is being created by
Auto-Tune, noting that "there is nothing natural about recorded music"
and that "T-Pain's deployment of Auto-Tune is a similar assertion of self,
no different in kind from the older, more traditional tricks of tape-splic-
ing, double-tracking the voice, and adding a little reverb."[47] Here I dis-
agree. No different in intention than the technologies mentioned by Frere-
Jones, and certainly an assertion of self, but indeed different in kind.
Frere-Jones's "more traditional tricks" of pop music production never call
into question the fundamental nature of vocal production. Other experi-
mental techniques have done so (vari-speeding vocals to produce wild, un-
singable effects, for example) but in popular music the essential "realness"
of vocal production, even when tweaked for pitch accuracy by the normal-
functioning Auto-Tune, has never been challenged in any mainstream and
widely accepted recordings. The Auto-Tune of Cher and T-Pain, and their
successors, opens new doors to the creative expression of vocal melody in
the same way that drum machines and sampled loops have in rhythm construction—and the same cycle from derision to appreciation to admiration
is in evidence.

The contemporary landscape is littered with conflicted ideas regarding
the vast new horizons of music creation, as well as with the notions of musical "fixing" and performance "cleansing." Although these new capabilities seem radical—and they are new—it is not difficult to imagine a future
when even much greater degrees of control over subtle elements of musi-

cal performance become available. Technologies that model all different kinds of performance subtleties including vocal resonance and timbre have already appeared. Along with these practices will come the aesthetic reactions to technologies, such as we see in certain popular music lo-fi recording aesthetics and in genres such as bluegrass that emphasize acoustic music and naturalistic recordings of live performances. Today's cultural terrain can accommodate many aesthetics at the same time, but the dominant trends in popular music suggest a continued reliance on the current flood of technology. Rap, hip-hop, alt rock, and even so-called world music ride the waves of technology and artifice that include Auto-Tune, Beat Detective, and DeBreath. Most of contemporary popular music presentation is the result of a process of construction, where music is built from all different kinds of materials, both new and repurposed. The house that music lives in is continually subjected to add-ons and additions; new furniture is moved into existing rooms, and old furniture is repaired to spiff up the environment. The musical house is repaired and scrubbed to meet contemporary living standards. What might be considered artifice—but what is better defined by a less pejorative term such as *construction*—becomes an increasingly pervasive tool in the production of music. What the musical model home of the future will sound like is, as always, unknown.

part two { Repurposing Performance

Introduction to Part II

Part II considers the musical performance as integrated into and transformed by the contemporary recording process. The temporal dislocation of music recordings from the listener has forever altered the nature of musical performance. The evolution of the recording process has been accompanied by an equally profound evolution in the nature and meaning of musical performance. Along with advanced technical capabilities has come an increased interaction between the recordist and the performer. In the following chapters many ways that performance has been repurposed as an element in the new recording paradigm are considered—from a futuristic collaboration that reimagines jazz improvisation to the unpredictable nature of recording that may allow for the capture of an intimate personal performance.

The application study (chapter 4) takes the spontaneous, improvisational nature of jazz and integrates elements of chance and imagination, while dramatically increasing the role of the recordist. It exploits the vastly expanded editing capabilities of DAW to elevate the role of editor to active participant as arranger and even composer. This process also inserts the recordist into the improvisational process of traditional jazz. The work here serves to "play against type"—to stretch the bounds of an existing idiom in unexpected and perhaps controversial ways and to blur the distinctions and deepen the collaboration between musician and recordist. This application study sets the stage for a discussion of the evolving role of the musician in the world of computer-based audio production.

The studio study (chapter 5) examines how one particular performance was recorded and how it captured an unexpected but treasured musical moment. The studio study furthers the notion that the performing musician is now, more than ever, a part of a network of participants and that within that network, technology has enabled an ever-expanding function for the recordist. In both studies spontaneity is the link between improvisation and the unintentional, and the intervention of the recordist is an essential part of making that connection. I challenge the reductive attitude toward reproduction that views recording primarily in its distinction from live performance.

In the conventional understanding of the terms, an artist is identified primarily with creation and an artisan primarily with craft—separating the two as a result. Is the composer an artist and the performer an artisan? For performers, what is the dividing line between interpretation and improvisation, and does this factor into some division between art and craft? Ellington may be nearly as canonized as Beethoven but both are primarily known as composers. In both jazz and classical music the performers—the interpreters—have also risen to a certain level of icon status, whether Rubenstein and Heifetz or Miles and Coltrane. In literature Barthes suggests: "The image of literature to be found in ordinary culture is tyrannically centered on the author, his person, his life, his tastes his passion";[1] at the same time, "to give writing its future, it is necessary to overthrow the myth: the birth of the reader must be at the cost of the death of the Author."[2] Whether Barthes is correct or not regarding the reader (or listener), in music there is the additional element of the performer to contend with. Does the rising control of the performer and recordist over so many compositional elements herald the "death" of the iconic composer before the music even reaches its audience?

Notions about where authorship ends and craftsmanship begins are further complicated by the nature of improvisation, and are all the more in question as composition and improvisation increasingly interact with the recording process. Issues surrounding musical form also get caught up in the collaboration between the composer, the arranger, the improviser, and the recordist. The arguments in the final chapter of Part II (chapter 6) do not attempt to answer the question of how we might distinguish between artist and artisan. Rather, they further the argument that such a distinction is moot.

four

{ Application Study
  Jazz Piano Trio

Conceptualizing the Recording Project

Early in 2005 I conceived of a recording project that involved a jazz trio of piano, acoustic bass, and drums. I wished to use the expanded capabilities of computer-based recording technology to explode the conventions of traditional, improvisational jazz, without the results being apparent in the final recording. I began with a jazz piano trio that had a history of playing together. We selected a familiar jazz standard, one not especially associated with a particular artist or recording. We agreed upon a basic arrangement of song sections and solos, and a tempo for the recording of this composition. I then recorded each individual musician separately, at different times and without the other musicians present. Each musician listened to a click track so there would be tempo consistency between all the performances. Because the horizontal arrangement was charted out for the musicians, the performances lined up as far as the chordal structure was concerned and each had an idea about what part of the performance he was in (e.g., statement of melody, piano solo, etc.). This consistency in rhythm and harmony ultimately allowed all of the parts to be edited together. I was the only person to hear the musicians play their parts or interact with them regarding their performances. I then constructed a version of the composition that drew from elements of multiple individual takes from each musician. Finally I sent the musicians the completed version of the recording and got their responses to the work we had done together.

The ability to conduct this project was completely dependent upon the new capabilities provided by the DAW. This technology provides potential for enormous shifts in responsibilities as well as providing vast new capabilities. This is summarized well by the producer/composer Brian Eno: "The technologies we now use have tended to make creative jobs do-able by many different people: new technologies have the tendency to replace skills with judgment—it's not what you *can* do that counts, but what you *choose* to do, and this invites everyone to start crossing boundaries."[1] In this process I have both replaced skills with judgment—from performance interaction to editing judgments; and I have shifted key portions of the creative work, from improviser to recordist.

I am crossing musical boundaries by borrowing from genres that are steeped in these new methods of constructing compositions and adapting them to the world of jazz improvisation. Of the popular genres, dance music is often pointed to as the ultimate in production where "musicians have become little more that raw material which is manipulated, transformed, and recomposed in the studio itself."[2] Jazz is usually considered to be at the opposite end of such studio construction, so my project challenges some of the basic assumptions of the idiom. A key difference between this project and dance music construction is that the final recording is not meant to sound constructed. It is not meant to point to its own process in the way that dance music announces its constructive nature; instead it retains the sound of traditional jazz.

This project also resonates with "found" music, *musique concrète,* and other avant-garde musical conceptions. It uses technology to create music in unexpected ways, in this case also seeking to "hide" this process from the listener. Ultimately the conceptual aspect is intended to shock and surprise the listener after the initial experience of the recording—as was sometimes true of these earlier uses of technology that stretched the bounds of music construction. Theoretically these practices are in line with DeNora's observations regarding the interaction between music and culture. She suggests that technologies may "structure use and users [but] artefacts do not *compel* users to behave in preferred or prescripted ways."[3] The freedom to break from traditions is a part of the gift of human imagination.

My project has particular significance in its relationship to one of the hallmarks of jazz—the practice of improvisation. My approach here bypasses the immediate temporal interaction and becomes a kind of improvisation of the imagination on the part of the musicians and an improvisation of construction (editing) on my part. To the extent that "patterns of perception, modes of attention, structures of feeling and habits of mind are inculcated in and through musical media"[4] these qualities are meant to be expanded by the notion of improvisation. And the qualities of improvisation are intended to be expanded here by escalating the importance of imagination and chance. In traditional jazz improvisation, imagination and chance play an important role but they are guided by the temporal exchange between musicians. Here the imagination must take center stage and the musician is forced into new modes of thinking about the progression of improvised ideas. With this model, it is the recordist, using the tools of the new audio construction, that guides the heightened imagination and the potential intersections of fortuitous musical connections.

Historically jazz has been a genre that has been resistant to technology, and in chapter 6 I go more deeply into the specifics of that resistance, as well as various ways that jazz musicians and theoreticians have embraced technology and contemporary modes of music construction. From the controversy over Lennie Tristano's use of fadeouts in his 1950s recording to the outcry over the use of technology in Herbie Hancock's seminal *Head Hunters* recording in 1973,[5] many from the ranks of both jazz critics and practitioners have attempted to restrain the adoption of recording technologies within the idiom. While my intention with this project is to press the boundaries of the entrenched jazz ethic, I don't believe that it steps so far beyond the tradition as to be irrelevant to the genre. Instead I see it as a part of the historical process that continues to bridge the gap from performance to recording and as a part of the process that has extended the primacy of performance in jazz to various interactions with the capabilities of recording technologies.

A (Fragmented) Day in the Studio

On August 9, 2005, I went to the pianist Dana Atherton's home studio and started setting up for the day of recording. Dana and I had consulted previously on a couple of occasions, and he had assisted me in planning out a strategy for the day. We had chosen a jazz standard and had devised a simple arrangement for each musician to follow. It was a standard jazz arrangement: statement of the melody, a piano solo that played twice through the song's chord progression, a bass solo that played once through, and some trading of four-bar sections between the piano and the drums before the restatement of the melody at the end. We chose an appropriate tempo that we would use for the click track. This would guide the musicians so that their performances would fit together on the same rhythmic grid, regardless of their position on the musical timeline. The song was simple—its chordal structure forms the basis of many jazz standards—so it would not present any special challenges to the musicians. It had been widely recorded, so it didn't have any strong associations with previous recordings. This particular trio had played the song together previously, but it wasn't a tune that they played frequently or one that had strong associations for them as a group.

We had decided to record the piano tracks first, then the drum tracks, and finally the bass tracks, but this was simply based on scheduling needs. Each musician would play his part in a vacuum, that is to say, he would not have heard any of the other performances when he played his part. However, I would be providing verbal instructions that might assist in how the musicians used their imagination as they performed. My instructions might also help to "glue" the performances together by describing general approaches that would ultimately be shared by all three instrumentalists.

I began by instructing each musician to imagine their fellow musicians playing along, as though they were improvising together. These three musicians had considerable experience playing together, so I suggested they imagine the particular sound of the other two playing along as they played their own part. I took multiple recordings of each musician playing through the composition so that I would have a variety of material to choose from in the editing process. For certain recording passes I asked for a denser, more aggressive approach, and for certain passes I asked that they play more sparsely. At times I expanded my instructions by responding to their playing in the way of a bandleader or arranger. I might suggest that they take another pass based on the way they had approached one section in the previous take: "Play the whole piece again using that legato feel you used on the bridge in this last take," for example—and I would play for them the part that had caught my attention to remind them of what they had done. For each musician I also took a couple of passes asking for a specific rhythmic approach—a reliance on figures that employ quarter-note triplets—as a means of getting some particular phrases that I might use to create an "unexpected" convergence of musical ideas.

It was certainly a new and different experience for everyone. The biggest struggle was keeping track of the arrangement without the reinforcement of the other players. I think this was a bit of a revelation for all of them—the extent to which they rely on each other for reinforcement of position in the song structure. This presented the most difficulties for the pianist Dana, because when he's soloing in this imagined trio environment he is not using his left hand to outline the chordal movement with bass notes or simple chords as he would likely do in a typical solo piano environment. With no bass player and drummer to signal transitions or parts, he would sometimes lose his way harmonically. There were some similar problems for the drummer, Jason Lewis, because he didn't have any of the usual harmonic signals. The song has a "B" section that comes around after three "A" sections in a typical AABA compositional scheme. Jason discovered that, while he knew a transition was made (they would happen every eight bars), he would normally rely on the harmonic movement of the other instruments to reassure himself when it was the "B" section. Maintaining the arrangement was the least challenging for the bass player, Dan Feiszli, because typical jazz bass playing outlines both musical time and chord changes. The classic "walking" style of jazz bass playing relies on a repeated quarter-note pulse that "walks" through the chord changes, providing simple rhythmic and harmonic structure. Dan's relative ease with staying within the arrangement reinforced the notion that the bass serves to bridge the rhythmic and harmonic structures in jazz improvisation and cues the other musicians, especially during flights of somewhat abstract improvisation.

Maintaining performance with the metronomic structure of the click also required some special attention from each of the musicians. None of them had much trouble maintaining basic timing while playing to the click, but they all noted that this required a certain amount of attention that was a distraction from improvising. When I did ask them to stretch the rhythm more, around the quarter-note triplet feel, there were more time problems in the performances, including the occasional dropping or adding of a beat.

As a result of the difficulties with maintaining structure and timing, they all said they couldn't really put too much attention on "imagining" playing with the two "missing" musicians. Yet when they listened back to their performances, without hearing the click and concentrating on structure, they were surprised at how natural the playing sounded to them. Because they do play together often I could hear a certain compatibility between all of the performances, before even beginning to edit them together. Despite the frustrations, the musicians all seemed to really enjoy the session and expressed great interest in hearing the final product. I told them I would be asking for their feedback once they heard what I put together and they all readily agreed to make comments.

One especially interesting anecdote from the day's session involved the tracks I recorded with the drummer, Jason Lewis. After his first take Jason noted that, because he wasn't hearing anyone else's parts, he thought he might be overplaying. Actually on later takes I think he played even more than on that first take—he was responding to the "space" created by the lack of other sounds. At the end of the day Dana and I had a conversation about Jason's musicianship. We both agreed that we loved his playing and, while we admired his great sensitivity and taste as well as his awesome technical chops, if we had one complaint it was that he tended to under-play, to be too tasteful (if there is such a thing). But in this situation he did play more than we were used to hearing and we both felt that it might have had a positive influence on his performance.

Several More Days with Pro Tools

Once the recording had been completed I began the editing process, which in this case was really more of a construction job. I wasn't just editing ele-ments; I was actually going to construct performances for each individual instrument and in combination for the ensemble. It is only because of the ease and depth of manipulation over individual audio elements provided by the DAW that this project was even possible. I was editing, arranging, and composing—constructing all the elements of music creation outside of the original, isolated, performance. The musicians were playing to a set arrangement at a set tempo so that by simply starting them at the same time they would apparently play through the song together. One form the construction could take was to simply choose which of each individual's complete performances to use. More elaborate musical choices could be made by selecting different pieces of each individual's performance from different takes, such as the piano intro from take 1 and the piano solo from take 2. However, because they were synchronized to a consistent tempo, and because the song contains many repeated cycles of chord changes, it was also possible for me to use elements from each performance in places other than where they were originally played. For example, I could use the first eight bars of the opening melody on the piano as the first eight bars of the closing melody instead, by simply cutting and pasting that part to its new location. This meant that there was a virtually endless number of pos-sibilities for creating a final composition from a relatively few original ele-ments—I had taken four or five complete passes through the song for each of the three instrumentalists. This is adapting current pop music produc-tion techniques to the world of improvised jazz.

My goal was to look for interesting combinations of performances that generated the traditional compositional sense of good jazz improvisation. I did not explore realms that started to stretch the limits of what sounded plausible within a traditional trio environment,[6] though these possibilities were certainly available to me. This approach helped to limit the extent that I would experiment with combinations of elements, given the staggering range of construction possibilities. There was also a significant element of chance that I could allow to come into play. By randomly combining complete performances (e.g., take number 2 from the piano, number 3 from the bass, and number 4 from the drums) I could then listen to the results and see where I thought particularly interesting interchanges between the performances had taken place. It was some element of chance that made these moments occur, though there were also elements of imagination on the part of the musicians as they anticipated the playing of the others. Then it was my responsibility to make judgments about what was "good" or "interesting" or "appropriate" as an "improvised" moment in the overall composition. Despite all those words in quotes, this is actually in line with traditional production responsibilities—the producer is often responsible for choosing the best take when multiple takes of jazz recordings are made. However, in this project the role of the recordist is being elevated to the level of active, creative participant to an extent never previously possible.

The actual construction project was creatively very stimulating, especially in the early stages. I would combine various of the three instrumentalists' takes and listen through to the results. When I heard a particular passage that I found appealing for whatever reasons, I would copy and paste that element into a composite playlist.[7] Perhaps something with particular synchronicity had occurred, as sometimes happens with improvisation—when two or more of the musicians spontaneously phrase things in a way that connects them in a particularly musical and conceptually harmonious way. Or they might just have played something that felt really good together, that "grooved"—or perhaps one musician had left a bit of a space and another had played an intriguing figure in that space. For whatever the reason, I would take the passages where things jumped out at me as interesting.

As I started to build bits of an overall arrangement, made from elements that I had chosen, I then had to consider the overall integrity of the composition and of each individual track. I began isolating each instrument and listening for continuity—placing and replacing various elements to make a more cohesive sounding progression of musical events. I would go back and forth between the individual tracks and the ensemble to hear how the parts were working together. I took great pleasure at finding the "right" bass track—at finding the "right" drum edit—and hearing a larger section come together in a way that seemed both musically interesting and plausible from a performance standpoint. I discovered that the transitions between sections were the most difficult to negotiate. Sometimes finding a way for each instrument to move from the "A" section to the "B" section required a lot of trial edits. In order to find something that was both internally coherent in terms of the individual instrument and sounded "correct" from an ensemble point of view I might have to experiment with parts that had come from different points in the overall arrangement. Dealing with coherency in the solos was also challenging at times. Interesting ideas from different takes did not always connect together in ways that made musical sense or sound as though they might be something that the musician would actually play. Of course I could have ignored such considerations and created a more abstract musical construction—and that would be an interesting project in itself—but my intention was to create something that had the "sound" of a jazz piano trio playing and improvising together—that the listener would believe could have happened in a traditional ensemble context—and I constructed parts with this idea in mind.

The process was fascinating but it was also very time consuming. I spent two hours putting together the first (of two) cycles of Dana's piano solo. During this process I also discovered that Dana's earlier passes were stronger and more cohesive than his later takes. I remembered this same phenomenon from having recorded Dana in more traditional recording environments—he's the type of musician that needs to be "caught early" in a recording session in order to get his best performances, usually in the first or second take. Some musicians need to warm into their studio performances and do their best work four or five takes into the process (not many people do much good work after six or seven takes). Dana's tendency to perform best in his first couple of takes held true to form in this "artificial" environment in which he was performing in a vacuum.

Construction of the final version of "A jazz 'improvisation'" (audio clip 11) took about sixteen hours and produced four minutes and thirty-four seconds of music. This flies in the face of conventional recordings of improvised jazz, which take the amount of time it takes for the musicians to play the piece! What is the value here? There is a whole additional level and layer of engagement with the music and the process on the part of someone outside of the performance process. This is very much in line with Brian Eno's suggestion that new technologies allow a whole new level of choice in music creation. This project crosses musical boundaries and opens new doorways where new paths to creativity are given an opportunity to grow.

Beyond Editing

After finishing the completed version I sent copies to the musicians for feedback. I wondered how they would respond—the extent to which it would sound natural or unnatural, obviously edited or plausible, to them. These are the things that I have struggled with in my own process, but I wondered how different the experience would be to those who actually created the original performances? I asked each musician for feedback in the most general terms—I didn't want to skew their responses by directing them in any way. I asked for their overall impressions of the recording, their personal performances, and the performances of their fellow musicians. I also suggested that they might comment, positively and/or negatively, on more specific aspects of the recording, or on particular passages.

In my initial conversation with the pianist, Dana Atherton, after he had heard the final version (March 3, 2006), his first comment was an expression of surprise over how cohesive it sounded: "It sounded like we were playing together." This reinforced my general sense that the experiment had been successful in its fundamental goal of re-creating a "natural" sounding traditional jazz recording in a most "unnatural" way. When asking for a more critical response, he indicated that to him the drummer's performance was the most problematic. Because the drummer is tied to rhythmic structure but not to harmonic form, "his limitations are fewer" and thus his performance seemed the least cohesive. Drummers are sometimes referred to as the "glue" of musical ensembles, and the lack of context may be the most challenging for the one trying to create the rhythmic connections. Perhaps we had not gotten so "good" a performance from Jason after all. Dana volunteered that some of the edits were obvious to him but some undoubtedly slipped by unnoticed. What he liked best about his own performance was that it was "nonrepetitive," in a way that he found refreshingly different from his typical recorded performances. For the pianist to discover something fresh in this constructed performance suggests ways in which a project such as this might uncover new areas of creative expression through an expanded collaboration. It is impossible for improvisers to completely break out of patterns and predilections in their own per-formances. While this represents the strength of individual expression, the ability to hear one's own ideas freed from one's own larger tendencies of construction might also be personally liberating and instructive, as well as creatively successful.

The email response from the drummer, Jason Lewis (March 13, 2006), was somewhat less positive. Perhaps this was a reflection of the greater difficulties mentioned by Dana—without the harmonic structure Jason was cut more adrift from the music experience. "My overall impression was that it sounded a bit like a science experiment rather than a cohesive piece of trio music," he wrote, but he did acknowledge that "Taken in small phrases it sounds like a trio playing together." In regards to someone else reconstruct-ing his performance his response was that it was more of an alienating ex-perience than one that might provide elements of discovery for his own playing: "It is surprising to hear how some of the edits have been put to-gether. It's like someone has taken my brain and hands and manipulated them for their own purpose." While not completely negative—"It is amus-ing to hear phrases that sound like my playing but put into places I wouldn't normally put them," I got the sense that by calling them "amus-ing" he was being generous and that "disturbing" might have been closer to his true response. I know that Jason enjoyed the day in the studio, but it was apparent that the final version provided him with little musical satisfaction and did not serve as a means of learning new things about his own perfor-mance or improvisational work. It was noteworthy to me that Jason's re-sponses focused on the way the ideas were put together, and not on the overall rhythmic "feel," which was apparently less problematic for him.

The email response from the bass player, Dan Feiszli (March 15, 2006), struck something of a balance between Dana and Jason and was the most detailed. Dan found some passages convincing and others not: "Overall, it's very interesting. Some sections sound more like 'normal jazz' (bass solo, some of the drum trading, the head out).[8] Others, especially the head in and parts of the piano solo (especially the breaks), sound like somebody's pulling the strings." Dan was more specific about what in the construction he thought made some of these specific elements sound like they were ex-ternally controlled:

> I think what makes it sound like that to me is the "on or off" nature of this kind of construction—we, individually and together, go directly from one idea to another and back, without the usual in-betweens that

occur in normal playing. We're either playing one idea or another, and in normal performance you can hear the ideas develop from one to another, sort-of allowing you to hear the performers think. Here things move very suddenly from one to the next.

This points to a concrete difference that may occur when more people are participating in the creative process. The condensing of ideas is a part of editing that is not usually a part of the improvisatory standard in traditional jazz. The process itself may bring a different general approach to composition. Dan is only offering an observation here, not a value judgment. One could argue that this new compositional sense brings a fresh approach to the spirit of improvisational jazz or that it defeats the primacy of individual expression.

Dan also noted a technical challenge that was unique to his position as an acoustic bass player.

> An interesting thing about the bass solo is the intonation—you can hear my pitch drifting in and out in large segments over the course of the solo. More of a technical thing having to do with me having no external audible pitch reference when I played; generally if (OK, when . . .) my pitch slips in and out over a solo, it's on more of a note-by-note basis than a line-by-line.

Neither the piano nor the drums have any control over pitch as part of the performance, so this was not an issue for them. Stringed instruments without frets and all wind instruments must be constantly adjusted for pitch as they are played. In a solo performance the variations Dan refers to would largely go unnoticed, but when they are later combined with an instrument with a fixed pitch reference—in this case the piano—these inconsistencies in intonation are revealed. It's interesting that this was only noticeable to Dan during his solo—his intonation was stable enough in the ensemble passages, even without hearing the ensemble. This bears a relationship to the observation that intonation tends to be more strictly defined when musicians are sight reading and looser when they are playing better-known or rehearsed pieces.[9] This might also suggest the need for further refinement of this process, such as regular sounding pitch references along with the click track as a part of the structure for the individual performances where adjustments in intonation are being made.

All three musicians agreed that the most problematic element in terms of cohesion was the edited version of the drum performance: "I'd say that

Dana's playing sounds the most natural, mine the second-most, and Jason's the least natural." Dan acknowledges, however, that this sense of what is "natural" may be highly subjective: "Dana's playing sounds more natural to me than mine, though this could be because he's the lead more often and it makes more sense for him to change direction often, or it could be because he likes quick changes in his playing naturally, or it could be just that I'm more sensitive to edits in my playing than his." This ambiguity in his ability to place the cause of his response reinforces the idea that this experiment is stretching the bounds of the creative process. While all three musicians enjoyed the challenge of making the recording, Dana and Dan seemed also to enjoy at least some of the results of the editing process as well. Dan especially notes that the "drum trading is cool, it sounds like a trio playing jazz where everyone's sort-of doing their own thing without any one idea dominating, which happens naturally in the real world as well." After getting their responses I wondered what would have happened if we had all four set about the editing process together. This was not practical because of the time involved (and the lack of budget!) but my sense was that even the difficulties with the drum performance could have been resolved and that a final version that was more stimulating and less problematic would have been the result.

I have played this piece for other colleagues who are either jazz musicians or jazz appreciators but I have not asked for any kind of analytical response. The casual listener, even if steeped in jazz recordings, accepts this recording as a typical product of a typical live jazz session. The project would have to be developed further, along some of the lines mentioned above regarding better cueing tracks and a more collaborative editing process, before I would want to ask for outside scrutiny of the final material.

For my own part this application study emanated from a desire to explode the traditional idea of a piano trio recording. As part of my larger explorations of the new paradigms of music construction it stretched the limits of the social structure of traditional jazz, which has previously been rooted in the physical connection between the improvising musicians. This project highlighted the computer-aided construction models that are capable of helping to free musicians from routinized musical behavior. It explored the potential for a deepening of the inexplicable and ineffable elements of musical connections between improvising musicians by moving that connection solely into the realm of the imagination of the isolated performer. At the same time it expanded the direct participation in improvisation to the domain of the recordist, and expanded the dialogic environment of musical collaboration. Such an expansion suggests some interesting implications for notions of community that are a traditional part of music performance.

The Community of Improvisation

The relationship between music and the social construction of community is deeply rooted. Chanan suggests the breadth of this connection: "music is always—among other things—an expression of actual or ideal social relations. There are certain affinities between the forms of music making and those of society."[10] Chanan has placed this observation in the context of the cultural and historical contingencies that are an important part of the subjective experience of music, yet they may be difficult to dissect: "The problem is that such external determinants are always symbolically coded, frequently in paradoxical ways."[11] It is these paradoxes that may obscure how contemporary expressions of musical networks continue to build social networks. What appear to be practices that are dislocating and fragmenting may also be socially active and constructive.

For some, the practices of contemporary composition, production, and consumption of jazz have tended to move the idiom away from its traditional capabilities of providing social structure and cohesion. Matthew Butterfield's writings seek to incorporate a greater understanding of the community aspects of jazz. He references Ingrid Monson's work, which has developed "a 'vernacular' theory for the interpretation of jazz"[12] that uses African-American cultural aesthetics as the starting point, as opposed to traditional tools of music analysis. Monson emphasizes the social processes of the music and situates them relative to the conversational kind of expressions found in black idiomatic linguistic practice. In the same way as conversation, then, Monson "shows how musical interaction in jazz not only represents, but actually enacts social values, which simultaneously operate as the core aesthetic values of the music."[13]

Monson's approach retains the solitary nature of analytical activity but encourages the analyzer to look beyond conventional analysis "for idiomatically appropriate and interesting social interaction through music."[14] My application project represents a previously unexplored version of this kind of activity. It not only looked for these elements in the music but also enacted them, along with more traditional musical constructive elements, through active, creative participation. Butterfield notes that Monson's model for analysis "thus acts indirectly as an agent of community formation, for it facilitates the listener's participation in the social life of jazz performance events."[15] My application project, while still solitary and thus operating indirectly, heightens the agency of community formation and expands creative participation by including someone who is not a direct participant in the performance of the music.

Butterfield wishes to expand Monson's mandate through what he terms "situational particularism." Through this analytical technique Butterfield contextualizes Monson's integration of musical and social structures by using the structure of the particular musical situation to set the terms for analysis. In focusing in this manner Butterfield observes the kind of interpersonal solidarity and vulnerability involved in the collaborative process of jazz improvisation.[16] I contend that a closely related form of collaboration is extended to recordists in the recording process, which extends the social structure of creativity beyond the immediate circle of improvising musicians. My application project involved collaboration at the beginning and dialogue at the end, but it could easily have incorporated more collaboration in the construction process, as is common in pop music production.

Ultimately Butterfield does incorporate recording into his model. He acknowledges some ways in which recordings free the consumer from certain constraints of live performance, but he doesn't touch on the collaborative role of recording engineers and producers. The studio demands the collaboration of recordists, and while their participation may vary in degree, contemporary recording practices have tended to increase their direct participation. My application project heightens this collaborative element and yet removes it from the commonality of place found between recordists and musicians in the traditional recording studio experience. It is true that when anyone works in isolation, that person is removed from "the erotic social potential of live performance events"[17] and thus their working process doesn't allow for the face-to-face social cohesion that may also be a product of live performance. Nonetheless, having extended the collaborative process of studio work, my project points toward ways in which Butterfield's situational particularism may be expanded to embrace the potential for social cohesion in contemporary music practice beyond face-to-face collaboration. I hope that such activity may reinvigorate and extend, if not the erotic social potential of live performance, the general social structure of musical activity through the intertwining of compositional, improvisational, and analytical activities in ways previously unimaginable.

Cook exactly anticipates my application project in describing the balance between a rehearsed part and a group performance:

> But it is not as if each player's performance becomes so fixed, so overlearnt, that they could just as well perform wearing headphones and hearing only a click track. . . . Instead, making music together means constantly listening to everyone else, constantly accommodating your performance to theirs, being sensitive to other people's states of mind, knowing when to follow and when to lead. In short, making music together is an enaction of human community, and the sound of music is the sound of community in action.[18]

I certainly don't wish to argue that performers—the performers in my application project for example—will perform just as well in the kind of isolated performing environment I created, but rather that this environment doesn't necessarily exclude them from the community-enabling process of music making. Cook's next point reinforces this understanding, as he, following Schutz's ideas regarding intersubjectivity, notes that "you do not need to be actually playing in order to participate in the intersubjectivity of music, you become a member of the musical community just by listening."[19] I believe that this community participation applies to the listener of recorded music as well as to live music, especially given the predominance of recorded music in the culture and the manner in which listening and buying habits influence music creation. And if the listener is experiencing this musical community while listening to recorded performances that were played in isolation, is it any less of a community? So, the question becomes, at what point does intersubjectivity enter the picture? Broadly argued, then, contemporary music practice allows intersubjective musical relationships that were never before possible, and the participants become a part of the musical enaction of community. Not only might the listener have this kind of intersubjective experience in listening to my constructed piece of music, but also I have had a profoundly intersubjective relationship with the musicians as I constructed the piece from their performances.

Porcello addresses Schutz's notion of intersubjectivity as part of his ethnographic study of contemporary recording sessions. On the one hand he contends that the studio process of construction of music that he observes, and that coincides with much of the studio practice that I describe herein, is characteristically postmodern—involving a fragmentation of musical process resulting in a simulacrum of a shared musical experience. "Nonetheless," according to Porcello, "the vast majority of musicians and engineers I have worked with strongly believe and articulate ideas of shared musical experience virtually identical to those described by Schutz."[20] Ultimately Porcello characterizes this "tension between the romanticized emic and the overly cynical postmodernist theoretical discourses"[21] as part of a broader tension that is characteristic of attempts at cultural representation. Although Porcello's observations are most telling, he doesn't provide much insight into the position of the "vast majority of musicians and engineers" that he references here, nor does he try to square those sentiments with the contrary sense of a scattered intersubjectivity that he has observed.

I would suggest that it is the breadth and depth of musical experience of musicians and recordists that is the cause of their resistance to the relegation of the process to mere simulacrum. Porcello lacks the countless hours of musical activity that create the backdrop of the contemporary recording process when engaged in by the kind of experienced professionals that he was monitoring. Porcello acknowledges the fluidity of roles between the musicians and recordists, as well as the varying degrees of expertise (some musicians know a lot about the technical elements, some less—some engineers know a lot about music theory, some less, etc.) but he still perceives the process as having substituted a simulation for a truly shared musical experience. And on the surface this is true. But the reason it is not perceived this way by the musicians and recordists is that there is a direct connection between this process and the most essential kind of live music performance—the thing that has apparently been "lost" in the highly convoluted studio process. Just as the composer or songwriter holds onto the notion of the final piece to be performed live somewhere in the fragmented process of composition, so musicians and recordists hold a connection to shared music-making throughout the similarly fragmented studio process. The nature and depth of the knowledge that provides the underpinning for this understanding is defined as tacit knowledge and detailed by Susan Schmidt Horning in "Engineering the Performance: Recording Engineers, Tacit Knowledge and the Art of Controlling Sound."[22] *This tacit knowledge is the subtext that glues together the apparently fragmented (and fragmenting) process of making contemporary popular music recordings.*

In regards to broader issues affecting music and technology Porcello concedes that cultural critics "often reinforce the sense that technology is problematic for music" and that this "early problematization of technology has cast a long shadow into the scholarship that grapples with music/technology relationships."[23] Though he argues that not all scholars see this relationship (music/technology) as problematic, he notes that even those who don't "usually find themselves arguing from a persistently defensive position."[24] Cook places his reflections on the community-building qualities of music in line with this same long history of writing about music that sets music in opposition to technology. By associating music with the positive attributes of community "instead of being technological, industrial, and alienating it became natural, human, and authentic."[25] However, Cook identifies this negative predisposition toward technology as suspect in the way that "anybody who has the slightest acquaintance with the literature of critical theory or deconstruction is immediately put on guard by invocations of nature, the classic stratagem by which writers further their own agenda under the appearance of just saying how things are."[26]

So, those of us positively disposed toward the ancient marriage of music and technology are free to embrace the idea that *the enactment of community continues in today's highly technologized musical environments.*[27] Even the dislocating application project at hand may produce music that constructs social relationships. In opposition to decades of writing about music in which music and technology are seen as being at odds, and in support of Cook's proposal that there ought to be "an indefinite moratorium on equations of analysis and value judgment, and indeed more broadly on equations of academic research and aesthetic approval,"[28] I embrace the playful and creative potential of the marriage of technology and music.

In a 1994 article about the Frank Sinatra CD *Duets,* the *New York Times* critic Hans Fantel reflects on the fact that the two singers in each supposed duet were recorded separately in both time and space. In the context of primarily negative reflections on what he prefers to call "sonic collages" rather than duets, he too anticipates my application project when he "wonders if a jazz group, fragmented in time and space and later electronically recombined, could match the musical cohesion and spontaneity of the Benny Goodman Quintet ecstatically crowding about a single microphone to cut their old wax platters."[29] The clear implication here is in the negative. Fantel's particular brand of technological phobia is interesting in its combination of speculation, nostalgia, and non sequiturs. Fantel wishes to stir the controversy, without committing to any real opinion about technological mediation or about the CD he is reviewing. His statement could easily be reversed to speculate on the advantages of technology—one could wonder how a reconstituted jazz performance might exceed the capabilities of live performance—and Fantel does make the obligatory allusion to Glenn Gould later in his piece as perhaps representing an opposing point of view. He acknowledges the success of the Sinatra CD but only fleetingly mentions its potentially gratifying musical contribution in the context of his questioning its fairness as a constructed performance. Fantel associates technology with an assault on musical integrity, but his assault is really nothing more than nostalgia for earlier technological mediation, such as single microphone recordings. Fantel speculates widely on the potential alienating qualities of certain technological capabilities, without balancing his view with their potential advantages.

If, as Martin suggests, "We are dealing, in short, with the relationship between individual inspiration and the expectations of the collectivity in which it must be expressed,"[30] then we need to look more closely at what constitutes such expectations. Chanan points to the breadth of the powers of music both to form and to represent the positive construction of community: "Music, at the same time a direct and a symbolic expression of social relations, retains the power of affirmation."[31] The expectations of collectivity may be more fluid than is generally supposed, and it is my contention that assumptions about the alienating qualities of technology are not as fundamental as they may first appear. *Music is able to expand its socializing message even when the technology circumvents the traditional social interaction, and people are able to expand their capabilities to create community beyond the face-to-face requirements of traditional social networks.* As this application study has expanded these notions of community, the following studio study explores realms of musical intention that reach beyond the traditional idea of musical study, practice, and performance. Together the two studies continue to extend the notion of what it means for musicians to be performing music in the contemporary technological environment.

five

Studio Study
Capturing the Unintentional Performance

Backstory

In 1992 I was working as the recording engineer on the Robert Cray CD that was released later that year under the title *I Was Warned*. We had been working for a few days and were getting ready to make the initial recording for what would become the title track. We were recording what is called "basic tracks." That is, we were just going for final takes of the bass and drum parts, even though Cray was playing guitar and singing along. Everyone in the band was playing together so that the "feel" for the whole song, with the whole band, was present. The assumption was that the guitar, keyboard, and vocal performances would be rerecorded later when more time and attention could be paid to them. For this reason Cray's guitar amp was boxed in a little isolation crate. This setup wasn't best for recording but it prevented the guitar sound from "bleeding" into the other mics. This would allow it to be replaced later without problems. Cray thought he was doing what is called a "scratch track"—something for the rhythm section to groove to but not something intended to be used in the final recording (eventually it would be "scratched").

To help with the "feel" Cray played a guitar solo during the section where he planned to redo his solo later, in the middle of the song, and he played a long solo in the vamp (the ending groove section that usually fades out). As it happened both solos, including the ending solo—the longest guitar solo on record for Cray—were so spectacular that as soon as the take was over everyone (except Cray) knew that both solos *had* to be on the final CD recording. In fact, not only did those solos appear on the record but the vamp solo was also featured in a subsequent radio special on the fortieth anniversary of the Fender Stratocaster guitar.

At first Cray dismissed the idea of actually using these original solos—he had assumed that it was a "scratch track" and that he would be doing them over again. Many artists are plagued by the notion that they can always do better, and it is especially hard for some to accept a performance when they thought they weren't even trying! It took some time—and the continued enthusiasm of all of us at the session—for Cray to recognize how good that performance had been.

In a recent discussion with Cray I asked him if he believed that this performance had something to do his assumption that it was "not for keeps." He now readily admits that it had a whole lot to do with it. Even after eleven CDs (including many international releases on major labels) Robert Cray is still affected by the "pressure" of the red recording light. Despite all that experience, what many consider to be his finest moment on record came from an unintentional performance.[1]

Producing Advice

Walter Benjamin did not miss the significance of unintentionality. In "The Task of the Translator" he focuses on the slippery slope of interpretation of intention. He asserts that the translator must strive for the "language of truth, the tensionless and even silent depository of the ultimate secrets which all thought strives for."[2] Tensionless indeed! Translation is an apt metaphor for the recording of a musical performance and tensionless is an apt word for describing the best of unintentional performances. So how do those of us who are involved in the translation from performances into recordings assist in uncovering the musical "language of truth"?

As a recordist one of my primary jobs is to put the artist at ease. There are many techniques for doing this. Beyond the need to make the technical part of the process as transparent as possible are the more psychological tricks that are meant to ease the artist's performance anxiety. Of course encouragement is basic, but most of the more subtle approaches speak to this issue of intentionality. One comment that I use frequently and that is surprisingly helpful for a struggling, self-conscious performer is: "I can hear you thinking. *Stop thinking!*" The humorous element softens what may be an uncomfortable request for less self-consciousness. Very often artists will recognize that they are "thinking" too much and that they just need to relax and "play." It's no accident that *play* is the operative musical term.

Along these same lines is the request for a musician, regarding the construction of her particular part, to "make it more remedial." This is a comment born of the tendency for musicians to overplay—especially in the studio. Overplaying is usually a symptom of anxiety and self-consciousness. Again, humor eases the request for an altered approach to performance—a request that may be fraught with undertones of criticism. For those of us who work regularly with studio performance, the difference between a self-conscious performance and an unconscious one is usually immediately apparent. "Usually" is an important qualifier and sometimes "reading" performances is difficult. And of course, there is much more involved here than a simple distinction between relaxed and overthought—there are considerations regarding musical execution and other subjective elements in judging performance as well. Nonetheless, a lack of self-consciousness goes a long way toward an outstanding musical performance.

The relationship between these performance considerations and contemporary audio practice yields an interesting snapshot of contemporary cultural values. A transparent recording is one that places the least amount of apparent mediation between the performance and the recorded audio. Transparency may be desirable, but as recordists we must keep focused on the more important objective—if naturalism is the goal, it is the performance that needs to be naturalistic more so than the recording. The widespread move of professional recording out of the commercial studio and into the home reflects this desire by trying to make the recording experience more familiar and more comfortable. So how does current recording technology play into the capture of unintentional performances?

The Unintentional Computer

The motivations of unintentional production are in sympathy with what one author characterized as "the freedom to write crap." The word processor page is a liberating medium: we can discard, erase, rewrite, and refine at will. Early recording technologies were very restrictive, and their lack of editing capabilities may have contributed to inhibited performances. What was badly done remained badly done. The great advantages of magnetic tape—its reusability and its editing capabilities via tape splicing—led to its refinement in the postwar period. Final musical performances began to be constructed by editing together different sections of tape from many different takes. The guitarist Les Paul invented multitrack tape recording, which provided the capability of layering performances together to create one master recording. This expanded the idea of multiple takes used to piece together recordings from individual parts.[3]

Multitracking revolutionized the process of making recordings but there remained severe limitations on the "freedom to record crap." The process of multiple takes and of rerecording by individual instruments and individual portions of compositions was liberating, but the destructive nature of the tape-based format still inhibited a variety of editing functions. DAWs have finally granted to sound and music a level of freedom similar to that of the blank page. The following three capabilities, each a product of digital audio technology, have liberated the recording process:

1. The virtually unlimited amount of nondestructive (nonerasing) recording and editing within any ongoing recording project.
2. The ability to make very high quality recordings for a relatively small amount of money.
3. The ability to easily alter both timing and pitch of musical performances.

The combination of nondestructive recording and virtually unlimited recording time[4] has really created the "freedom to record crap." Previously, agonizing decisions over attempts at retakes often had to be balanced against the price of losing (erasing) the previous take. In the digital environment any number of takes may be tried without concern for track and tape limitations. This can create a nightmare in the quantity of editing chores later on, but it can also allow experimentation and risk-taking on a level previously inconceivable.

The ability to have very high quality recording at a very reasonable price has enabled a whole new paradigm of musical process. Traditionally, because of budget constraints, the demo recordings of songs and song ideas were created at home or at inexpensive studios. In these environments the quality of recording was not considered acceptable for commercial release. This meant that if the opportunity arose to create a commercial recording of the same song the entire recording had to be started again from scratch. This led to endless hours of frustration as artists and producers attempted to re-create things they especially liked about the feel or performance of the demo recordings. This process was sometimes referred to as "chasing the demo." In my experience we were *never* able to satisfactorily reproduce the things we loved the most about the original demos.

With a DAW it is possible to purchase one or more channels of "signal path" (the complete chain of recording from microphone to final analog to digital conversion into the computer) that matches the general quality level of top commercial studios. For the relatively small price of a few thousand dollars per channel one can record very high-fidelity audio at home. With a single channel of signal path the all-important vocal tracks can be recorded at one's leisure. Once the investment is made all subsequent recordings, whether serious attempts at final takes, or middle-of-the-night experimentations with vocal approaches, may be suitable for final commercial release.[5]

A typical scenario in today's DAW environment is reflected in the process for a recent record I made with the songwriter Bonnie Hayes.[6] Hayes had recorded many of the songs as song demos in her DAW. We started working on the final recordings right in the same Pro Tools[7] files as the song demos. Most of the elements were replaced eventually, and live drums and bass were recorded to replace the drum loops and keyboard bass she had used for the song demos. However, many of the vocal performances remained from those early recordings. Try as we might, we could never recapture the freshness of those first vocal takes, many done immediately after the song was written. They expressed the enthusiasm, immediacy, and energy that accompanied the inspiration that was necessary to write the song in the first place. Because these "demo" recordings were done in the same recording format, with the same level of high-quality signal path that we used for all the other "final" recordings for the CD,[8] not only were we able to use these early recordings but there were no technical compromises in doing so, and thus the "first take" vocal that was an essential part of the composition of the song has become the "final vocal," just as Robert Cray's "scratch track" guitar solo continued on to the final version. The unintentional performances were seamlessly integrated into the historical legacy that is now a commercial release. This process dissolves many of the complications associated with previous methods of moving from creation to performance to permanence.

The new functionality provided by computer-based recording and processing has resulted in other gains in relation to the capture of recordings of unintentional live performances. For example, throughout the history of multitrack production of popular music the drummer has been the one least able to really take advantage of the flexibility of the technology. This is because drum kits are very complex instruments—actually a combination of many instruments including both drums and cymbals—that are very different in sustain and timbre. For the most part the drum track was needed as a basis for the other performances, and it was usually not possible to replace parts of a drum track because the myriad of resonances (especially from the cymbals) prevented the seamless insertion of a new piece of a performance. As result, the normal process of overdubbing—and especially the further refinement of "punching in" (replacing small parts of a performance while retaining the remainder)—has not been available to drummers. Typically they had to play their part as one complete take. The nondestructive aspect of computer-based recording, combined with the editing power of cross-fading between digital recordings, has given the same flexibility to drummers previously enjoyed by the other players in most pop music production. San Francisco bay area drummer John Hanes expressed it this way:

> The Pro Tools revolution has had an enormous effect on drummers, inasmuch as it is no longer crucial to get the bitchin drum take for everyone else to overdub onto. Now I can record like the real musicians—go for a take, fuck up a little, and punch in. This has freed up my playing significantly.[9]

Other DAW capabilities have allowed us to keep performances that previously would have had to be discarded. The ability to fix timing and certain pitch aspects of recorded performances has revolutionized studio production. Sometimes great musical performances have some simple flaw that previously rendered them unusable. It may be a single note that is slipped out of time in an awkward-sounding fashion, or it may be the pitch of an otherwise inspired vocal performance that goes slightly out of tune at the very end of the last note in the line. We may now fix these undesired aspects of an otherwise brilliant (perhaps unintentional) performance through tools in the digital domain. I have had to erase many great musical moments because of some small flaw that could not be fixed and that the artist found unacceptable—this is no longer the case. Of course, this may be taken to extremes, and many have bemoaned the excessive fixing and polishing of recordings, sometimes taken to the point of sapping all of the life from the original recording. *No matter how the technology and the user conspire to manipulate sound via recordings, ultimately it's the listeners who must decide whether they are the beneficiary or the victim of these practices.*

Value and Judgment in Musical Performance

For all the expansion in production capabilities, what is the true value created in the process? Are we gaining from the capture of a vastly expanded number of performances, or are we fulfilling a legacy implied in the newfound "freedom to record crap?" Suffice it to say that this really lies totally within the domain of the subjective. It is easy to side with Greil Marcus when he articulates the distinction between a good and bad record as follows:

> Now, by a good record I mean one that carries surprise, pleasure, shock, ambiguity, contingency, or a hundred other things, each with a faraway sense of the absolute: the sense that . . . someone (the singer, guitarist, the saxophonist) wants what he or she wants, hates what he or she hates, fears what he or she fears, more than anything else in the world.
>
> By a bad record I mean one that subverts any possibility of an apprehension of the absolute.[10]

The invocation of the absolute suggests the realm of the unintentional performance. I suggest that some quality of unintentionality is an essential part of the kind of performance Marcus wishes to celebrate here. Marcus's sentiment also reminds us of the importance of the relationship between the artist and audience. The ultimate effect of the unintentional performance requires travel on the two-way street implicit in Marcus's observation. It speaks to a reciprocal relationship between expression and the reception of that expression. For a performance to be judged as good it must be judged—that is, it requires the listener's participation in response. Yet, while I maintain that unintentional performance may be an essential element in accessing that sense of the absolute, these judgments remain primarily subjective, applicable only on a per recording / per person basis.

Other authors have arrived at similar conclusions regarding the personal nature of the experience of music. As previously cited, Roger Beebe observes that "Because 'authenticity' is for many authors merely the best metaphor for a certain kind of pleasure, there may be as many authenticities as there are pleasures."[11] Thus the argument that some know what is authentic simply continues the authenticity myth by "insisting on a false opposition between critics/academics ('fake') on the one hand, and fans/musicians ('authentic') on the other, as if it were impossible for someone to occupy all these places at once."[12]

Similarly musicians are not necessarily interested in or capable of making judgments about their own performances. In relation to the application project above, jazz musicians often rely on producers to pick among various takes. Cray initially rejected the idea of using his "scratch" solos on the final recording; his own expressed sentiment regarding these solos is thoroughly in line with the conclusion that "musicians are often surprised at what they create and often only retrospectively comprehend what they were attempting to articulate."[13]

I have focused here on a single performance by an accomplished musician. One may debate the relationship and relative merits of skillful and unintentional performance, but as noted in the following from Marcel Proust, the bliss of ignorance also needs to be recognized on its own terms:

> That bad music is played, is sung more often and more passionately than good, is why it has also gradually become more infused with men's dreams and tears. Treat it therefore with respect. Its place, insignificant in the history of art, is immense in the sentimental history of social groups.[14]

Good or bad, music is changing, and the activities and capabilities described here raise many questions regarding some of the fundamental relationships in musical performance. The final section in this chapter tackles questions regarding the evolving relationship between composition and improvisation, the nature and meaning of musical form, and a continuing discussion of rhythmic "feel."

six

{ Artist or Artisan?

Improvisation and Recording Subvert Categorizations

My application study and studio study in the preceding chapters indicate some of the new possibilities that recording technology offers for capturing and constructing musical performances. They also raise questions about how we define composition and improvisation. There is a natural correlation between recorded music and composition. Because recordings have a repeatable permanence, they bear a close relationship to a musical score and thus to composition. Live performances require a unique physical manifestation for each presentation. Popular notions of art versus craft or artist versus artisan have followed along similar lines—composition and authorship are aligned with art, whereas performance may be relegated to craft.[1] The application and studio study present examples of how these categorizations are becoming increasingly blurred in contemporary musical practice.

The interpretation of live performance from a score is still easily distinguished from authorship and, because of its dependence on composition and its physical manifestation, may be associated with craft rather than art. These two paradigms, the craft of live performance versus the art of composition, are somewhat undone by the very notion of improvisation. Improvisation is a kind of live composition—performance as a kind of authorship—that is less easily separable from composition than interpretation from a score. Solo improvisations aside, improvisations are distinct from compositions in their collaborative nature, but this too is somewhat undone by the very notion of recording. Recording begins to weaken the dominant position of collaboration in performance and independence in composition, and contemporary computer-based music construction practices subvert the positions completely.

Contemporary recording practices relieve ensemble performances from the necessity of real-time collaboration, allowing recorded performances to share in the off-line construction model that composition has always employed. Recorded ensemble music may be created from disjointed and time-shifted performances through multitrack recording, overdubbing, editing, repurposing previously recorded audio, and so on. As a result, recordings of ensemble music may be the work of a singular author/performer. The application study in this chapter further extends and destabilizes the models of improvisation, composition, and collaboration. The jazz piece I created removes both ensemble performance and improvisation from real-time performance and from collaboration. At the same time it creates recorded ensemble performances by applying the model of the solitary authorship of composition. There is no ensemble collaboration involved in creating the final ensemble performance as presented in the recording. This is a further step removed from the common practice of ensemble recordings built from performances recorded in isolation at different times, but where the performers are listening and responding to the previous performances.

One might argue that this new compositional model brings a fresh approach to the spirit of jazz or that it defeats the primacy of real-time, collaborative improvisation. In any event it breaks the traditional improvisational mold. Berliner details many of the qualities of improvisation, including some of the most challenging elements. He notes "the intensity of struggling with the creative process under the pressure of a steady beat,"[2] and the musicians in my application study struggled with this in unique ways because they were performing in isolation. However, Berliner also points out that "the consequences of their actions are irreversible,"[3] and it is this quality of improvisation that has been undone by my application project. The musicians were improvising but the final ensemble performance was created using the compositional model—a single author (me) with control over each element (prerecorded, isolated performances). This resulted in the positive response from the pianist to his fresh improvisational structures and the negative response from the drummer, who reacted to his sense that someone had manipulated his performances with their own purposes in mind.

Just as we now have time-shifted noncollaborative ensemble performance, we also have real-time collaborative composition. The idea of com-

positional collaboration has been active in jazz for a long time. It sometimes emanates from accidental occurrences in improvisation: "Should
musicians regard such unanticipated results of their interaction as successful, they can incorporate them into their formal arrangements as fixed or
composed features."[4] This approach borrows from the real-time collaboration of live performance improvisation and "ports that over" (to use the
common phrase from cross-platform computer application development)
to composition. This allows collaboration to fertilize composition and improvisation to reach beyond its status as a single performance. Even in its
simple form, as described above by Berliner, the evolution from improvisation to composition suggests the difficulties in tracing the influence of
collaboration on later works.

Cook points to the many features that improvisation and composition
share, with specific musical elements of planning and spontaneity a requi-
site of both activities. Nonetheless, Cook suggests that there "is a simple
and fundamental difference, one that admits of almost no borderline cases,
which is that improvisation takes place on-line (in Schutzian inner time)
while composition takes place off-line (in outer time). . . . For this reason
it seems to me that improvisation's more significant other is performance."[5] This is a variation on the distinction just drawn between real-
time and time-shifted performance of ensemble music. It also hints at the
distinction between collaboration and singular authorship, without privileging either.

However, Cook's distinction between the temporality of improvisation
and performance is only intended to apply to the activity, not the product
of these activities. There are points at which recording activities blur many
of the distinctions between performance, improvisation, and composition.
When improvisations are rearranged in the off-line editing process, what elements are then improvised and which composed? As compositions are
lifted from on-line performances, which part is considered improvised and
which composed? Perhaps the played portions (*the music itself*) rightly retain the moniker "improvised," but the edited aspect of the final recording,
or the elements later extracted as composition, is "composed." This too is
good in theory but it becomes a fine job of splitting hairs to separate the elements. This is especially true when the editing process takes on the kind of
broad intervention of my application project. After the process is complete
and memories begin to fade (and old files won't open in new programs),
there is no longer any reliable way to distinguish between the improvised
and the composed. In this way even the on-line/off-line distinction be-

comes difficult to hold on to. It still exists in theory but in practice the elements cannot be differentiated. This coincides with Cook's broadest conclusion: "in the reality of life as actually lived, binary distinctions—such as between the literary and the aural/oral, or between improvisation and performance—are rarely as impermeable as they are made to appear."[6] Similar binaries between authorship and collaboration, and ultimately between art and craft, would seem equally porous.

Improvisation and Composition Are Both Constructed

Another (false) binary understands composition as a means of making music concrete and improvisation as a fluid expression of musical ideas. Barthes suggests that the fluidity of improvisation may be subsumed back into composition out of the desire to fix meaning. In speaking of film Barthes notes that "all images are polysemous,"[7] and certainly the same could be said for all music, even for each musical passage or phrase. By attempting to explain film or music the linguistic message becomes one of the ways society seeks to "*fix* the floating chain of signifieds in such a way as to counter the terror of uncertain signs."[8] Whatever one's opinion of jazz, any written critique may be motivated by a desire to "counter the terror" of the unknowns of musical improvisation. Barthes argues that there have been historical disagreements but contemporary researchers (and Aristotle) agree on "giving primacy to the logical over the chronological [and thus] the task is to succeed in giving a structural description of the chronological illusion."[9] Barthes's language suggests the impossibility of such a task. The illusion of the perception of time ("time flies" versus "time stands still") speaks to the difficulties in separating composition from improvisation. Composition and improvisation have complex relationships to time that cannot be logically fixed, nor can they be isolated from each other. The "chronological illusion" breaks down the simplistic notion that defines composition as off-line and improvisation as on-line.

Certainly improvisation is not tantamount to pulling wholly new musical performance out of nowhere. Improvisers are working from their trained musical skills, they are drawing from a vocabulary of musical ideas that they have mastered (just as authors draw from their linguistic vocabulary), and they are usually operating within a musical tradition that has very established modes and parameters of expression.[10] Certainly improvisers may be involved in spontaneous creation, but that is only one element of what they do, and spontaneous creation is an element in composition (or writing) or any supposedly off-line creative endeavor as well. Improvisation as elaboration within a sociological context also places it in closer proximity to composition than the simplified belief that improvisation is wholly spontaneous or unplanned.

Improvisation may lean closer to composition in ways that fall outside the typical understanding of musical models of construction employing Western rationalist thought. Bruno Nettl describes a Native American musical tradition that isn't "planned ahead" and thus would normally be considered improvisation.[11] However, once this spontaneous music gets played it tends to remain rather fixed. This really brings it closer to the compositional model—a kind of spontaneous composition—than to the traditional ideal of improvisation where each playing is its own unique expression. However, when recorded, sometimes improvisations—ones that were intended as a unique constructions created in the moment—become fixed. This is because they are heard repeatedly by listeners, including other musicians, and sometimes even relearned and reperformed by the original improviser.[12] In both these examples the lines between improvisation and composition are very fluid.

Nonetheless, Nettl contends that "art music is correlated with discipline, art for art's sake, reliability, and predictability, while the opposites of these characterizations apply in the case of jazz."[13] This description of the qualities of these genres does not necessarily stand up to close scrutiny of the genres in actual practice. Commentators such as Johnson have pointed to the philosophy of aesthetics that has created these stereotypical notions of the genres: "The centrality of performance rather than prior composition also destabilizes the mind/body hierarchy that underpins high-art aesthetics."[14] And contemporary musicology seeks to reclaim performance as central to the Western art tradition just as it recognizes the long-lasting influence of recorded improvisations.[15] Again, binaries such as mind/body not only fail to encompass the broader process of music making that incorporates composition and performance together, but fail to describe each supposedly unique element in the process. Composition must include spontaneity just as improvisation must include planning.

Attali adopts his own revised definition of composition to highlight the hopeful direction he wishes for musical activity—encompassing improvisation by positing an approach to composition that is based on intention as opposed to control. For Attali compositional control is an illusion and its ascendancy as the essence of creativity that eclipses improvisation is a historical anomaly. Attali seeks a fundamental shift "in which man has conquered power [and] the relation to technology and knowledge changes, because the relation to the essential has changed."[16] Certainly we have seen this shift relative to technology and knowledge in the world of music creation—a paradigm shift toward the construction of music that hinges on "a general availability of new tools and instruments"[17] just as Attali suggests. Whether his further suggestion, that the intention of the artist has changed such that the goal of creative labor exists for the sake of the act itself rather than the results of the act,[18] is a more difficult case to make. In a much more modest proposal I would suggest that our ability to capture the unintentional performance, such as in the studio study above, has elevated our ability to experience elements of the essential in musical performance. However, such examples hardly augur a wholesale shift in the artists' relationship to the essential as described in Attali's hopeful new compositional model.

These various formulations confirm the ways in which composition insinuates itself into the basic structure of an improvised performance. Nonetheless, the jazz critic might wish to downplay the centrality of composition almost to the point of eliminating it:

> In classical music, it is considered that how a work is performed is never as important as the work itself. In jazz, the work itself is never really as important as the way it which is played. Jazz, then, is not a composer's art; rather jazz is the art of the performer, the performing ensemble, and the arranger. The quality of the art is dependent upon their creative ideas.[19]

While this reinforces the orientation of improvisation to performance, it also, perhaps inadvertently, reinforces its dependence on the off-line compositional model. Though improvisation leans heavily on real-time performance, even this attempt to minimize the role of traditional composition contains a piece of the compositional model by including the arranger in the list of primary participants in the creation of jazz. Arrangements are made in the same manner as compositions—off-line—and the distinction between composer and arranger is often blurred. Nonetheless, both arrangements and compositions—and all of music—must be realized *in* time in order to be heard, whether it is a live performance or an elaborately constructed recording. The structural description that Barthes notes as part of the attempt to contain the terror of chronological uncertainty must ultimately be abandoned when music is finally played.

Writing in the same volume as Nettl, Stephen Blum expands the intersection between composition and improvisation in ways that reinforce positive elements in both my application study and my studio study. As noted, the pianist in my application study was most interested in the ways that my edited version of his playing allowed him to hear himself outside of the kind of repetitious tendencies he battled to overcome in his own improvisations. Blum suggests that "If improvisation has often been described with respect to the expectations and responses of listeners in a familiar milieu, it can also be treated as an art that enables performers to control their dependence on habitual responses."[20] The improvisers' reliance on repetition and habitual response[21] reminds us of the ways improvisers lean on compositional elements within the improvisational context, despite their attempts to control these dependencies.

Yet none of this is intended to diminish what it is about improvisation that thrives on the spontaneous, and we may still embrace the notion of improvisation as part of the imaginative process that produces music that is created in the moment. This links improvisation to the kind of unintentional performances I detail in my studio study. While this reinforces the fluid element in improvisation that is part of what distinguishes it from composition, the joy in *capturing* these spontaneous elements is part of what recording provides. This then reconnects even the most spontaneous improvisation to the fixed quality of composition. As recording makes the fleeting musical moment concrete it further blurs the lines between improvisation and composition.

Recording Redefines Improvisation

Brian Eno suggests that because recordings allow repeated listening, improvisations "become more interesting as you listen to them more times. What seemed like an almost arbitrary collision of events comes to seem very meaningful on relistening."[22] This transformation of significance is one way improvisations begin to evolve into more formalized compositions: "So they were listening to things that were once only improvisations for many hundreds of times, and they were hearing these details as being compositionally significant."[23] It's a short step from compositionally significant to actual compositions, as detailed here by Berliner: "Guitarist John McLaughlin and violinist Shankar, of Shakti, would record their informal improvising. After evaluating the taped sessions, they sometimes extracted the most cohesive segments to combine and reassemble into original compositions and arrangements."[24] The act of transcribing an improvisation, only possible through the ability to analyze a performance by repeated listening to a recording, may also move the improvised performance closer to the realm of composition. But recording serves to reveal and expand the idea of composition in more than just this kind of simple progression from played to replayed to transcribed to composed.

The ambiguity between the passing improvisational moment and the compositionally significant musical idea is no more evident than in the playing of the jazz saxophonist Ornette Coleman. In Coleman's case the notation of his improvisations only serves to complicate what the ear might hear as significant over repeated listening. Coleman's revolutionary compositional approach breaks down musical conventions such as regular meter and harmonic tonal center while maintaining a free flow of musically satisfying (compositionally significant) ideas. Cook uses the analogy of the flight of an arrow to describe Coleman's playing. Just as we are unable to describe the flight of an arrow (only its position at any given moment)—so with any of the flights of Ornette's solos (many of his notes make no sense when viewed statically) notation cannot truly describe the flights of his improvisations.[25] We experience Coleman's playing as having compositional integrity, but when we try to codify the notes as composition they seem to belie the experience. Similarly Crouch uses a comparison to Picasso to describe Coleman's improvisations: "In Coleman's case, that form has great plasticity, protean possibilities, but it arrives in music quite like the Picassos that mix the figurative with abstraction."[26]

This idea of plasticity, which is most often associated with filmmaking, brings to the fore questions regarding the nature of composition in the context of improvisation and recording. In its traditional form composition uses the plasticity of notation, but in its contemporary form it is at least as likely to use the plasticity of recording instead. And the extended capabilities of recording make for compositional approaches that move beyond the formal structures of notation, encompassing new structural conceits—from simple splices to the kind of heavily reconstructed formats of my piano trio recomposition. Yet recordings that emerge from an improvisational context of great plasticity may take on all of the qualities of composition and bypass the structural process of either recording or notation. Cray's unintentional performance, which was expected to be discarded but has risen to the level of career-defining performance, emerges as musically defining for the artist in a way typically associated with the legacy of compositions. As with the experience of many Ornette Coleman performances, the recording has transformed Cray's improvisation—created completely in the moment and seemingly removed from the formality and off-line model of notational composition—into what becomes a compositionally significant experience for the listener and a historical legacy for the artist. In both cases the recording serves the process by providing the simple capability of multiple listenings, without the constructivist practices of recording or notation.

The fluid relationship between process and product that characterizes recordings of improvisations blurs the notions of composition and performance and breaks down the composer-centric orientation. Jazz musicians often work backward from improvisation to composition, transferring "the swooping shapes, rhythmic subtleties, and intensities of jazz improvisation to the written page,"[27] further blurring the distinctions between playing and writing. Sometimes solos "acquire independent lives as compositions"[28] and sometimes soloists have to relearn their solos from recordings to satisfy their audience. Ultimately, jazz allows these various activities—playing, listening, and writing—to blend into one fluid creative process that may be thought of in terms of composition in the broadest sense: "jazz improvisers fundamentally devote their lives to music composition. This remains true whether they store, edit, and revise musical ideas by ear, visual imagery, and instrument, or carry out similar procedures with the aid of writing or recording."[29]

The interweaving of writing and recording is becoming more complex—sharing more connections while also becoming broader in the ways that they are implemented. Recording encourages interaction between composing and improvising—because it allows the reflection born of repeated listening. As a result, the "solo" that sounds more like a composition than an improvisation (sometimes called "through-composed" solos) is a common element in popular music and increasingly prevalent in jazz as well.[30] Because of the expectation of repeated listening improvisers have tended to orient their playing to more of the internal structure and logic associated with composition. Recording also facilitated the selection of solos of this type by allowing for repeated takes from which selections can be made. However, the technology of recording has not only encouraged the use of solos of this type but it has enabled the construction of such solos through editing. As with my application project, improvised solos may be edited and thereby reimprovised, or more accurately recomposed (because this is done off-line). Such editing can significantly alter the sense of an improvised solo from one that has the more abstract elements of improvisation to one that has the more formal sense of the through-composed solo. Here again the intervention of the recordist (with or without the collaboration of the original performer) has a compositionally significant effect on the final recorded "performance."

In a most basic way, recording itself is now so thoroughly a part of musical practice as to have changed the essence of how music is composed and then performed. "If thinking of classical music as reproduction leaves too much out, in the case of most other musics—popular music, jazz, non-Western music—it leaves practically everything out."[31] Simple reproduction of scores as the musical performance paradigm is not just inadequate, it is now thoroughly inaccurate. And in much of constructed contemporary music, thinking of recordings as simple reproductions of musical performance is utterly mistaken as well. Recordings now blend and blur improvisation and composition and adapt and repurpose audio into a performance constructed from a mélange of sounds and techniques.

Live versus Recorded Improvisations

In the relatively new field of Performance Studies "performance" gets identified in the broadest of terms by Richard Schechner: "Performances mark identities, bend time, reshape and adorn the body, and tell stories. Performances—of art, rituals, or ordinary life—are made of 'twice-behaved behaviors,' 'restored behaviors,' performed actions that people train to do, that they practice and rehearse."[32] This broad understanding of performance certainly encompasses both live and recorded musical improvisation, including the performance of the recordist who constructs musical recordings. However, in jazz there are significant differences in both theory and practice when it comes to live versus recorded performances. How profoundly are the "twice-behaved behaviors" of live jazz improvisation altered by recording?

For many jazz critics live performance is central to the practice of improvisation. The unifying moments in improvisation that take place in live performance are understood to encompass the performer, the listener, and the physical space that the performance takes place in.[33] Recording, on the other hand, is frequently seen as an impoverished version of the "complete" experience of improvisation that live performance provides. Derek Bailey suggests that the dislocation from space is the most damning part of the attempt to translate the live jazz experience to a recording: "But much more important than the limitations of the technology is the loss during the recording process of the atmosphere of musical activity—the musical environment created by the performance—'the matching of music with place and occasion,' as Peter Riley describes it."[34]

Is it even possible then, through recordings, to extract improvisation from the audience and environment? One interesting development in recent compositions is an indication, as a part of the musical directions made by the composer, of the space of the performance. Pope observes: "I am most intrigued by several pieces that I have heard in the past that introduced themselves as specifically intended for performance over home stereo systems, or via headphones, or solely for performance in large halls with expensive sound projection systems."[35] Note that here there is also a technological element that interacts with the acoustical space. Chanan takes this idea further: "if . . . music is frequently composed not only for particular performers but also to fit particular kinds of acoustic space, then the truth is that acoustic spaces have their own history and create their own expectations."[36] This reminds us that recording studios also have a history and set of expectations that may interact with performance, both positively and negatively, so Bailey's reference to the "dislocation from space" cannot be wholly accurate.

One may argue that yes, the environment that studio recordings take place in also interacts with the performers, but it is the addition of an audience—in combination with performer and physical environment—that creates the privileged improvisations of the live experience. Here again, though, there are related elements in the process of recording. Recording musicians often speak of performing for the select audience of the recordist(s) in the control room, and musicians frequently comment on their relationship to the microphone (a relationship that is carried from live performance to the studio and back again in most circumstances). I am not suggesting that the performance/space/audience dynamic of live performance is mirrored in studio recordings—only that it is not lost in them.

Not even the harshest critics of recordings deny their value,[37] at least as a source of some elements from musical occurrences; yet the tendency is toward considerable qualifications regarding the value of jazz recordings. Berliner states flatly that "they are not equivalent to live performances."[38] While most might accede, along with Rasula, to the value of recordings in the preservation of the tradition—"the historian setting out to compose a written history of jazz will find that history already composed, and made audible in recordings"[39]—this carries a very limited status. In this sense the improvisations remain extracted and isolated from the live music experience, with the recordings only retaining value as historical documents. It is the fixedness of recordings that allows for their extraction from audience and environment—they have become a kind of remembrance of performance where their cultural presence may be debated along the lines of Benjamin's "aura" although their historical influence is undeniable.

Though the experience of improvisation may be limited in recordings because of their relative isolation, it is enhanced in other, significant ways. Sometimes these limitations produce unexpected and beneficial results, as documented by Berliner. He tells of George Duvivier's efforts to master a bass solo from a particular recording. To master the solo Duvivier had to develop a new fingering technique only to discover, when he saw the band live, that the "solo" was actually a duet, with the drummer playing along on the bass strings with his sticks.[40] This somewhat happy accident for Duvivier is a direct result of the physical separation of recording from performance.

Another effect of jazz recordings on improvisation that is widely acknowledged is the educational opportunities they provide. As materials for study they offer clear value as documentation of performances despite their perceived limitations. Recordings provide the opportunity for both the preservation and the continuation of many of jazz's legacies. Chanan observes that recordings communicate "what cannot be indicated in any score, the nuances of articulation and timbre which are central stylistic concerns of jazz."[41] Also, thanks to recordings, we can hear seminal performances that would have been lost to all but the minuscule number of those who were present at the original performance. This is certainly a net gain. It is through recordings that access to these performances has provided generations of jazz musicians the opportunity to develop the musical genre, benefiting from having learned from these earlier performances. But it isn't only access to such a broad spectrum of performances that is brought about by recordings. In regards to the subtleties of musical execution, recordings provide access to a much broader spectrum of performance detail than can be captured by score or transcription.

Contemporary recording techniques may further encourage negative reflections on the relationship of recording to improvisation. Butterfield clearly indicates his assessment of the specific practice of overdubbing parts in the following anecdote about a recording made by the well-known guitarist John Scofield and the legendary jazz saxophonist Wayne Shorter:

> What is telling here is that neither Scofield nor his interviewer Zan Stewart express the slightest surprise or embarrassment that Shorter

never actually played his part with the other performers—the practice of overdubbing has become that mundane. Listeners, on the other hand, are still supposed to experience the recording as though the musicians were all co-present during the recorded performance. The final product thus effectively masks from public view a radical transformation in the social relations of music performance.[42]

But is the practice of overdubbing really masked from the listener, and is it truly a concern? Most members of contemporary audiences are aware that these kinds of studio practices are common, and yet they are thoroughly willing to accept the musical experience as presented. Butterfield makes a valid point about the transformation of social relations, but that this should cause embarrassment or is tainted as somehow "masking" something from the public suggests nostalgia for a time before recording technology had transformed everyone's relationship to the musical experience.

This combination of nostalgia with an unwillingness to grant contemporary audiences a heightened understanding that technology is a partner in both musical creation and consumption leads others to lament the effects of recording on improvisation. Derek Bailey finds the fundamental techniques of recording to be anathema,[43] and he quotes a variety of jazz artists speaking negatively about the recording experience, including Lionel Salter, who opines: "I'm not at all sure that recording is useful for anything more than reference."[44] Despite this, Bailey ultimately acknowledges that "Records simply supply a different listening experience to listening 'live'; for the majority of people, apparently, a preferable one."[45] This final admission reveals that those who are unwilling or unable to come to terms with the relationship of improvisation to recordings are left out of the primary discourse of contemporary jazz.

But it is not just the grudgingly acknowledged historical or educational opportunities that jazz recordings present, nor the undeniable passion for recorded music that audiences demonstrate with their dollars, that give recordings meaning for the jazz tradition. Recordings provide inspiration for musicians as well. Though impossible to quantify, it can be argued that much in the evolution of jazz, much of the innovation and leaps in creative expression, are fueled in large part by access to recorded performances. For the musician and the listener, recordings often transcend their status as commodity.

Nonetheless, the relationship of the work of art to the commodity that art often becomes has long been a point at issue. A firm distinction is sometimes drawn between the two, following John Dewey's school of American pragmatism and his book *Art as Experience:* "The *product* of art . . . not the *work* of art."[46] This is explored in regards to improvisation by Keith Sawyer, who defines improvisation as a live event in which "the creative process is the product; the audience is watching the creative process as it occurs."[47] So improvisation, as defined by Sawyer, displays an "emphasis on creative process rather than creative product."[48] Some might say that with the product of recordings, this principle of improvisation is automatically betrayed. Although Sawyer differentiates between product creativity and improvisational creativity, he links the two because product creativity is often the *result* of improvisation. He uses the example of the Henri-Georges Clouzot film[49] showing Picasso's process of improvisation that ultimately leads to a "product" (a painting) but he could have as easily used any recording of a jazz ensemble. Crouch uses Picasso to illustrate the same thing, though he ties it directly to the improvisations of Louis Armstrong: "Armstrong made the musical performance a work in progress much like a series of nudes or bathers in Picasso's work, where there is no correct version, only the variation or variations that most move the individual."[50] The existence of multiple recordings of jazz improvisations—for example, the whole phenomenon of the commercial release of "outtakes" from historic jazz recording sessions—participates in this same continuum from process to product.

A distinction can be drawn between a jazz recording intended for commercial release and the act of improvisation because the result of the former is a product—it is fixed and is therefore no longer a process.[51] More and more layers of production continually complicate the continuum between process and product. In the new era of musical construction, however, the process has extended far back into the realm of the fixed product. What used to be fixed may now be another part of a new process, even potentially a new improvisation. Recordings are no longer fixed in the same way, no longer a simple end to process; instead they may be a new starting point for a new process that leads to a new product as part of a continual creative cycle.

The expanded notion of process that is made possible by contemporary recording techniques may provide the depth of experience that some critics seem to miss in traditional jazz recordings as opposed to "live" jazz. It can't replace the subtle relationship between performer, place, and audience, but it can provide different levels and layers of creative expression.

The constructed performance of my application study is an example of how the fluid relationship between process and product, or live and recorded, may be extended. Improvisational expression may be made new by innovative types of collaboration that are not possible in live performance. Certainly recordings give their audience an experience not available to the audience of a live performance. Whereas recordings have limits in contrast to the gestalt of a live performance, they have expanded the boundaries of musical form and process.

Improvisational Form versus Compositional Form

The increasingly fluid relationship between improvisation and composition also encompasses developments in musical form. Robert Cray's unintentional guitar solo, created in the moment and without thought that it was ever to be used, ended up extending the form of the song by adding a lengthy, unrehearsed "vamp" to the end. Although Cray was improvising, his soloing is very structured sounding, progressing from section to section in a way that carries the logic of a composed form. Of course he is playing to the chord changes of the song, so there is underlying harmonic form, but the structure he creates is much more "formal" than simply outlined by the harmonic structure. We can think of this as improvised composition, or "through-composed" soloing, and we have noted its long-standing place in jazz improvisation. The link between improvisation and composition is heightened in this case by the unintentionality of the performance. This musical moment is as fleeting and spontaneous as we might imagine—a purely improvised performance—yet because it is etched in stone thanks to the recording, and because the formality of its musical construction is so memorable, it achieves some of the status of a formal composition. And over time its compositional status increases as it becomes a formal part of music history—transcribed and then studied by an ever-increasing number of people.

The construction of the jazz track that I created for the application study might be thought of as "reconstructed" or "recomposed" form. This is the kind of newly acquired access to form that is the result of the editing capabilities of the DAW. In recomposing these individual improvisations I have taken many liberties with musical form. Twice, as I assembled the final piece, I found the progression of the performances I had chosen suggested to me that the rhythm section should stop for two bars and allow the piano to play solo into the following section. These breaks occurred in two different places in the overall song form. This kind of two-measure break is a fairly common device in jazz arrangement; however, it usually subscribes to a certain formal logic (such as at the end of the final "A" section of the melody as a lead-in to the piano solo) and that wasn't the case in my construction. My "breaks" had a natural feel to them—they are idiomatic—but didn't adhere to this specific convention of form. Instead they were randomly placed in a way that would probably not have been planned as part of an ensemble arrangement.

This kind of seemingly random construction in musical form has attained much greater acceptance in the arrangements of a lot of contemporary hip-hop. The combination of free-form lyric writing approaches and DAW construction techniques has encouraged changes in traditional song forms such that apparently random, nonrepeating elements have become routine. Song sections may also vary widely in their length (number of bars) in contrast to the traditional song form where verses and choruses are usually set to a standard length of eight, twelve, or sixteen bars. These more randomized constructions of musical forms have not prevented large parts of the population from embracing this genre. Most rap and hip-hop is created using the editing techniques available in the digital audio workstation. The flexibility of DAW editing encourages a random quality that is not found in traditional popular music form and reflects an evolving cultural response to music—part of the evolution of the culture's musical ear.

The musicians' responses to my "recomposed" version of their playing point to differing reactions to issues concerning musical form. What Dana liked best about his own piano performance was that it was "nonrepetitive." He did not comment on the two somewhat randomly placed "breaks," but they might have added to his perception of a more varied improvisational approach. Just as the culture seems to be able to embrace less repetitive musical forms, so Dana enjoyed the less repetitive approaches to his own improvisational playing. It is worth noting that it is my intervention through recomposition that assisted him in achieving what he considers to be a desirably less repetitive performance in his improvisation.

On the contrary, it was precisely issues of form that the drummer responded to negatively. Jason focused on the way the ideas were put together, and not on the overall rhythmic "feel," which I had expected to be the area that would be most problematic for him. The reordering of elements felt to Jason like an intrusion on the flow of ideas that he would create in an unedited performance—though he did not comment specifically on the random two-bar breaks. Berliner suggests that it is balancing compositional form with rhythmic freedom that allows an improvising musician to maintain a sense of place within the structure of improvised jazz: "It is only after developing command over the forms of compositions and the diverse rhythmic modes of jazz that they can engage in creative rhythmic thinking without losing their bearings."[52] Perhaps it is the upending of the constructed set of "bearings" that is the reason that Jason found the reordering of his performance intrusive.

Although Berliner affirms that jazz improvisation requires both compositional form and rhythmic and harmonic modes, the status of structure in jazz remains at issue. Historically structure is associated with musical score, and Chanan describes how the status of notation generates a reaction to alternative structures: "Under the hegemony of notation, the Western psyche came to fear the embrace of what is repressed, and responded to any music which manifested this repressed material as if it were a threat to civilization."[53] Avant-garde musician and composer George E. Lewis has insisted that cultural power resides with the creators of structure, and he reiterates this hegemony of the structural status of notation: "The structure inevitably arrives in the form of a written text, a coded set of symbols, intended for realization in performance by a 'performer.'"[54] This is set in contrast to jazz, which instead follows the less formalized improvisational model. However, it is more than simply different: "the dominant culture informs [us], in myriad ways that are continually reinscribed across the breadth of daily experience, that 'improvised' is a synonym for 'unstructured.'"[55] These messages maintain the dichotomy between highbrow and lowbrow, though they may be less apparent than previous pronouncements that separated Western art music from jazz. As an antidote to this hegemony the jazz critic may wish to emphasize the sophistication and spontaneity of content in jazz over the supremacy of the reductive form of musical text.

LeRoi Jones venerates the African tradition and Afro-American music in the occurrence of accident and circumlocution, placing content above form.[56] Stanley Crouch, on the other hand, wishes to redefine the distinction. Rather than accepting "that formal attention is some version of Western imperialism dressed in aesthetic armor," he insists that "it was the ability to create logical music on the wing, responding both to the structure at hand and to the invention of his fellow players"[57] that truly distinguishes the great jazz improvisers. That is to say, while it is still form that sits atop the musical hierarchy, the form created in the jazz context deserves the same status and represents the same level of achievement as composed form. In this sense it is impossible to distinguish between the forms that are cemented in notation versus the forms that are invented in improvisation (and cemented in recordings).[58] Recording is central to this breakdown in the distinction between improvisational form and compositional form. The codifying of improvisations through multiple listening of recordings and through transcriptions of improvised performances reinforces the formal aspects of jazz improvisation.

New Directions in Performance and Composition

Classical music creation is also engaged in the techniques that have transformed popular music construction, although there remains considerable cultural capital in the idea of the score (along with the supremacy of the composer) as a marker of status for Western art music. As noted, Lewis contends that "cultural power clearly rests, for the moment, with the 'bringers of structure.' In Euro-American art-music culture this binary is routinely and simplistically framed as involving the 'effortless spontaneity' of improvisation, versus the careful deliberation of composition—the composer as ant, the improviser as grasshopper."[59] But many in the classical world wish to elevate the joys of improvisation and spontaneity into the realm of both classical composition and performance. There have been subtle developments beyond the standard level of performance interpretation—such as contemporary conductors' propensity to release tempo control briefly to orchestral soloists[60]—but there are also many classical composers who seek a much closer affinity to the improvisational ethic of jazz. Michael H. Zack contends that listening to jazz improvisation—especially of the freer kind—is partly "a matter of tolerating ambiguity and equivocality [and finding] it to be a source of beauty, exhilaration, and creative freedom."[61] Composers in Western art music are seeking to make similar demands on their audiences.

The avant-garde in classical music has long incorporated elements from mass culture, and contemporary computer-based musical experimentation finds some of its most interesting applications within the classical ranks. Certain elements of jazz improvisation, as well as a fascination with the unintentional, have inspired recent interaction between classical musicians and computers. Zack quotes Ryle's description of improvisation and suggests that "the pitting of an acquired competence or skill against unprogrammed opportunity, or obstacle or hazard seems to be right on target. The contention is around what we mean by 'unprogrammed opportunity.' "[62] A new genre within contemporary classic music, sometimes called "interactive composition," incorporates computer capabilities and borrows heavily from jazz and the notion of "unprogrammed opportunity."

The participants in this new genre are using the computer to actively break down the roles of composer, performer, and audience. Modern composers from Stockhausen to Cage have written "composed improvisations" where the abstract instructions require considerable improvisation on the part of the performers. Initiating the debate on where composition ends and improvisation begins was one of the motivating factors behind such scores. Contemporary composers are using computers in interactive ways—that is, the computers are programmed to respond to musical performances—so that musical input results in a response from the computer in the form of musical output. This inspires a response by the performer, thereby triggering new computer-based responses and on and on in a riot of artificially intelligent improvisation. The result, further pressing those boundaries between composition and improvisation, is the "interactive composition."[63] Where one draws the line between composition and improvisation is less important than the motivation, which is to shift the emphasis from the composer or performer to collaboration between the two. This is a motivation that resonates with many popular music forms that are also blurring the distinctions between all of the various elements that go into a musical performance or recording.[64]

An excellent description of the activities that are pressing the boundaries of improvisation, composition, and computer-oriented music interaction comes from Lewis's account of the process involved in creation of his composition *Voyager:*

> *Voyager* . . . is a nonhierarchical, interactive musical environment that privileges improvisation. In *Voyager,* improvisers engage in dialogue with a computer-driven, interactive "virtual improvising orchestra." A computer program analyzes aspects of a human improviser's performance in real time, using that analysis to guide an automatic composition (or, if you will, improvisation) program that generates both complex responses to the musician's playing and independent behavior that arises from its own internal processes.[65]

Here Lewis explains his intentions regarding the categorization of musical activities:

> *Voyager*'s unusual amalgamation of improvisation, indeterminacy, empathy and the logical, utterly systematic structure of the computer pro-

gram is described throughout this article not only as an environment, but as a "program," a "system" and a "composition," in the musical sense of that term. In fact, the work can take on aspects of all of these terms simultaneously—considering the conceptual level, the process of creating the software and the real-time, real-world encounter with the work as performer or listener. Flowing across these seemingly rigid conceptual boundaries encourages both improvisers and listeners to recognize the inherent instability of such taxonomies.[66]

The breadth of Lewis's formulation is telling. The computer continues to act as a primary tool for breaking down categories of musical creation and performance. Part of the way that it does this is the ease with which the computer allows fixed musical recordings to be repurposed in both composing and performing environments. My application study takes recorded elements and uses them in both recomposing and reimprovising the initial recorded performances—providing further examples of the way contemporary practices may participate in Lewis's notion of the instability of fixed musical taxonomies. My studio study shows the ways recording may capture some of the most intimate musical moments, moments that would likely never have occurred in live performance, where the performer's intentionality is constantly reinforced by the presence of the audience. Contemporary musical practice generates a fluidity of musical performance that helps to dissolve hierarchical distinctions between creation and execution, between artist and artisan.

part three { Repurposing Participation

Introduction to Part III

Part III explores the changes in the ways that composers, musicians, and consumers are participating in the musical process as a result of the expanded capabilities provided by digital audio. I began by undertaking a project built around a traditional African piece of musical folklore. The recording I have constructed consists of a re-creation of an African musical story called "Milee Yookoee." I use only samples of previous recordings that are repurposed to create this version of "Milee Yookoee" (audio clip 12). I describe both the musical foundation and the technical procedures used to create this piece of audio, and I draw on this for a broader discussion of contemporary musical process. Key expressive elements from African music have become fundamental to popular music construction and supply the context for a better understanding of contemporary music culture. I explore the complex relationships between music, community, and technology within the context of both historical and hybridized music cultures that are continually adapted within contemporary music.

The studio study (chapter 8) reaches into these notions of participation and community within the technologized music culture of the West. I propose a paradigm shift in the dynamic between the composer, performer, and consumer of music. These relationships are changing as people interact with technology in ways that provide new expressions of social value through participation. I investigate the drive toward creativity that emanates from the pervasive consumer technology of the iPod through to the consumer-oriented compositional tools made available by the music construction software GarageBand. I argue that *the new capac-*

ities created by repurposing of audio elements feed new expressions of partici-
pation and community.

In the final chapter I look more closely at how creativity operates in the contemporary world, where music recordings are often made by constructing repurposed audio. Fundamental changes in the creative process are balanced against universal qualities of creation and participation. Repurposing is seen for its creative potential, notwithstanding its more obvious role in overhauling our notion of where music comes from. In this way the distinctions between elements such as original and copy—including even the reciprocal relationship—begin to dissolve as musicians participate in the new paradigm of construction via repurposing. Finally, two prominent contemporary practices that emanate from the use of repurposed audio—file sharing and cultural appropriation—are briefly examined within this larger context of music participation. These discussions allow me to expand from the specifics of "Milee Yookoee" and the African folkloric tradition into a broader consideration of cross-cultural musical encounters.

seven

{ Application Study
African Folklore and Music Communities

Musical Assembly versus an Assembly of Musicians

Some years ago I studied and played in ensembles with Kwaku Dadey, a master drummer from Ghana who lives and teaches in the San Francisco Bay Area. One of the classes I took with him involved learning traditional folklore pieces from the Yoruba tradition. This music is part of the West African storytelling practice in which the drum pattern is linked to lyrics, in effect telling the story through the drumming. As we studied these various pieces I became interested in transcribing them, and I worked with Kwaku on making transcriptions. Of course there are innumerable difficulties in transcribing any music that doesn't begin as a notated composition. There is a lot of subjective interpretation required to get from a musical piece as it is performed to the necessary reductions of pitch, rhythm, and dynamics needed to create a notated version. Nonetheless, I began the current project of creating a recorded version of the piece "Milee Yookoee" by referring to my notated rendering of the music.

At the foundation of the composition is a typical African approach to polyrhythm. The fundamental rhythmic underpinning involves the subdivision of a basic pulse by three imposed over a subdivision by two: this is technically called *hemiola* but generally referred to as "three against two" in musician's vernacular. In order to create a Western popular music context I began with a strong pulse to set up the subdivision by two, over which I could superimpose the subdivision by three. I used a sample of a single bass drum hit to establish the repeating pulse. This created the same fundamental rhythmic structure used in a lot of dance and electronic music, the "four on the floor" underpinning that began with 1970s disco. "Four on the floor" is a play on words that references four evenly spaced beats per bar played by the bass drum (the drum usually placed on the floor in a typical drum set configuration), though the term originated as an automotive reference to a four-speed manual transmission operated by a floor-mounted shifter. By using this as the basis I have removed the musical context from a traditional African musical setting (which would not employ a straight pulse underpinning) and given it a recognizable popular music context.

The "three against two" polyrhythm was structured over the course of a half-note in 4/4 time. Because the bass drum pulse was made up of quarter-notes, it was outlining the "two" subdivision—two evenly spaced bass drum notes in each half-note. To establish the contrary "three" subdivision I created a track of hi-hat (closed cymbal) sounds and placed them to create an even three pulse over each half-note (quarter-note triplets). I then repeated the bass drum pattern and the hi-hat pattern over a stretch of about three minutes to provide a working foundation.

For the story line I constructed the rhythm pattern from my transcription of the piece as I had learned it from Kwaku. I took drum samples from a collection of drum recordings that I had made of single drum hits. I arranged each appropriately pitched drum into the rhythmic pattern of the story, against the grid of the bass drum pulses that I had previously constructed. This particular piece requires some intricate rhythmic construction, including several phrases where four evenly spaced notes are played in the space of three beats (four against three). I constructed the rhythms mathematically so that all notes were placed in their fractionally correct position against the musical timeline. I listened to the playback, adjusting the levels of each individual element until the whole sounded balanced.

I then went to a sample download website to search for samples to use as accompanying rhythmic substructure. There are many websites that offer royalty-free samples that are searchable by musical genre, instrumentation, key, and tempo. These are typically short loops made of instrumental segments—the building blocks of many typical popular musical recordings. *Royalty free* indicates that the musical sample purchased is not encumbered by any copyright, and the purchaser is free to use it without any royalty payment consideration.

I searched the sample websites under submenus "world music/ African/drums and percussion" and selected tempos within plus or minus 10 bpms (beats per minute) of my original tempo. I auditioned the samples available, listening for samples that contained the polyrhythmic underpin-ning that I wanted to accompany the "melody" (in this case the single-note drum pattern that is the story line of "Milee Yookoee"). I selected one two-bar sample that seemed like it might work well as accompaniment. It con-tained a percussion ensemble of a variety of instruments with an underly-ing pulse that incorporated the "three against two" feeling that I wanted outlined. It was played at a slightly slower tempo than I wanted for my piece, so I time-compressed it to the desired tempo. One of the newly ac-quired capabilities available when using digital audio is this ability to ex-pand or compress (make slower or faster) audio tempos without altering the pitch of the original element.[1] This is a tremendous advantage when creating sample-based compositions such as this, as it allows easy synchro-nization of material that was not originally played at the same tempo.

Once I had this two-bar percussion phrase at the desired tempo I looped it to play continuously under the entire piece. I then worked on a second two-bar percussion phrase, consisting of a different percussion en-semble playing in a similar style. I adjusted the tempo of this phrase by us-ing the time compression function and looped it to play continuously. The two loops worked well together, providing a dense, polyrhythmic bed of percussion. I then worked on a third percussion phrase using a lighter-sounding ensemble of wood block sounds. After adjusting the tempo and looping this phrase I began to construct an arrangement from the various elements.

I built an arrangement without trying to emulate any traditional mod-els. I started with the two contrary pulses—bass drum and hi-hat—added the first loop and then played the story of "Milee Yookoee" using my drum samples playing over the percussion bed. At the conclusion of the story line I started a second loop, creating a more dense underlay of percussion. After eight bars I further developed the polyrhythmic percussion bed by adding a snare drum pattern that I created from a snare drum sample. This pattern reinforced the tradition African bell pattern.[2] I let that play for eight more bars and then added the third percussion loop, creating a very dense and highly polyrhythmic percussion ensemble. I then broke the piece back down to the original loop with the bass drum pulse. After four bars I added the hi-hat pulse back in, and four bars later I repeated the story of "Milee Yookoee" as it had been programmed using individual drum samples. Once again, at the end of the story line, I started the sec-ond loop—this time letting the percussion groove for a few seconds and then slowly fading the music out. Arranged in this manner the entire piece was slightly over two minutes long. Please refer to audio clip 12 to listen to this piece and follow the arrangement I have described here.

The piece of music that I have created employs only preexisting samples of recordings that have been repurposed to create this version of "Milee Yookoee." That is to say, I did not actually "play" a single note in the traditional sense, yet I am responsible for the existence of this version of this piece of music—*I constructed it.* Although created in isolation, this music can be shared as a listening experience, it can be considered as a technical process, and it can be treated as a musicological reference to the traditional folkloric story line. Through this application project I explored the bond that may occur through musical creation regardless of the cultural context, and the many elements in that bond that cross widely divergent cultural environments.

The essence of a musical experience is inevitably tied to social and cultural integration, a part of the historically and culturally contingent nature of musical experience that we have been repeatedly reminded of as we have explored musical effect. Therefore, the specific musical manifestation—the individual piece of music—may be experienced very differently by different people (especially those from different cultures or at different times). Yet there are numerous elements that remain consistent regardless of the musical, cultural, or historical specifics. These include the expression of creativity, which is an amalgamation of the historical and cultural history with the unknowns of individual expression; the interaction between the musician and the tools of creativity, where we find the intersection of the human and technical in that pursuit of creative expression; and the experience of music as taking an active role in the construction of society and culture.

Later in this chapter the larger issues revolving around isolation and collaboration will be discussed within the context of the African music tradition. Essential cultural expressions of community and creativity will be considered in their musical context, balanced between their representation in the African tradition and their parallels in the world of digital audio. The relationship between art and technology is primarily a social process, a cultural dynamic. In light of the contemporary social network of audio experiences I will consider a possible reversal in the conventional hierarchy of production and reproduction. The use of repurposed audio through sampling technology allows for new compositional models where the copy achieves a status that may overtake the original. This also speaks to the increasingly important and varied role of the recordist as a more di-

rect participant in musical creations, and to the idea of the recordist as au-
teur. In this creative environment musical and technological elements become more intertwined than ever before. While these new relationships
proceed helter-skelter in the practices of the music community, there is
the need for them to be more fully examined within the larger context of
cultural expression.

Before exploring these ideas further it is valuable to first look more
deeply into the African music tradition. In doing so it may seem that my
application project (the constructed "Milee Yookoee") and the tradition it
draws from are light years apart, if not diametrically opposed. However, if
we break down assumptions about both the computer age and traditional
musical expressions, a more balanced picture of the impact of contemporary audio technology may be found.

African Rhythm and Values

Music is deeply woven into the structure of traditional African culture, and
rhythmic expression is at the heart of traditional African music. John
Miller Chernoff maintains that despite the great variations in the manifestations of music and culture throughout Africa, there remains a sufficient
thread of truth in the above statement to render it useful for discussion.[3]
The extent to which music is deeply embedded in the *structure* and *function* of African folkloric culture is reflected in the widespread participation
in musical practice. While we identify these as distinguishing features of
African folkloric culture, at the same time we must recognize that the
African and European musical traditions share a great many elements,
both musically and culturally.

Kofi Agawu observes that most ethnomusicology focuses on the differences between African and European musical traditions, and this distorts
the myriad ways in which they are the same, which might be of equal interest and importance.[4] Agawu focuses on musical sameness, while acknowledging musical differences. What follows here focuses on musical
differences that have evolved into sameness through the adoption of elements from African music in the West. In line with Agawu, none of what
follows should be interpreted as essentializing difference between African
and European traditions, and ultimately the focus here is on the sameness
of musical cultures as apparently divergent as African folkloric music and
high-tech Western popular music. What follows is also a representation of
African music that, while drawn from anthropological research, is not to

be understood as a totalizing account of the complexity or diversity of musical expression within Africa.

As Christopher Small explains, African music is "not set apart in any way from everyday life but is an integral and essential part of it, and plays an important role in all aspects of social interaction and individual self-realization."[5] The intention of musical activity revolves around the practicality of functions. Amiri Baraka describes these functions as consisting of many of the most essential human activities, including courtship, labor, rites of passage, spiritual pursuits, battle, leisure, and so on.[6] Fundamental to African musical culture is the assumption that everyone is musical: "Musicking is in fact thought of as being as basic a form of social interaction as talking."[7] This doesn't mean that all Africans are equally gifted or skilled; it simply means that the universality of music practice is central to the cultural identity. Most African languages are tonal and the connection between the rhythms and melodies of language and music is very strong. "A cursory comparison of transcriptions of speech and transcriptions of drumming reveals striking similarities between the two domains."[8] Thus the status of musical expression in Africa "can be used to challenge the privileged conceptions of both language and writing as preeminent expressions of human consciousness."[9] This is an indication of the level of importance that music attains in African culture. Indeed, the African cultivation of music encompasses the ethical and aesthetic values of both community and individual.[10]

These expressions of structure and function in the African musical tradition coalesce into a highly evolved rhythmic concept. As such the intricacies of rhythm operate on many different levels of complexity: "rhythm is the most perceptible and the least material thing."[11] David Brackett quotes Olly Wilson as saying that "Africanness consists of the way of doing something, not simply that it is done"[12] and thus reinforces the need to delve into the specifics of African music construction. Mark Katz also uses Wilson to extend this idea one step further. He quotes Wilson as asserting that the African and African-American traditions seek a "heterogeneous sound ideal," and he suggests that using loops as I have done in my project may participate in this same ideal.[13]

Repurposed audio, in the form of loops from audio taken from a variety of sources, is a natural extension of the ideal of heterogeneity. Thus loop-based music, which has emerged from the African-American music traditions, is a contemporary expression of music's interaction with social function, utilizing recent developments in audio technology. This is not to suggest that the varieties of contemporary musical participation are equivalent to the range of expressions of participation in the African folkloric tradition, but to further the exploration of these relationships it is valuable to consider some of the ways that African music is manifest in the West. This encourages us to recognize that musical expression is much more than simply the music that is played, but most significantly, the *way* that it is played.

"It Don't Mean a Thing If It Ain't Got That Swing"

Musical notation provides a means of "recording" essential information about musical performance. However, notation is very limited when it comes to subtle elements of expression. Digging deeper into the language of music yields many layers of expressive capabilities. Burrow through the strata of harmonic theory, and myriad complex relationships emerge: passing tones, implied key changes, and ambiguous tonal centers all surface as tools of expression. These are all readily analyzed within music's theoretical bounds. Peel the rhythmic veneers and similar elements are encountered: the backbeat, syncopation, and odd time signatures expand the range of musical exposition within a widely understood theoretical framework. Dig further into harmony and rhythm and unearth a set of expressive tools that form a whole range of expressive techniques that are not so easily quantified—a whole musical subtext.

A major portion of this subtext is a product of purposeful deviations from notational values.[14] In melodic terms this means played or sung notes that intentionally vary from an adherence to precise chromatic pitch. In terms of rhythm this means a divergence from strict metronomic timekeeping. This is far from "Can't keep a beat," however. In fact it is the opposite. Consistent placement of notes that subtly deviate from metronomic time is a powerful form of musical expression. It is widely practiced in African folkloric music and has been integrated into much of the popular music in the West. American popular music is directly indebted to African music in the adoption of syncopation and backbeat. This is widely recognized. What is less understood is that we have actually learned different ways to *feel* rhythm by adapting the African model of variations in note placement within our popular musical forms. *Africa has taught us how to "groove."* This is different from expressiveness in Western art music because of the consistent nature of the purposeful nonmetronomic note placement. In Western art music variations in note placement are used to interpret phrases and passages independently and often include variations in tempo. Groove derived from African music functions as an autonomous, omnipresent layer of variations in note placement relative to a stable tempo.

An outstanding description of the various expressive elements that are integral to African folkloric music and have found expression in American music is the following list of components of the American spiritual from Samuel A. Floyd Jr.:

> These included elements of the calls, cries, and hollers; call-and-response devices; additive rhythms and polyrhythms; heterophony, pendular thirds, blue notes, bent notes, and elisions; hums, moans, grunts, vocables, and other rhythmic-oral declamations, interjections, and punctuations; off-beat melodic phrasings and parallel intervals and chords; constant repetition of rhythmic and melodic figures and phrases (from which riffs and vamps would be derived); timbral distortions of various kinds; musical individuality within collectivity; game-rivalry; hand-clapping, foot-patting, and approximations thereof; and the metronomic foundational pulse that underlies all Afro-American music.[15]

From a purely rhythmic standpoint Floyd hints at the depths of complexity contained in the African musical tradition. Syncopation, backbeat, and small-scale rhythmic repetition form easily analyzable elements that have been recognized as gifts to American music from African sources. The concept of offbeat phrasing represents an expressive element more difficult to define in the traditional language of European musical analysis. Western music tends to create rhythm based on a regularity of rhythmic subdivision, employing units of equal value called bars. My use of "four on the floor" as a means of putting "Milee Yookoee" into a popular music context imposes a European sense of rhythmic construction. Traditional African music imagines rhythm as a looser conglomerate of both musical and physical expressions (dance). Agawu faults much analysis of the rhythm tradition in African music for not incorporating this "choreographic element."[16] Beyond this difference in conceptual organization the African tradition also focuses on minute variations in note placement (off-beat phrasing) in order to create what is now commonly referred to as musical "groove."

Attempts to understand "groove" have been hindered by limitations in technical ability as well as limitations of language. Attempts at such analysis have also become confused by the needless addition of value judgments such as the following: "scientific analysis of rhythmic components of a given groove would be meaningless if the analyst (or the analyst's 'informants') could not distinguish between a 'good' groove and 'bad' one."[17] The experience of musical groove is exceedingly personal. A musical groove may be considered good by any individual who is drawn to it. Nonetheless, there are communal elements of groove that are traditional to cultures and have been long admired by fans and analyzed by musicians and musicologists. Many of the most prevalent, admired, and mystifyingly complex grooves have come to us from the African tradition. Among these is the widely beloved groove identified as "swing." Part of the mission of musicians and musicologists has been to discover better ways of analyzing and understanding musical groove.

Along the way the meaning of the word *groove* has become confused. Here, and throughout this work, I am using *groove* to refer to the rhythmic interpretation or "feel" of a particular performance—a "feel" that is dependent on a repetitive interpretation of note placement and accentuation. This is the most common use for the word among musicians in the world of popular music. Musicologists have come to use this word to include a combination of what I would call arrangement and groove. Such is the case in an essay from Lawrence Zbikowski entitled "Modelling the Groove: Conceptual Structure and Popular Music." Zbikowski lays out a structure for groove analysis that has the potential to encompass both arrangement and interpretation. However, the essay proceeds to interpret several pieces of popular music strictly from the standpoint of arrangement—of how musical elements are put together as opposed to the "feel" of how they are played—and in my experience most musicians would not identify this analysis with the primary notion of what comprises groove.

The popular musician's meaning of groove becomes clearer when it comes to judging the value of a groove. Zbikowski, as with Brackett, asserts that "listeners know a good groove when they hear it,"[18] though he immediately identifies this as a problematical statement. The problem for Zbikowski is not the value judgment but "the status of the knowledge behind these actions: what is it that listeners know when they know a good groove?"[19] He goes on to suggest that the difficulty in assessing this knowledge is that neither the listener nor the musician has a good idea about how the judgment has been made. He complains that if you ask musicians, "what makes for a good groove," they "often as not become vague, refer to things like 'feel,'"[20] and generally skirt the issue. He then proceeds toward his structure for modeling groove (which again, could incorporate elements of "feel"), and his analysis focuses solely on arrangement. But the "vague" musician's reference to feel is actually at the heart of the meaning of groove that is always rooted in "time feel."[21] Any of the examples that Zbikowski explores could be judged as "good" groove or "bad" groove depending on how they're played. The most funky James Brown arrangement, in the hands of the wrong musicians, could be judged as utterly "grooveless" by musicians familiar with that music—yet the parts played could conform to the notationally correct arrangement of the original James Brown recording. Thus the value of a groove is completely dependent on "feel" and to analyze only the arrangement aspect of a piece of music is essentially to bypass the groove component.

The world of popular music vocabulary usage isn't quite so clear-cut as this would suggest. I have also heard musicians refer to arrangements as "grooves," so the meaning of the word is, to some extent, ambiguous. However, I have never heard the word *groove* used in practice, when it is intended to carry the weight of a value judgment, without the primary reference being to "feel" and not to arrangement. A good groove is always a "felt" groove. And feel is not "vague" but quite specific and increasingly analyzable. A transcription of a performance does not represent a good groove; it can only present the opportunity for being a good groove if it is played with "groove."

Contemporary manifestations of groove have followed along a progression that began with the purely communal expression of musical ensembles. In these cases the inner time of musicians is shared through individual musical articulations,[22] but the group is also under the direction of one individual. In African ensembles there is a master drummer who sets the tempo and focuses the groove—in small rock and jazz ensembles this task falls most frequently to the drummer. In larger ensembles the conductor or bandleader directs the groove. In loop-based musical construction the groove is selected from previous performances, previous manifestations of groove, and it is the builder of the piece that is ultimately responsible for the final groove. All of the elements I describe in the "Milee Yookoee" project—from selecting to modifying and combining elements—coalesce into a new groove. The computer environment has directly entered into the groove-making process, and while African music taught us how to groove, the computer has extended the ways that we may apply those lessons.

Thus, with loop-based music constructed in a DAW it may be that "no performers are required; indeed, there is no 'performance' in a conventional sense."[23] But does this mean that there is no intention, no activation of groove aesthetics? Construction of music through building blocks of elements creates the notion that music is less something that you do and more something that you know.[24] But whether it is through doing or knowing, there is still judgment; with loop-based music construction, people are making the original grooves, but it is people who are remaking them as well. And, as with Brackett's quest for "good" and "bad" grooves, people are making judgments about these grooves regardless of whether such judgments are the product of "knowing" or "doing." Zbikowski goes farther in acknowledging the historical and cultural basis for value judgments about grooves. This is appropriate as such judgments vary within different cultural contexts and ultimately must be reserved for each individual to make. There can be no universal judgment of the quality of any musical groove. This is directly in line with Allan Moore's broader observation that "No sooner do we suggest that a music is 'better,' than we have to ask 'better at what?' and 'for whom?'"[25]

Elements of the Diaspora of African Rhythm

It is valuable in the context of Western technology to note some of the key aspects of the diaspora of African rhythm and to see how new technologies reinforce some of these elements. The use of call-and-response and repetition are hallmarks of African folkloric music that have been tremendously influential in American music in the past two centuries. Ultimately the confluence of African rhythm and European harmony forms the basis of a great deal of the popular music tradition in America.

Call-and-response is so essential to African-American music that it has been called the "trope of tropes" and proposed as the musical equivalent of Henry Louis Gates's identification of "signifyin(g)" in the African-American literary tradition.[26] From spirituals through gospel, and from R & B to hip-hop, the call-and-response model has been a central characteristic of African-American music. Closely related is the tradition of musical repetition. The distinctively African expression of musical repetition involves extended, small-scale phrase repetition and includes elements of simple variation through improvisation. Both of these practices distinguish the African musical tradition from traditional European musical construction. Agawu is careful to qualify the extent to which this practice represents significant difference: "What perhaps distinguishes the African usages is the degree of repetition of the constituent patterns, the foregrounding of repetitions as a modus operandi. If this counts as a difference, it is one of degree, not of kind."[27] In Agawu's eagerness to emphasize sameness—certainly a worthy endeavor—he has perhaps succumbed to overstatement. The distinction between the foregrounding of repetition in African usage and the occasional appearance of such repetition in the history of Western art music must be considered a significant difference.

James Snead elevates repetition "to a position of ontological importance as a distinctive marker of 'black' and 'European' cultural difference."[28] Snead further asserts that black culture accepted musical repetition as a form of beauty, whereas European culture, especially in the nineteenth century, avoided repetition in favor of accumulations.[29] While Snead may be debated on this point—consider baroque dance music (and Agawu's general objection)—the African practice of lengthy, small-scale repetitions with variations has hardly been central to Western art music until its quite recent (and quite influential) appearance in the works of composers such as Steve Reich and Philip Glass (both of whom readily acknowledge the African roots of some of their music). In the meantime this style of repetition has become a fundamental musical principle in American popular music from the earliest appearances of the blues.

In a technical sense repetition is a necessary element in the more elaborate improvisations that have become the basis for most American jazz. The improviser relies on repetition for the harmonic sequence, but often even more specifically for the ostinato of the accompaniment. On the social level both call-and-response and this African form of musical repetition reinforce the integration of music with the fabric of society, providing structure and supporting social functions. Call-and-response does this through direct participation and message reinforcement, while repetition, which allows individual expression through variation, supports small-scale freedoms within a tightly structured community. Both elements also provide support for an emphasis on communal, participatory music making. Ultimately it is the marriage of these African rhythmic elements with basic harmonic elements from the European hymns spread by colonialism that yields the early missionary hymns in America. Together the two traditions forge the fundamentals of American popular music.[30] The triumph of the fundamental American form, the twelve-bar blues, derives "in roughly equal measure from African tribal call-and-response chants and the simple triadic chords of missionary hymns."[31]

This evolution is reinforced by the blending of the primary motivations that compel these traditions. These forms that merged to create American popular music, the African and the European, reflect the cultural heritage whereby "more participatory musics are more rhythmically complex (and harmonically simple); more contemplative musics are rhythmically simpler (and more harmonically complex)."[32] This analysis in no way reinforces the racist portrayal of the African musical tradition as simple (body) and the European as complex (mind).[33] Quite the contrary, it acknowledges the deeply complex and yet complementary roots of both of these traditions. And thus, along with these rhythmical complexities, American culture gets a dose of the central qualities of structure, function, and universal participation that come with them.

It is noteworthy that other aspects of African rhythm have not made significant inroads in American music. The highly integrated practice of polyrhythm—multiple rhythms expressed with roughly equal weight over an entire piece of music—traveled from Africa to Cuba and South America but has never had a significant impact in European or North American music.[34] This may be traced to essential differences in religious philosophy if one accepts the case for a parallel "between the aesthetic conception of multiple rhythms in music and the religious conception of multiple forces in the world."[35] The structure of African religious belief incorporates a multiplicity of spirits that are both independent and also considered manifestations of a supreme being. The many rhythms of the music might be considered expressions of the spirits. Such a philosophy finds sympathetic expressions in the indigenous cultures of Cuba and South America but is at odds with Euro-American monism. Such a simplistic concordance as this breaks down, however, when other musical attributes are considered. Counterpoint, for example, might also be understood as an expression of multiplicity but it is prevalent in the much of Western art music.

The "Milee Yookoee" project adopts the practice of repetition—heightened and made more rigid while at the same time more accessible to a Western audience through the use of sample-based compositional construction—while incorporating the much less common use of a highly integrated and consistent expression of polyrhythm (hemiola). Is it possible that the more formalistic tendencies of loop-based construction might ease the sense of dislocation created by this type of polyrhythm for those steeped in Western pop music? It certainly makes such construction more available to a much wider range of composers, for it removes the skill element required for performance—the "doing" as opposed to the "knowing." It has also made the integration of different styles of music much simpler, and thus loop-based construction has been a prime factor in driving the current hybridization of different forms of music—a process the merit and meaning of which are still very much debated (see chapter 9 for more on this).

Community and the Process of Participation

Contemporary cultures are very different from the cultures of the nine-teenth century, and one of the most profound areas of difference is in the nature of community. Nineteenth-century patterns of community were much more significantly bound by geography, while any good definition of community in the contemporary urban world must include structural and functional elements that are not defined by territory. There are the ex-plicit communities of geography and of primary institutions such as churches and schools, but there are also the implicit communities of func-tion or process that draw people together through secondary interests and activities. It is these implicit communities that have been the most pro-foundly affected by current technologies. Mass media and now the Inter-net have made for communities of interest that are truly transnational, and some of the most conspicuous are established based on musical interests.

At the end of the nineteenth century the experience of music in the West had already begun to be transformed from the direct participation of previous societies to the passive audience of the concert hall. The develop-ment of audio recording then began its transformation of musical recep-tion into an experience that was secondhand, the experience of reproduc-tion rather than of live performance. Benjamin argues that mechanical reproduction of music, which has the destructive element of "the liquida-tion of traditional value of the cultural heritage,"[36] is nevertheless positive for the masses because social emancipation requires the dissolution of tra-dition that binds people by class. Of course social divisions also played a large role in earlier societies, but this does not alter the fundamental con-nection made when communities interact directly through music and dance. The participatory nature of live music performance, and the social cohesion that it engenders, allows a quality of integration that is simply not possible in "virtual" communities. Even real-time interaction over the Internet is clearly not the same thing as a musical experience where indi-viduals are physically present together.

The alienation and fragmentation that are so much a part of contem-porary culture are reflected in a certain dislocation between music and its reception, but mechanical reproduction is not necessarily the primary cause that may work to strip this connection. To place such dislocation at the feet of reproduction is to miss many of the broader sources of the contemporary cultural condition such as the dislocation of families, the crowded urban environment, the automobile, and so forth. As previously noted, it may be elements of the process of reproduction that are responsible for *restoring* some of the integrative forces within the postmodern experience. Just as Benjamin saw both positive and negative value systems reflected in mechanical reproduction, so might we note the positive and negative effects on community building that mechanically reproduced music may have.

Is it fair to conclude that the Western cultural experience of recorded music denies community? Is it appropriate to taint mechanical reproduction as a force of social isolationism, and deny its own forms of participation? Jonathan Sterne models recording technology as part of an essential social network. From the earliest forms of audio reproduction "these technologies were understood as having the potential to break down social boundaries and at the same time to help enforce social norms."[37] There is a complex relationship, based on shared values and assumptions, that builds a "social correspondence" between the performing musician and the sound that is experienced coming from a radio or CD player. Louis Meintjes sees the mediation of the recording studio as essential to the way that music creation not only transfers elements of cultural identity but also transforms them.[38] This parallels Sterne's network of musical creation, but Meintjes is speaking from a directly African perspective. In her ethnographic study of a South African recording studio she chronicles ways in which contemporary technologies of music making cut across international and pan-cultural influences: "I show how global and national dynamics interface with local and individual struggles to reshape social life by reworking expressive forms."[39] This is not to deny ongoing differences between Western and African music culture, but it does affirm the shared qualities of the community-building network in contemporary music creation.

The recognition and acceptance of contemporary music construction practices as retaining a connection to community building requires a broader recognition of the function of music in culture. Sterne acknowledges the false dream of a vanishing mediator but replaces it with the practical relationship between the network of sound reproduction and the consumer.[40] Where Sterne sees the practicality of current networks as having maintained the role of music in culture, Attali sees the need for a more profound alteration before music's position might be restored to its standing in earlier eras. Attali's vision of contemporary culture, where the de-ritualization of music has left it with only a "hereditary memory [of] music's power of communication,"[41] chronicles the increasing mediation between music and culture with much less apparent hope for its healing. Music is still there, but it has lost its connection to ceremony and thus to the "logic" of the process of communication. It is no longer focused within cultural institutions. According to Attali, "when this happens, music can no longer affirm that society is possible."[42] Attali concludes that "in this sense, music is meaningless, liquidating, the prelude to a cold social silence in which man will reach his culmination in repetition. Unless it is the herald of the birth of a relation never yet seen."[43] Ultimately Attali's hopeful model of a new understanding and practice of "composition" returns music to the role of societal building block.

But is Attali's pessimism warranted? Beyond the conflict between his interpretation and Sterne's more generous notion of community building lies an acceptance of music's role that is more broadly understood within its social context. There is a lot of contemporary music—from Eno's ambient music explorations to the smooth jazz radio stations that play in office waiting rooms around the world—that is intentionally dislocated from the traditional role of musical engagement. This music's meaning is clearly tied to its social landscape in ways that are profoundly affected by the cultural climate. Recognizing this helps to remind us how music can change our experience of things. Conversely, how music is experienced in different cultures may be significantly different. For example, in the African folkloric tradition rhythms are understood as a sequence of beat groupings added one after the other, whereas in European music rhythms are understood as structured within a preexisting metric system of beat groupings. Whether it's the notion of ambient music or the context of rhythmical understanding, if we lack the cultural context, we may well mistake the true intent of the musical enterprise.[44]

The true intent of the musical enterprise includes social interactions, which are reflected and advanced in musical interactions. The way musicians and audiences must cooperate with one another in order to complete the musical experience provides positive models for the way people must cooperate in order to create community structures of all kinds: "Music, then, reveals with singular clarity just how people can work together, and how it is possible to design a framework within which they will do so."[45] More specifically: "Participation in music is like a flight simulator for social life: listening to others, developing your sensitivity to them, experiencing different relationships with them as the musical lines interact with one another—all these constitute a kind of crash course in interpersonal relationships."[46] This constructivist view of art described by Nicholas Cook means that music doesn't just reflect a cultural condition but may actually change it. Whether or not we are able to distinguish music's significance in any particular culture we must acknowledge music's power to participate in and directly influence that culture. Cook uses as an example the new South African anthem and notes that "It doesn't symbolize unity, it enacts it."[47]

Matthew Butterfield also examines the power of the social interaction that is enacted in musical play, placing it within the context of larger social events. He uses this broader understanding as a structure for musical analysis that he calls "situational particularism." Butterfield contrasts this with standard musical analysis, which analyzes musical content outside of its larger context: "Instead of examining music apart from the real situations in which it is encountered, it considers how the structure of a given situation determines the social and cognitive relevance of musical details."[48] Butterfield's situational particularism is more restrictive than Cook's constructivist model in that it privileges live performance as the preferred means of enacting social structure from the social interaction of musicians. He notes the dislocation of recorded performers both from the audience and from each other, as in the case of performances on a single recording that are recorded at different times. Butterfield suggests that "Technological advancements have thus altered the social meaning of performance as it takes place in the recording studio. Musical interaction is largely mediated; as a result, it loses much of its erotic social potential."[49]

Butterfield's project focuses on jazz performance, so it is perhaps understandable that he emphasizes the ways in which recordings separate musicians from their audience. In the case of my "Milee Yookoee" project (and similar musical constructions that are common in today's contemporary music) the detachment from the original performances is key to the social construction of the particular musical experience. It is true that the musicians are removed from this social interaction, but they were actually removed as a part of the original construction of the musical piece, which repurposed their performances in an entirely new context. The very indirect relationship of the original musician's performance to the final musical construction is an essential part of the new musical creation. This is key to the nature of my "Milee Yookoee" project because, while it draws from a specific performances of African music, it is a contemporary expression of music construction. Although the music is created in a social vacuum, it may be encountered in a highly social setting as a shared listening experience. Recordings may be shared in very social environments, both face-to-face and in the virtual communities of the Internet: "today's isolated fans can find like-minded friends on the Internet."[50] This community experience may activate ways in which the music's social construction influences larger cultural and interpersonal relationships—it is a contemporary expression of social interaction. This is the kind of social exchange that participates as a constructivist force as it might in any culture. This suggests an inclusionist understanding of all forms and technologies of musical expression as participants in the constructivist model.

Technology Releases Musical Community

It is most appropriate to view the differences between musical cultures as simply ideological rather than comprehensive, as per Baraka: "Ideology functions, at least in part, to fix the individual in a certain place at a certain time by organizing the world. The individual constructs reality from a position already inside that reality."[51] This ideological position encompasses the social, the political, and the economic; it is expressed by production and articulation that emanate from a unique cultural location. Cultural ideologies are bound by history and location, and we may look beyond them to discover the similarities in musical communities.

Floyd understands that the differences in musical expressions are not fundamental to humanity, only to specific human cultures—what he terms "cultural memory." The limited cultural memory of an individual may cause them to condemn any unfamiliar tradition unfairly. The listener must "possess the knowledge, perceptual skills, emotional histories, and cultural perspectives appropriate to the various genres."[52] Thus some misinterpret the blues and call-and-response traditions as "shameful relics of the American past," whereas others who see an orchestral work as "'dry,' 'scientific', or 'unemotional' do not appreciate the aesthetic values of European-derived musical expression."[53] The differences in the specifics are eclipsed by the similarities in the essential musical objectives of personal expression and communication. Music specifics are culturally based, but the greater musical "project" is the same in all communities. Certain composers are able to create a new paradigm; Duke Ellington, for example, did so by "making use of the myths and the mythic constructions of African-American culture and by treating African-derived myth and ritual within the context of European-derived myth and ritual."[54] Ellington successfully bridges the two cultural communities. Community is created and re-created within a cultural context, and we are continually integrated and reintegrated into that context.

The digital age of sound reproduction corresponds to the age of the Internet and the promise of transnational, distance-based communities. The Internet has greatly expanded the ability to experience and share music instantaneously and to create music in a "virtual" community. Musicians create recordings together without physically being together—the digital audio being transmitted in real time over the Internet.[55] Some artists are using the Internet to provide individual elements of their music for those who might be interested in manipulating and reprocessing it in differing forms—allowing fans to become partners with the artists in the creative process.[56] Thus, as the anthropologist Clifford Geertz indicates, the cultural resources become the building blocks of the culture and the technology is a central participant, just as the more traditional elements of communication always have been: "Words, images, gestures, body-marks, and terminologies, stories, rites, customs, harangues, melodies, and conversations, are not mere vehicles of feelings lodged elsewhere, so many reflections, symptoms, and transpirations. They are the locus and machinery of the thing itself."[57] The communities of music live within the context of the entire range of cultural relationships. As Geertz insists, this time with the help of Michelle Rosaldo:

> "[If] we hope," Rosaldo writes, with the groping awkwardness this sort of view tends to produce, given the ingrained Cartesianism of our psychological language, "to learn how songs, or slights, or killings, can stir human hearts we must inform interpretation with a grasp of the relationship between expressive forms and feelings, which themselves are culture-bound and which derive their significance from their place within the life experiences of particular people in particular places."[58]

Although it may be typical to note that "for preliterate peoples everywhere, music was an important aid to structuring thought,"[59] it really is thus for all people in all cultures, including cultures after literacy. In fact, early childhood studies tell us that "music is constituted as an integrative human process right from the start of our lives in the world,"[60] and this goes for all of us.

Yet the value of music extends beyond music's contribution to the culture—its cultural capital—to its real value in economic terms. Too much music analysis tries to separate the broader cultural interaction of music from its simple commodification. At the same time we have seen forms of cultural nostalgia and determinism demonize contemporary forms of technological mediation. Musical expression is not independent of the network from production and distribution through to consumption,[61] and technologies provide ever-changing commodity environments for music within the larger network of contemporary culture. Our understanding of musical participation must embrace all of these elements while recognizing the contradictions that such an embrace might entail.

One can detail any specific historical genre and discover the ways it which it furthers sociability, how it strives for community. At the same time the mediation of technology or the demands of commodification may supply narratives that seem to contradict traditional notions of musical practice or musical community. I have sought to position my re-creation of an African folklore piece in line with more traditional musical creation despite the fact that I didn't play one note. I also claim it as a part of the process that sustains musical community despite the fact that it was created in isolation. Frith documents a similar process in regards to contemporary folk music—noting the ways that it presents itself as naturalistic rather than musically sophisticated, and communal rather than commercial. Yet the striving for community is present even though it "seems to rest on an essential self-deception—that which is worked hard for is presented as coming naturally, that which is commodified is presented as communal."[62] But isn't there a subtext to every artistic cultural interchange that might represent a kind of deception about the effort needed to achieve what is presented as natural, or that seeks to hide the exchange of capital (cultural or otherwise) behind the experience of community? Part of the profound connection of music to community is its ability both to be part of an apparent deception and at the same time to engage community on a fundamental level.[63]

The nature of musical participation in cultures is separated by degree, not by essence. In *Music and Technoculture* Lysloff and Gay confirm the contribution of technology itself to community building while reiterating the potential dichotomy: "the technological device, whether it is a quill pen or a personal computer, gains meaning through human agency. Because of human agency, technology can be politically oppressive yet also liberating; it might build community while simultaneously causing social alienation."[64] One could add the ancient African talking drum to the list of technological devices, and this might help to remind us how intimately technology and music making are connected. Outside of the voice[65] music is *always* expressed through technology, and the DAW stands in line with the wooden flute as essential elements in the cultural exchange.

The level of integration of music with fundamental human qualities such as wisdom, reverence, and social code is exemplified in the African folklore tradition. This music represents an elemental force in the culture, and to recognize this level of integration helps one consider the interaction between technology and contemporary musical practices as it provides a benchmark for the interaction between music and community. As a means of further exploring the way contemporary music practices reflect similar qualities, I propose an evolving relationship between consumption and composition. The iPod introduces new modes of music consumption, and GarageBand offers a new breed of recording studio tools. Together the two provide a possible model for the future of music participation that shares elements with the African folklore tradition as well as with Western music culture prior to the advent of recorded audio.

eight

{ Studio Study
From iPod to GarageBand

Art and Artifice Encounter Technology

Much has been written on questions surrounding art, craft, amateurism, authenticity, and meaning in cultural artifacts. This studio study concentrates on the relationship of these broader ideas to the shifting dynamics of participation between composer, performer, and consumer of music. I propose that we are witnessing a paradigm shift in the music consumer's relationship to music creation. This is a circular proposition where the technology that facilitates new forms of music consumption is also returning consumers to the act of musical creation. To begin I follow researchers struggling with the implicit cultural hierarchies that seem to rank these successive elements—composer/writer at the top, performer attempting to interpret her own or others' compositions, and the consumer struggling to participate within the context of what is often described as the diminished experience of recorded versus live music. Where are we now in this relationship between the technologies of reproduction and the notions of art and artifice? And most critically, what is happening to that lowest of status participant, the listener? This continues my work from chapter 3, which first explored the dichotomy of art and artifice, using it to frame discussions of determinism, the musical network, and authenticity.

In a great deal of cultural analysis we find the effects that are attributed to music recordings getting the short end of the stick. Walter Benjamin famously declares that as a result of mechanical reproduction of an original work of art "the quality of its presence is always depreciated."[1] Since then, other significant voices have chimed in with similar sentiments. Here's

Roland Barthes's relevant comment: "Today, under the pressure of the mass long-playing record, there seems to be a flattening out of technique; which is paradoxical in that the various manners of playing are all flattened out into perfection: nothing is left but pheno-text."[2] Jacques Attali attacks on similar grounds, describing what he perceives as excluded in recorded performance:

> Little by little, the very nature of music changes: the unforeseen and the risks of representation disappear in repetition. The new aesthetic of performance excludes error, hesitation, noise. It freezes the work out of festival and the spectacle: it reconstructs it formally, manipulates it, makes it abstract perfection. This vision gradually leads people to forget that music was once background noise and a form of life, hesitation and stammering. Representation communicated energy. Repetition produces information free of noise.[3]

Edward Said comments on (and sides with) Adorno:

> Some years ago Adorno wrote a famous and, I think, correct account of "the regression of hearing," in which he emphasized the lack of continuity, concentration, and knowledge in the listeners that has made real musical attention more or less impossible. Adorno blamed such things as radio and records for undermining and practically eliminating the possibility that the concertgoer could play an instrument or read a score. To those disabilities we can add today's complete professionalization of performance.[4]

These accounts discredit recordings as diminished versions of musical performance and the effect on musicians as restrictive; Simon Frith points out that in the 1960s "the classical music world was wary of musical perfection achieved through studio 'cheating.'"[5] One frequent argument is that the musicians themselves, upon hearing their performances played back to them, are driven by an ethic of perfection to save themselves the embarrassment of sloppy or theoretically "wrong" performances. Playing becomes divorced from the emotional connection to a live audience and is diminished by this ethic of perfection. In this way, from the simplest technology of reproduction through the increasing complexities of creating final commercial recordings, the recording studio process is often defined in these negative terms—sterile, artificial reproductions of contrived performances constructed through a form of musical deception.

In a recent article on music and technology the *New Yorker* critic Alex Ross concludes that one cannot conclusively pin this "phonograph effect" on musicians' response to hearing themselves recorded, but he acknowledges that a strong case can be made for such an effect.[6] Certainly there was, and continues to be, pressure from recording companies on musicians to create products that can bear up under the scrutiny of repeated listening. While the true nature and extent of the phonograph effect cannot be known, it has certainly been a factor in the evolution of musical performance. Despite this, many artists from all genres have found recordings preferable to the concert hall or the stadium, most famously Glenn Gould and the Beatles. And more contemporary voices of analysis have purposefully painted a more complex, balanced view of art and artifice, original and copy, personal expression and technology.[7] In any event, the march of technology is not slowed by these negative evaluations as it interacts with the cultural dynamic. Certainly technical innovation is not to be halted by fears that it might diminish experience. Music sounds themselves most often originate in the technology of musical instruments—the piano, for example, is a technological marvel. Even live musical performance is now most often dependent on state-of-the-art technology. This phrase "state of the art" is itself very revealing regarding the cultural relationships of technology, art, and artifice. In previous times *state-of-the-art technology* might have been considered an oxymoron, but it is currently the standard currency[8] of technological consumption. Art and technology have become increasingly and inextricably connected.

This connection suggests that it is no longer credible to center discussions of art and artifice around technology. In the context of a debate between sound engineers and the musicians in a rock band, Frith comments that "nature is pitted against artifice, 'true' music ('live' music) against 'false' (studio or electronically manufactured) sounds."[9] But that was referring to a particular moment in early rock-and-roll history: the idea of the sound engineer as the traditional enemy of the musician in the "natural versus artificial" debate no longer has resonance when the majority of musicians are sound engineers themselves.[10] Almost all popular music musicians are involved in the technology of recording now, and if they're not, then they are probably anxious to ally themselves with someone who is, because they recognize that the life of their music in the world is dependent on technology. Similarly, in Western art music the once thriving contest between Nimbus recording and multimicrophone studio recording has receded as the multimic approach dominates all current releases. While historically of interest, the contemporary landscape points to the obsolescence of the debate.

As is clear from my application studies, current recording capabilities have rendered the notion of "performance" problematic.[11] From Britney Spears and Ashlee Simpson caught lip syncing to the Milli Vanilli debacle,[12] there are endless examples of how performance is rendered problematic by the current technology. Even live performance is subsumed by the culture of recorded music. As Charles Keil points out, "the normative recordings intensify live performance as something extraordinary, abnormal and magical as well."[13] This view privileges live performance but it does so by acknowledging that the recordings are now the base experience—the "normative" for music consumption. But beyond this, the proliferation and devotion to mass-produced media indicates that in contemporary culture the copy is often preferred to the original.[14] Sometimes the reproduction is even more "real" than the original—such as when a "live" event is being staged for ultimate presentation on TV, or in a live music performance where most eyes are fixed on the large-screen video projection. In this context it's clear that technology is a direct contributor to the creation, execution, and experience of art.

Frith, at a meeting of musicologists, makes the following appeal:

> The implication of our discussions was that rather than speculating how technology will change music culture, we should be studying music culture for clues as to how technology will be used and shaped. Popular music has its own long history of relations between the local and the global, the licit and the illicit, craft and entrepreneurship, machines, sounds and careers. It is these relations that we most need to understand.[15]

We continue then to detail some of the ways that current technology is being used to shape the creation, presentation, and experience of music. At the same time we can draw parallels between some of these practices and the fundamentals of the musical experience prior to recording in the form of structure, function, and participation. The composer, performer, and consumer categorizations provide interesting insight on the ways music has participated in prerecording cultural life and on how technology has been used and shaped to create social value.

Technological Parallels to Prerecording Music Culture

Twenty-first-century technologies provide composers with new structures, performers with new functions, and consumers with new access to participation. These expanded capabilities indicate how traditional roles within music culture have influenced technologies, compelling social and creative interaction. Technology also assists in breaking down these categorizations, further driving the contemporary experience in directions with more parallels to prerecording music culture. While, as Chanan maintains, it is no doubt still true that "In surviving oral cultures the relations between musical senders and receivers is much more fluid and symbiotic than in modern Western society,"[16] it is also true that technology is a partner to forces that are driving an increasing fluidity and symbiosis in contemporary musical relationships.

The composer finds new structural models through an expanded interaction with various audio elements. Instrument samples provide access to unlimited musical instruments and sounds, either played or programmed from a keyboard or a computer. Remixing techniques use source material to create completely new arrangements of previously recorded material. My "Milee Yookoee" is an example of a composition created entirely from previously recorded and then repurposed audio. Repurposed audio samples from previous recordings provide a structural link to music history. Mash-ups—wholly new compositions created from the (often unlikely) combination of elements from disparate recordings—offer yet another new compositional model. The most famous mash-up to date is DJ Danger Mouse's *The Grey Album,* which combines the vocals from Jay-Z's *The Black Album* with reprocessed tracks from the Beatles' *White Album.* Such activities as these clearly link new compositional approaches to broader cultural connections.

Compositional models are also radically altered in structure as a result of recordings functioning as the new musical "score." Compositional sketches may be created by one musician through recordings of multiple parts by a single individual. Ultimately, one musician may create fully realized compositions. I created "Milee Yookoee" in isolation, though audio elements were drawn from Internet resources and the final recording/composition is being shared over the Internet via download. Recordings capture compositional structure along with performance, thereby more closely linking the two functions. As a result, the once solitary pursuit of composition may occur within the socialized environment of performance, integrating structures in ways that provide greater opportunities for collaboration.[17]

The performer finds new functional capabilities in technologies that promote more subtle expression, the same technologies that are often implicated in separating performers from their audience. Amplification allows a greater dynamic range in performance. Video projection at larger venues allows understated expressions to be experienced in a "live" setting by large audiences. The combination of large-scale concert experiences with an increase in perceived intimacy between audience and performer reinforces fundamental cultural functions such as cooperation through shared experience. It is telling that a number of the large popular music festivals are given names such as "A Gathering of the Tribes" or "Tribal Stomp."

Studio performance has become much more malleable with the development of recording technologies. Increased control over final versions of recorded performances began with the ability to edit multiple performances into a single version, extending control over recordings to outside the timeline of the original performance. The advent of multitracking and overdubbing allowed construction of recordings from a variety of individual performances created at different times and even in different places. Combined with the new tools of composition, such as repurposed audio, these capabilities further conflate notions of composition and performance. The "Milee Yookoee" project uses multiple tracks in order to accommodate the use of a large number of audio elements that function both as repurposed composition and repurposed performance. The fixing of recorded performances, including timing and pitch elements, allows easier creation of music that conforms to professional standards.[18] In this way the professionalization demands created by nineteenth-century specialization are made functionally accessible to a much wider population. Advances in the price and performance ratio of recording equipment have meant that home recording allows the capture of more intimate and raw performances that still match fidelity expectations of the consumer. This has also meant that access to recording and distribution technology provides creative leisure that is more integrated with community building and sharing. For example, I am able to (and have) shared "Milee Yookoee" with many friends and colleagues through email of mp3 attachments, and I now have it available on my website. All of these elements combine to have a freeing effect on the demands of musical performance and participation.

The consumer finds new levels of engagement in the musical process that fosters a sense of cultural participation. Technology allows increased access, intimacy, and fidelity of musical experience for the consumer. Improvements in the quality of audio reproduction have increased sonic detail in both live and recorded performances. Recordings have generated enormous opportunities for access to music from around the world as well as providing the opportunity for repeated listening. Music is made more compelling through repeated listening as the listener has the opportunity to adapt to the experience. For example, the polyrhythmic structure of Milee Yookoee begins to sound more natural when it has been heard repeatedly. These new levels of access, intimacy, and fidelity provide a stronger connection to the experience of listening to music and thereby reinforce the social connections binding music creation to music reception.

The consumer's participation includes creation of individual musical "space" by enhanced control over playback of recordings. The consumer controls all of the following:

1. What is played (with easy access to music from all over the world)
2. When it is played (now including broadcasts via Internet access or podcasting)
3. Where it is played (with all music now completely mobile via iPods and the equivalent)
4. How it is reproduced (from earbuds to audiophile)
5. The order it is played in (often from one's entire library via iPod/iTune type technology)

This participation encourages a greater interest in music given the opportunity to take part as a "performer" of the listening experience, and thus as an active collaborator in the creation of the musical experience.

In this dynamic between technology and the continuum of music creation through consumption, most analysis focuses on the two fundamental relationships: the relationship between the composer and the performer, and the relationship between the performer and the consumer. Relative to composer and performer the recorded mode of music delivery has cemented the ability of the composer to *be* the performer, sometimes to the extent of elaborate arrangements where the composer performs all of the parts separately. Recordings may be preferred over live performances by composers as well as by performers and consumers. As long ago as the 1960s Milton Babbitt suggested that recordings offer many advantages over the "intellectually trying, socially trying, physically trying conditions of the concert hall,"[19] and one can picture the Beatles, Steely Dan, and many other popular music artists nodding in agreement.

But it is largely with the second primary relationship that I am concerned here, between the performer and the audience, as recording technology ties the two more closely together. Consumers are taking a more active role in many aspects of how they consume and share their experience of recorded music. This in turn changes the way performers imagine their relationship to their audience. As Gould pursued his very elaborate recording projects, he was motivated, in part, by his belief that recordings make for "a new kind of listener—a listener more participant in the musical experience."[20] As we shall see, new technology has continued to feed this listener participation, now encompassing music creation and performance.

Twenty-First-Century Compositional Musicking

Are we indeed entering a new period of cultural practice in which greater numbers of people are once again practicing music, as they did before the advent of recordings? Are computerized compositional capabilities making the creation of new music a more widely practiced cultural phenomenon? From Gould to Frith I have traced some of the evolving acknowledgment of the broader role of the music listener, facilitated by the various technologies of recording. Is digital technology partially responsible for driving a greater quantity of individual musicking[21] that encompasses composition? Tracing analysis of the cultural condition into the twenty-first century yields further speculations and observations regarding the emergence of an even broader cultural participation in the compositional aspect of music making.

Timothy Taylor documents a contemporary shift toward musicking that is intimately tied to the technology of music. Taylor begins by noting a relationship between Attali's stages of music and the development of music technologies. In faulting Attali for missing the connection, he furthers the contemporary model of reciprocity as the primary mode of understanding music in culture: "Failing to theorize the technological aspect of these stages means that Attali slips into a deterministic model of technology in his book, as if each of these new sociotechnical systems simply produced new musics rather than being caught up in complex webs of music technology, society, and history, all of which presuppose each other."[22] Nonetheless Taylor uses Attali to acknowledge the current potential for a new level of broad cultural musicking: "Still Attali's optimism about 'composition' is infectious. With digital technology, there is some hope that people—at least those who can afford computers—will begin to make music for themselves again using their computers and cheap, easily available software; it isn't even necessary to buy much hardware anymore."[23]

At the same time Taylor is quick to severely qualify such "hope" by noting that, as regards the democratizing potential of technology, "such arguments are frequently so hyperbolic as to take one's breath away. . . . claims for the democratizing potential of almost any technology have been around for a long time."[24] Taylor also explicitly explores the relationship of contemporary practice to that of music making in the era before there was recorded music, managing both to celebrate and to problematize the contemporary potential for new paradigms of widespread musicking. He notes how the phonograph for the most part turned the same people who had previously made music into consumers of music, and thus

> people who might have once made their own music learned to buy it instead. Concepts such as genius, talent, and masterpiece that inhibit many people from making music became even more instantiated in Western European cultures. The rise of the hip hop and dance music DJ, however, redefined the function of the turntable: no longer simply a reproductive device, it became a productive one as well. Human agency struck back.[25]

While Taylor acknowledges the potential of agency here he doesn't really speak to the broad spectrum of people who now buy rather than make their own music—DJs, after all, occupy a small portion of the cultural landscape. To what extent, then, has individual agency actually struck back? Similarly, in acknowledging the access to compositional tools, he does so in the context of the isolating nature of the "music on the computer" experience:

> Before the advent of recording technology and radio, people made their own music most of the time, but what is radically different today is that it is now possible to create entire worlds of sound all by yourself with your computer; it is no longer necessary to be with other people. Music as social activity is becoming a thing of the past for many of these musicians.[26]

The interconnectivity of the Internet provides some potential for relief from the solitary nature of the music maker at the computer. Ultimately Taylor sees some possibilities for "at least a simulated social environment that animates [these musician's] agency in the face of the potentially dehumanizing nature of digital technology."[27] Taylor sees "potential," but the context of his analysis might inspire one to judge the brave new world of democratized musicking as "damned by faint praise." To emphasize the simulated nature of connections made via the Internet downplays the potential for meaningful social interaction. But *more recent developments and activities are animating more optimistic views on the interconnectivity of larger populations with musical content creation.*

In a 2003 volume of essays edited by René T. A. Lysloff and Leslie Gay, entitled *Music and Technoculture,* further claims for the progression of broad-based musicking are chronicled. The widely reported observation that the Internet opens up distribution channels is detailed in referencing bands that are unaffiliated with record companies: "They circumvent the established recording industry altogether by making 'the world your hard disk [and] everyone a publisher,' says David Post."[28] In a separate article Lysloff traces one particular community—the mod trackers—who "do more than just share prerecorded music; they are active as composers, manipulating sound samples with virtual mixing boards to create their own mod files."[29] These are emanations from small communities, but they might be more suggestive of a cultural phenomenon around musicking if it weren't for the fact that most of the websites where he has observed this activity were, just three years later in 2006, no longer active. As with Taylor, we get suggestions of broad-based compositional musicking but little that backs up these anecdotal observations.

Bill Ivey and Steven J. Tepper present a much broader case in *Engaging Art: The Next Great Transformation of America's Cultural Life.* This volume theorizes a true paradigm shift in the cultural participation in music making. In an introductory article, entitled "Cultural Renaissance or Cultural Divide?" Ivey and Tepper outline their thesis of a large-scale cultural shift. First they trace the earlier history of a professionalized culture, fed by nonprofit arts organizations. Arts were presented locally but the development of artistic performance and style were part of an international standard. Media and distribution technologies fed this elitist standard of arts presentation until "the amateurs at home were overshadowed by the new class of creative 'professionals,' and audiences were increasingly socialized to be passive consumers, awaiting their favorite radio broadcasts or sitting in darkened theaters and concert halls, applauding on cue."[30]

Along with a number of other media and culture commentators that they reference, Ivey and Tepper suggest that there is a new revolution in amateur arts creation, driven by what one commentator calls the "Pro-Am Revolution" populated primarily by "weekend warriors." This is understood as a shift that harkens back to the nineteenth-century vision of the piano in the parlor and the necessity of amateur music making in the world before recordings. However Ivey and Tepper add that "What sets the new participatory culture apart from the older local participatory culture of the 19th century is that amateur art making is taking place in the shadow of giant media. Moreover, there is now an explosion of cultural choice made possible by new technologies and a renewed mingling of high and popular art."[31] Ivey and Tepper cite the reduced cost of digital technology (especially in music and movies) and the availability of new distribution channels via the Internet as fuel, and the explosion of home recording studios and a threefold increase in sales of guitars in the last ten years as some of the evidence. This new participatory culture is predominately populated by males, in contrast to the piano in the parlor culture, where the amateur pianist was typically female.

Not all of the elements in the evocation of nineteenth-century musicking hold up. Cook notes that the professionalization of performance was not simply a twentieth-century product of music reproduction or a result of the participation of the state-subsidized nonprofit organizations.[32] The demands of virtuosity that had arisen since Beethoven had already firmly entrenched the professional in the world of musicking, as witnessed by the traveling musicians of eighteenth- and nineteenth-century concert hall performances. Cook also brings up the washboard craze of the 1930s and the Fostex eight-track of the 1980s as examples of a continuous line of musicking that one might draw from the nineteenth century to the present. The folk music revival of the 1950s and the rock band culture from the 1960s to the present also belie a viewpoint that suggests a twentieth-century abandonment of personal music making. But these expressions of musical participation don't really challenge the dominant paradigm that had placed music recording beyond the reach of the vast majority of people. Perhaps Ivey and Tepper do not sufficiently distinguish between musicking (from the piano parlor to the home recordist's bedroom) and musical recordings that can be easily shared internationally via the Internet.[33]

There *does* appear to be a real difference in the participatory cultures of the digital world of musicking and that of the analog past. Ivey and Tepper point to new developments that are dramatically changing the cultural landscape. The capabilities of digital technology have not only transformed the compositional paradigm to the new constructive model that I have described, but the practice of amateur musicking is also being transformed by the widespread availability of free and low-cost computer recording software along with mp3s and Internet streaming that provide an enormous expansion of distribution capabilities.

The Rise of the Consumer: Technology Supports Participation

The Sony Walkman was introduced in 1979, and the era of personal, portable playback technologies was launched. The history of the Walkman is usually told in the context of it having "forever changed the way consumers listen to music"[34]—a phrase that comes from Sony's telling of its own history. Today, if one searches Google for this phrase, it appears most frequently in the context of the iPod. The portability and flexibility of the iPod has further entrenched recordings in everyday experience, greatly expanding the consumers' control over their listening experience. The cultural penetration of the iPod is indicative of parallels, if somewhat indirect, to the entrenchment of music into the structure of prerecording musical cultures. The more casual and participatory nature of music performance in those earlier cultures and the social cohesion that it engendered are both mirrored and amplified by the iPod's prevalence in everyday life activities. The level of participation that the iPod affords the consumer in the scale of access and the many ways that it allows users to share their experiences far outstrip the technology of the Walkman.

Although a playback-only technology, the iPod expands the personal interaction with music in relation to time, place, activity, and access. This dynamic drives listeners into a more creative relationship with their experience of music: redefining participation for the digital age. One might even suggest that this is a "purer" relationship, as it creates autonomy from the constrictions of time and place. At the same time music becomes more embedded in the structure of, and participant in, the functions of the individual's cultural experience. Interaction with the iPod ranges from the most basic kinds that were introduced with Walkman technology—such as walking or riding on the bus—to the more elaborate, necessarily digital expressions, as listeners construct more and more of their personal musical space and are able to share that space with a broad virtual community over the Internet. This is further amplified on the Internet via many of the social media sites. The early popularity of one such site, MySpace.com, was built in large part out of people's desire to list their favorite music. These activities begin to mirror aspects of composing popular music as they take on a personal form of composing identity. The constructive nature of making iPod playlists mirrors the constructive nature of popular music creation. Music on the iPod may also be a buffer against the assaultive urban landscape, allowing a closer connection to self when confronted with the anonymity of mass culture.

The iPod allows vast amounts of music to be available from one instantly accessible source, and this yields much greater interactive capabilities, most notably in the use of the personal playlist. The playlist capability of CD players was noted in the late 1980s as an important step toward consumer engagement with recorded music, along with mix tapes and even the originator of the personal playlist—the jukebox,[35] but they all pale in comparison to the iPod playlist. The iPod allows the listener to easily construct sequences of material from the entire library of material on it—which may include thousands of selections. With iPod technology consumers now control many more aspects of the recorded music experience than they possibly could over the live music experience. Thus consumers may be much more engaged in their relationship to the recorded musical performance. We decide what songs to listen to, in what order to listen to them, and when to skip tracks or switch playlists. When we are more interactive in the listening experience we are more active musical participants. This dynamic has increased dramatically in the age of the iPod.

Personal musical tastes create strong personal identification with musical artifacts. An impulse toward self-definition via record collections has long been a staple of cultural expressions made possible by audio reproduction—the forerunner to "composing identity" on MySpace and Facebook. Ivey and Tepper point to what they call the "curatorial me," which refers to this kind of advanced engagement with one's personal library of cultural artifacts. They mention TiVo—the digital selection and recording device that assists with consumers' archiving of television shows—which has some interesting parallels to the iPod's playlist.

Playlists may reflect this inclination toward the "curatorial me"—music sequences that are personalized by the listener—but they may also be generated randomly by choosing "shuffle mode," which assembles haphazard sequences. The iPod shuffle mode represents one of the most interesting ways in which this technology has broadened the consumer's encounters with music. These randomized playlists can forge links[36] between pieces of music that may never have previously been in anything but the most remote kind of contact. This is a passive choice in one technological sense (the machine, not the operator, makes the choices), but the choices come from the listener's own library of music, offering what can be surprising insights into one's own musical preferences. In any event, choosing to access this feature may create a very active and different kind of participation with music on the part of the listener. It is my general contention here that this activist attitude on the part of the consumer has inspired the appearance and use of new music construction programs such as GarageBand, and so we have come full circle in the process of music creation.

None of these capabilities provides the consumer with any understanding of the fundamentals of music theory, and it's true that the formalities of music escape the vast majority of consumers—they don't understand music theory or even the idea of the musical note. They are more likely to hear musical intervals, chords, counterpoint, and the like as impressions of sound.[37] However, the listener is becoming more and more aware of the technology of popular music creation. The division between consumers and recordings is breaking down primarily in that consumers understand the constructive nature of popular music. They still may not grasp "notes" but they do understand that music is constructed in pieces, over time— not in one lump in real time.[38] As Frith has observed, the notion of multitracking is familiar to most people now, so the consumer hears "the music being assembled."[39] This is part of a new kind of "aural training" for contemporary music consumers. Combine this training with the iPod model of participation and the community capabilities of the Internet, and the stage is set for widespread participation in the construction of music recordings.

The Rise of the Consumer: Technology Drives Creativity

GarageBand—the consumer-oriented music construction program that comes free with all Macintosh computers—represents a final encircling of the musical continuum from composer to performer to consumer back to composer. Recently there has been an increasing acknowledgment of the reciprocity between creator and performer and then between performer and audience.[40] Music doesn't just flow hierarchically from author through the performer to the consumer; there is an interaction in each exchange. However, I believe we are now at the threshold of a new dynamic that extends beyond reciprocity to circularity. Cook has pointed toward this dynamic in describing the changing role of the musician's participation in music production: "What makes a musician is not that he knows how to play one instrument or another, or that he knows how to read music: it is that he is able to grasp musical structure in a manner appropriate for musical production—the most obvious (though of course by no means the only) example of such production being performance."[41] There is a current crop of musicians who "grasp musical structure in a manner appropriate for musical production" without coming anywhere near performing on a traditional musical instrument. These are the successful musicians that create on the computer using samples, preassembled loops, and other bits of sound. The composition may be built in ways that almost completely bypass the need for any of the conventional musician's skills. *This is the new paradigm of music construction.* GarageBand is a program designed to bring these techniques to the public at large[42]—a chance for the greater community of music lovers to join this new community of music creators. Life's natural creative impulses are engaged through the interaction with music construction provided by this kind of consumer software.

GarageBand makes all the musical elements easily accessible through samples and loops, with a minimal amount of musical knowledge and no ability to play an instrument required. The user is guided through simple steps that ease the process of assembling musical fragments into new musical constructions. These prerecorded elements can be combined with live recording into GarageBand for more sophisticated and personal compositions. The easy interface and the extensive library of musical building blocks, along with its free distribution with new Macintosh computers, separates GarageBand from previous music construction software. Elements of GarageBand have appeared before in consumer software, and they have been surpassed for some time by professional software, but the overall package represents a new plateau in consumer access to music construction.

GarageBand takes the ethic of participation from the iPod and combines it with the consumer's understanding of the constructive nature of audio recording. GarageBand then places the tools of contemporary composition into the hands of the consumer in the simplest possible manner. The reach of the consumer thus extends back into the realm of the composer. This closing of the circle of musical practice represents the further disintegration of the formal roles occupied by the composer, performer, and consumer of music. Because the consumer is already aware of the artifice, aware of the construction, aware that music is put together in pieces—and already puts together the listening experience piece by piece on their iPod—it is a relatively short step, the step to GarageBand, that circles the consumer back to the role of composer. This does bring tangible practices into Attali's predictions regarding widespread, democratized composition which he identified at the time as a kind of "abstract utopia."[43] Attali correctly identified the manner in which the coming surge in homegrown composition reveals the direct relationship of music to technology and knowledge: "In composition, it is cartography, local knowledge, the insertion of culture into production and a general availability of new tools and instruments."[44]

One might think of the iPod as at the Baudrillardian edge between active and passive: "*That is where simulation begins. . . .* not into passivity, but into *the indifferentiation of the active and the passive.*"[45] The iPod's isolated and passive listening experience is activated by a whole new realm of opportunities for choice to be made by the consumer. Chanan suggests that through reproduction technologies "music becomes literally disembodied [and this represents]—in a word, the negation of *musica practica.*"[46] Yet he also notes that "*musica practica* cannot be put down . . . *Musica practica* is an authentic object of popular pleasure, an embodiment of the human need for community."[47] While the iPod technology may be viewed as a drive toward community and connection or as a part of the postmodern experience of dislocation, GarageBand brings us back firmly to the realm of active participation, to *musica practica,* in a directly creative enterprise (and the program's community-oriented, grassroots name is no accident). Though the recordings themselves might be considered occupants of Baudrillard's world of simulacra, this hardly disqualifies them from the contemporary experience of community. The consumer engages the composer and performer more directly by controlling various aspects of their musical experience via the iPod—but GarageBand provides the tools to connect the individual directly to the experience of musical creation.

So instead of Frith's "confusion between musician and technician, between aesthetic and engineering sound decisions,"[48] we are moving toward an integration of these roles, a more fluid circularity in all musical functions—creation, production, consumption. As Attali has argued, technology is driving "the insertion of culture into production"[49]—where culture is here represented by the creative impulse. This integral role of technology means that it is sharing in community-building impulses just as the integral role of music shares in these same impulses in the African folklore tradition. And, as in this particular African music where drums and flutes predominate as the technological tools of music making, the creative impulse here drives the technology back to our own preferred tools for creation—which in the case of contemporary Western culture means programs that run on the personal computer. Théberge recognizes the extent to which consumer-based technologies have grown to become a part of the musical landscape, marking "consumer audio technology as a significant enabling factor, operating at a number of levels, in a wide range of essentially participatory, social and musical practices."[50]

These cultural currents, this drive toward participation, also support the production of live performance, which is why CDs and the iPod haven't killed the concert hall, the dance hall, or the nightclub. In fact live performing revenues have supplanted record sales as the primary income source for many musicians.[51] As Byrne suggests:

> I don't think fewer people go to live shows as Sousa and others have suggested. Not where I live. Not significantly anyway. The social and communal aspect of listening to music outweighs any negative aspects of the poor sound and imperfect reproduction at most live shows. It's about being with other people, relaxing, feeling a common bond. Of course we all try and do our best as performers to overcome sound re-production problems and make the music sound good, it is a constant issue, but maybe it's not as important as we think it is.[52]

While the fundamental relationship of the audience to live music remains, there have been wholesale changes in professional recording over the past ten years. Even before the proliferation of creative, compositional tools emerged, the ability to make professional recordings had moved firmly into a realm that was accessible to the consumer. While as late as 1996 Frith was still referring to the "disparities of home and studio sound technology,"[53] now huge portions of commercial recordings are recorded, edited, and mixed in homes and apartments (including my own) around the country. The disparity in audio quality between home and studio has almost completely broken down in the last ten years. And along with this we have the recognition of the new dynamic being created by composition techniques wholly based on new technologies—observed here by Jonathan Tankel: "Remixing *is* recording. . . . It is *prima facie* evidence of Benjamin's contention that to 'an ever greater degree the work of art reproduced becomes the work of art designed for reproducibility.'"[54] From here, almost two decades later, I extrapolate further on the Benjamin dictum: the work of art forged from the ever-expanding capabilities of reproduction becomes the work of art created by anyone and everyone. Certainly Benjamin would have approved of this kind of leveling of access to the tools of creation. It is more difficult to imagine how he might have responded to the contemporary blurring of original and reproduction, though his populist tendency would suggest that ultimately he might embrace this as well. Whether he would have ever progressed to the point of finding repurposed audio capable of producing a reproducible aura would involve pure speculation.

Frith acknowledges the power of technology but wishes to place some limits on its ability to affect musical meaning. He argues that in dealing with the big questions "technology doesn't so much resolve the politics of musical meaning as change the context—the sense of musical time and space—in which traditional arguments take place, the arguments about the transcendent and the contingent, about the freedom of artistic intention, the freedom of listener response."[55] At this point Frith warns against going too far with either "technological determinism (machines make meaning)" or "technological fertility (everything now possible),"[56] and his point is well taken. However it leads him to this observation: "What is most startling about the history of twentieth-century sounds is not how much recording technology has changed music, but how little it has. If music's meaning have changed, those changes have taken place within the framework of an old, old debate about what musical meaning can be."[57]

It seems to me that Frith opens two questions here, one of musical content and the other of musical meaning. Relative to musical content the very architecture of musical composition is undergoing radical transformations. And yes, the debate is old, but access to the musical experience is broadening exponentially for consumers, as they create more and more of their own musical meaning, and indeed, their own music. As Frith acknowledges, the technology has changed the context. Where I would differ is in gauging the scale of this change. From my perspective, speaking at the beginning of the twenty-first century as opposed to the end of the twentieth, the contemporary context has created startling changes in both musical content *and* meaning as people with all different types of musical skills participate in the revised musical architecture of the early twenty-first century. Such enthusiasm needs to be tempered by the recognition that we live in a stratified society where access to what might be considered the basic tool of contemporary music making—the computer—is hardly universal, and critical questions of access still reflect the ongoing digital divide created by the economic stratification in contemporary culture (more on this in the following two sections). Nonetheless, as I explore below, the new musical context of participation is reflected in social and communal activities that are enabled by technology.

GarageBand in Action

Evidence of consumer use of GarageBand abounds in online forums, user groups, and discussion groups. The usage figures from some of these sites indicate the breadth of activity. The GarageBand discussion group at the

Apple site boasts almost 80,000 messages and about 107,000 "hits."[58] The GarageBand Users Forum at the Mac Idol site notes: "We have 4,045 registered users. Our users have posted a total of 51,044 articles."[59] A typical posting sums up the assessment of the program (GarageBand is easy to use), the status (amateur), and the attitude (friendly) of one user who goes by DrasticDragonfly:[60] "I bought GB and you can hear my songs at sound-click.com. I imagine this is what a motivated hardworking amateur can accomplish in a few months with the software. Thanks for reading this post, have a nice day." These amateur music makers are as interested in sharing their work as the users of MySpace.com are in sharing their musical preferences. Soundclick.com, which is a free mp3 posting site, claims 4,198,057 registered users, who have made 3,967,174 postings to their forums.[61] This site contains commercial as well as amateur mp3 postings for legal download. They don't list overall numbers but they claim more than 50,000 new songs and 6,000 new bands added to the site each month.[62]

Another typical posting comes from the blogger THespos:[63] "I started messing with GarageBand and couldn't believe how easy and intuitive it was. A riff popped into my head and I hacked it out on guitar. Within 10 minutes I had drums, bass and a rock organ backing up the guitar riff." This user goes on to complain about how frustrating it had been when he had tried to use professional audio software and he had spent all his time trying to get everything set up right: "I know this is an entry-level application for recording, but it's definitely going to help me get a lot of songs out of my brain and onto a hard drive. What I really need is another week off, so I can mess around with this stuff unmolested for hours at a clip." The frustrations of the "weekend warrior" are clear, but apparently not a deterrent to the creative impulses.

Sometimes posts hint at larger issues, such as the friction between amateur and professional music creators. Here Rolo[64] lays into the group Fort Minor (really the side project of rapper Mike Shinoda from the rock group Linkin Park):

> OK, I'm pissed because Fort Minor uses a stock garageband loop in his song "believe me" as the main sound of the song.
>
> If some of us want to use that loop in a song we will be accused by tons of people of copying the guy!
>
> I know he is free to use all the loops he want, but like this [*sic*] i feel he is taking tools away from amateurs like most of us.
>
> Shame on him!

This amplifies the way the amateurs may be frustrated as they try to clear some creative landscape for themselves. The flip side to the access and connections made possible by Internet communities is the turf wars that are still dominated by commercial interests. When amateurs and professionals compete for attention (as on soundclick.com), the commercial interests will certainly dominate the bandwidth. Programs like GarageBand may provide access to creative tools but competition for creative and commercial space will still favor the big players.

Online reviews of GarageBand reinforce the contention that it is capable of a very broad reach. This reviewer, from synthtopia.com, details the GarageBand features while sounding pretty much like a commercial for the product (much of this probably comes from a company press release, as do many product reviews): "GarageBand turns your Mac into an anytime, anywhere recording studio packed with hundreds of instruments and a recording engineer or two for good measure. It's the easiest way to create, perform and record your own music whether you're an accomplished player or just wish you were a rock star."[65] It also touts GarageBand's interconnectivity—increasingly a watchword for product relevance:

> One of the greatest things about GarageBand is the way Apple integrates it with other Apple apps. You can make some new background music, and then add it to your iPhoto slide shows, burn it to a CD, or use it as a score for an iMovie and burn it to a DVD. You could grumble that GarageBand doesn't have some features that pros have come to expect, but it is a minor miracle that Apple has made a music studio that mere mortals can use. This may turn out to be one of Apple's hottest innovations yet.[66]

Another aspect of GarageBand, and one that might ultimately be the most important to its cultural integration, is its use in the classroom. I found many references to GarageBand as a classroom tool, along the lines of this synopsis from a University of Wisconsin class that trains middle school teachers (so the students in this case are actually teachers):

> The students will be learning about the Digital Music program Garageband. They will learn what Garageband is, how to incorporate it into the classroom, and how to use it. The students will be working in small groups at computers. The instructors will lead a short discussion on how to incorporate Garageband into the classroom then give an overview of how to use Garageband. The students will then be given

time to experiment with the program. The lesson will close with an
open discussion about the pros and cons of Garageband.[67]

I received a written account from a colleague who was teaching
GarageBand as a summer camp program to at-risk middle school children
in San Francisco. His experience was that "GB is pretty understandable for
kids" and that they found the basics pretty easy to navigate. I asked him if
he thought they would continue to construct music at home after their
camp experience and he responded: "Because of the outreach component
of the camps, only about 35% of the children have access to garage band
outside of the camps. Of this 35%, my take was that they all would be using the skills they got at home." Although Apple computers do not have a
large part of the market share, this nonetheless suggests that access to computers still represents a breaking point in the cultural divide. It also suggests that such access is central to the ability for the underprivileged to
break out of the cycle of poverty—music creation being one avenue for the
underclass to move into more productive economic conditions. While it is
wrong to simply posit computers as the cure for poverty, the use of computers in music construction continues the model whereby access to technology (previously in the form of musical instruments—pianos, electric
guitars with amplifiers, and so on, are also complex and expensive) continues to pose obstacles to entrée into the world of music participation. The
greatly increased access to recording technology may be changing the paradigm for the vast middle class, but the underclass is still largely cut out
from this new participatory model.

My colleague's broader comment here suggests the ultimate power of
programs like GarageBand to both engage children in music creation and
change the paradigm of such creation:

> My general take on the program is that it enables kids to produce songs
> at amazing quality and feel good about their creations even though
> they may have little or no musical experience. Each camp had very dif-
> ferent issues and strengths, as did the kids, but they all had something
> to contribute and were able to see it materialize into something cool.

Even to an experienced musician, the paradox of the new paradigm of music creation is not necessarily apparent. The teacher marvels at how much
music is created by these children with "little or no musical experience,"
but that is exactly the point. The musical experience now consists of a different set of skills and draws more from the listening experience, without
the need for as much traditional music education or music instrument

skills. These children actually *had* a lot of transferable music experience. Music construction on the computer more closely follows the model of music consumption and becomes accessible to children through basic computer skills such as cut, copy, and paste. This is a reflection of the continuum now stretching from consumption back to creation.

Whither Compositional Musicking?

Ivey and Tepper do not explicitly suggest a link between the "curatorial me" and the "Pro-Am Revolution" though they recognize the two as part of the same cultural movement. As argued above I believe the interaction to be significant, that the curatorial impulses are part of what is driving the more explicitly creative activity. Digital technology has broadened the ability to manipulate audio such that these structural connections can be made. Music that is created in GarageBand can be exported to iPod for listening along with one's library of songs; and songs, snippets of audio, sound effects, or any other sound files can be imported into GarageBand for use in one's musical construction. In these digital environments there is synergy between curatorial impulses and compositional musicking, both drawing on the desire for creative personal expression.

Ivey and Tepper trace the economic challenges that stifle the emergence of a true cultural revolution in creative production. They suggest that a variety of forces, especially those familiar to many aspects of contemporary economic activity that encourage consolidation and centralization, are creating greater roadblocks for new and emerging artists to find audiences. The nonprofit performing arts organizations "have also narrowed the gates, attempting to maximize attendance and contributions by advancing conservative, repetitious programming choices."[68] But are these economic conditions truly stifling all of the democratizing potentials of the current milieu? Ultimately Ivey and Tepper ask:

> Who is right? The cultural optimists (a thousand flowers are blooming, we are drowning in a sea of possibility, and we are surrounded by a new creative ethos) or the cultural pessimists (the market is too restricted, people are suffering from a dearth of cultural opportunities, and demands of the new service economy are leaving many workers with little time or energy to engage with art and culture)?[69]

And they answer "Both sides are right; each sees a separate side of the cultural coin."[70] That coin represents the age-old divide between the haves and the have-nots—those with resources and thus access, and those without—resulting in the current division of cultural elites versus the cultural underclass. Finally Ivey and Tepper propose that the challenge today, for educators and artists, is to find a way to broaden that access to a larger segment of the population. The experience of my colleague with the Garage-Band summer camp for at-risk children reinforces this notion.

The optimist's view suggests that we must adjust our notion of musicking as we observe its interaction with the technologies of audio construction. This brings us full circle to the prerecording model of music integration into the foundation of community practices. Are there elements from this model that might be feeding the emergence of a broader spectrum of cultural musicking? Did such models really disappear in the professionalization to an international standard that marked twentieth-century art production? The fact that recordings have become the primary vehicle for music consumption is not as damning to the cultural community as has often been portrayed. Technologies are helping to drive the culture back to some of the traditional cultural models where music is more closely tied to structure, function, and the assumption of participation. Technologies may advance alienation and separation but they may also combine with the human need to support participation and creation. Together they generate new forms of and new opportunities for compositional musicking.

Paul D. Greene also suggests that a "new modality of human music making has emerged"[71] and it is thoroughly wrapped up in the new technologies of sound construction. Rather than the economic dangers, Greene considers the potential negatives of the globalization of musicking that may represent "a worldwide assimilation of music making practices and a dissolution of meaningful distinctions among musics, aesthetics, and practices."[72] He proposes that what he terms wired sound "is thus culturally and politically charged: listeners and musicians around the world invest sound technologies and studio recordings with anxieties on the one hand, and desires on the other."[73] The anxieties revolve around a loss of cultural identity, but the desires embrace the expanded opportunities for musicking that technology brings. Ultimately Greene suggests a more positive interpretation of the current tensions created by these worldwide technological practices: "Might assimilation and differentiation both be underway at once?"[74]

Given these new models for musical participation it is appropriate to look more closely at the new models of creativity. The advent of repurposing has shifted the nature and meaning of the creative musical endeavor, both expanding and blurring its outlines. At the same time, as implied by Greene's observations, these new creative models have raised questions regarding intellectual property and cultural appropriation. The iPod is built on technology that has also fueled copyright infringement through illegal downloading. Ivey and Tepper suggest that some of the challenges to the "great transformation" that they identify are issues that surround intellectual property. My African folklore project raises questions about music appropriation from other cultures. How might we best evaluate both the positive and negative elements of this process of cultural reinvention? The following section explores these and other questions in the context of cultural practices.

nine

{ Integration or (Dis)integration?

The Musician's Creative Process

The relationship between the art of recording and the musician's creative process is widely debated. Some observers take a reductive attitude toward reproduction, viewing recording primarily in its distinction from live performance. Benjamin observes, regarding acting, that "the film actor lacks the opportunity of the stage actor to adjust to the audience during his performance."[1] While true, it ignores the different, though perhaps equally profound, internal process by which film actors or recording artists may adjust their performance for their future audience. The recording performer may have direct feedback; this is the role of the producer in the studio, but it is not equivalent to audience feedback. In fact the objective of that feedback is rarely to re-create a live performance that may be experienced in a similar way to a traditional performance in front of a live audience. For most recording artists this is not the primary goal; they recognize that listening to recordings is a different experience than attending a live performance. In making the recording both the goals and the performances are altered for the sake of the recording, not as an imitation of a performance in front of a live audience. Many artists have abandoned live performance while maintaining active recording careers. Most performing artists now treat the recording process as split from their performing careers, often using different musicians and recording different material than they play in live performance. Modern recording practices represent *fundamental changes* in the essence of music making rather than re-creations or bastardizations of live performances. As we have seen, the contemporary recording process often involves conceptualizing and creating music in ways radically different from live performance. At the same time recording has become the dominant mode of musical creation.

Chanan critiques the effects of the contemporary, multitrack recording process on musicianship. He argues that this kind of recording practice dislocates the musician from the temporal requirements of live performing such that "the essential activity of the musician, the performance of the music, becomes more and more fragmented."[2] He maintains that this fragmentation "induces a simplification of musical elements, a reduction in musical complexity, since the artist is relieved of the need to master anything more than basic skills."[3] While certainly true for some of the commercial popular musicians that Chanan is describing, this should be balanced against Gould, Les Paul, Jimi Hendrix, and the many other pioneers of modern recording techniques who almost certainly believed that their musical virtuosity was enhanced by the recording process. Is what Chanan describes necessarily fragmentation, which suggests a loss of cohesion, or might it also be specialization, which suggests an adaptation? Isn't the "brutal objectivity of the microphone"[4] as much a challenge to instrumental excellence as it is an excuse for excessive reduction? Might one see the expanded flexibility and capabilities of reproduction as liberating—as an expansion of creative potential? As Frith has said, "Recording . . . has extended the possibilities of expression in all pop genres."[5] Recording technology may *redefine* musical skills rather than reducing the need for them. The fragmentation of the recording experience described by Chanan may be understood as a new technologically mediated synthesis of skills rather than as an inferior simulation of live performance.

The cultural and historical legacies of a musician's process helps to mitigate Chanan's suggestion of the erosion of musicianship. There is a tendency to romanticize cultural histories and non-Western cultures in the face of the apparent complexities in contemporary Western culture. Small points out that the African cultural focus is on "learning how to live well in the world rather than mastering it"[6]—an attitude that does not agree with the scientifically minded European view that the world must be mastered first in order for one to live better. Small is quick to add that this is not to say "that Africans are in any way better, more instinctively moral, artistic, religious or, especially 'closer to nature' than any other human people,"[7] and that this attitude is simply a response to the natural limitations of the African environment. So it is with the creative process—the specifics vary but the process is universal. The culture and the environment define the specifics so each musician's creative process is unique, but it is ultimately guided by the universal imperatives of communication. As the cultural environment changes and interacts with the technological opportunities we witness transformations in cultural expression, but this is not to be confused with a diminution of creative activity.

In describing his lessons in African drumming, Chernoff uses the word "smart" to translate his drum instructor's comments to him regarding the physical mastery of his instrument. That is, "Your wrist is not as smart as mine"[8] means that Chernoff doesn't have the correct approach or sufficient relaxation in his wrist to play fast passages properly. Facility is key, so increased facility allows greater creativity—it is "smarter." Chernoff compares the evolved rhythmic concept of African folklore music to an evolved verbal ability: "The many ways one can change a rhythm by cutting it with different rhythms is parallel to the many ways one can approach or interpret a situation or a conversation."[9] Increased facility equals a greater range of expression and yields the potential for greater creativity. The specifics of the facility may be physical, mental, or technological, but they all feed the creative potential. One can extend this analogy for how musical function instructs other cultural functions to the heightened facility that the iPod is giving to the construction of the listening experience, or that GarageBand offers to composition. As these tools help to provide the culture with a more musically integrated experience, they assist us in using the functions of music interaction to educate us in other ways. Musical "play" instructs all of life.

Musical creativity reflects the basic struggles of life. The cycle of the human struggle/fulfillment model is transformed by music into an abstract representation that uses the language of emotion. "Art organizes and idealizes life, which, in reality, is often unharmonious and capricious . . . in musical works and performances, control is exercised over contrived events, relationships, refinements, and idealizations,"[10] according to Floyd. This may be interpreted as the power of African-based music in America, but it could easily be read as a validation of the evolution of computer-based recording as well. The ability to shape and control musical events is the essence—the manner in which control is exercised varies in its specifics.

Creation and (Re)creation

Creation, production, and consumption form the continuum of artistic cultural expressions. There is the potential for dislocation in this process as a result of the widespread use of digital samples as building blocks for contemporary audio construction (formerly known as composition). How does the practice of using repurposed audio affect the notion of creativity? Who is the creator and what is the status of that creation when elements are repurposed by one artist that were originally created by a different artist?

Chanan addresses this practice, which had emerged as widespread practice as a result of the digital domination of sound manipulation and was relatively new at the time of his writing. He cites the theorists of postmodernism:

> They concur . . . that an altered state of cultural consciousness is involved, in which traditional meanings and values have been set adrift. The flux created by the reproductive technologies of previous generations is merely the precondition for this new state, which adds to the sheer proliferation of cultural products the technical ease with which they can now be recycled and placed in entirely novel contexts; a state, therefore, in which all active traces of the traditional relationship of signifier to signified disappear, as everything becomes a semblance or a simulation.[11]

This final reference recalls Baudrillard's notion of simulation in contemporary culture. Baudrillard cites the example of a visit to the Alsace caves, where there is now a replication built 500 meters from the original—you peep in at the original and then visit the replica. Thus "the duplication suffices to render both artificial."[12]

The question is not how we might discount Baudrillard, but rather how we might accept his point of view without coming to the conclusion that traditional meaning and values have been set adrift. We can start by positing that subjective or "fictive" accounts can be a valid part of musicology.[13] The movie *I'm Not There* from director Todd Haynes about Bob Dylan is an example of contemporary music commentary told through fictionalizing actual people and events. While this is discounted by some reviewers as a pointless exercise in obscurity—"To capture the essence of a sometimes pretentious, occasionally unfathomable artist, Haynes has made a sometimes pretentious, occasionally unfathomable film"[14]—other reviewers hailed the film as perfectly suited to the monumental figure from popular music because in the end "Haynes makes a portrait not of the singer but of our perceptions."[15] Certainly this was a speculative venture, but it found widespread acceptance among fans of Dylan and certainly represented a part of an ongoing shared musical experience, a form of intersubjective agreement. As musical biography it would not have found much support "within the culture of objectivity that characterized much postwar musicology and theory,"[16] but our twenty-first-century sensibilities have carried us beyond reduction as the most valid means of describing how the world is.[17] Chanan's postmodern theorists, as quoted above, are involved in a reductionist exercise that seems to denigrate the use of repurposed audio as a contributor in a process that sets adrift traditional meanings and values. Chanan himself challenges this notion by recognizing that "In the new phase of postmodernism, the techniques of reproduction look set to become a parallel agency of cultural production, and threaten to nurture new creative potential of their own."[18] I argue that such a threat is now very much a reality. An approach that acknowledges the power of shared experiences allows for an inclusive account regarding the ascendancy of repurposed audio.

Some of the negativity that arises around recording technologies stems from an attachment to the notion that music is "natural"—a notion that I set out to debunk in the first chapter of this book. Understanding the larger cultural interactions that are a part of musical meaning works against the appeal of a natural musical presence. Tia DeNora's work is often occupied with analyzing the everyday participation of music as part of the social process. In one essay she approaches music production in a context in which musicians' reputations, musical subcultures and individual tastes combine to create a subjective social construction.[19] DeNora's larger point is that musicology that incorporates social construction "opposes itself to traditional understanding of what is 'natural' in music."[20] And just as DeNora unpacks this construction for standard modes of production, so might we unpack the current repurposed modes of production. When we adopt DeNora's framework of seeing music as active in culture rather than simply as a product of culture, repurposed audio production becomes a predictable consequence of the interaction between the widespread dissemination of recordings and the creation of new recordings. Contemporary uses of repurposed audio are elevated past the morass of Baudrillardian simulacra into "natural" musical entities in their own right. *Creativity is an essential part of the repurposing process.*

Cook notes that while music is often designed for reproduction by virtue of its having been composed, this is only a part of the picture: interpretation is still always necessary.[21] And though here he may have been imagining interpretation as a constituent contained in performance, we may include the same notion in the manner in which samples are used to construct new music. Recording technologies have become tools for new music creation as much as or more than devices meant for recording—in the sense of documenting—performances. Théberge points to the transformation of the turntable from "a quintessentially reproductive device, into a *productive* one, a musical instrument of the first order."[22] These technologies represent the ongoing continuity between composition and production—not their dislocation.

In specific applications, repurposed audio clips may incorporate a legendary quality. Take, for example, the often-repurposed "funky drummer" clip from James Brown's drummer Clyde Stubblefield. Mark Katz notes that it "enjoys a promiscuous, chameleonic existence [in that] something of the original sound is maintained, yet its meaning changes in every new setting."[23] Here the notion of interpretive performance has been extended to the reuse of previously recorded audio. This becomes heightened when the clips used refer to some familiar, even iconic, moment in recording history. These clips take on a kind of mythic status and this further informs the experience of the new musical creation. Katz refers to this as a kind of "performative quotation"[24] though I prefer the phrase *interpretive repurposing* to emphasize the importance of the new context over the reference (or original "text"). The referential quality of the repurposed audio is important, but the new context—the active interpretation—extends the meaning beyond the reference.

Recognizing this mythologizing capability as a part of the world of repurposed audio helps us to place it in the larger cultural context. Cook wishes to expand music analysis to include metaphor and fiction, and in doing so he compares this approach to myth, for it renders things "negotiable [by] formulating them in terms of the experiences that are familiar to any member of the culture in which the myth originates."[25] That is to say, "mythopoeic explanation takes place entirely within a culture: it explains things to culture-members in terms of culture-specific knowledge."[26] This is why the Dylan movie works. And this is why these iconic music clips speak volumes to culture-members who share the experience of the original recordings. Repurposed audio is capable of communicating far beyond the surface content of the music, the performance, or the recording that has been repurposed. Ultimately it is capable of broadening encounters with the entire history of music.

Reciprocity Abolished

I have argued for an essential reciprocity between human agency and technology, original and copy, and live performance and recording. Although reciprocity is supposed to be indicative of equality—an equal mutuality—it is difficult to release the tendency to privilege the first in each of the three pairs mentioned above. Yet in contemporary Western culture there is evidence that sometimes the mechanical reproduction is *preferred* over the original. This reversal of the typical hierarchical status in these relationships reinforces the true reciprocity between them. However, applications of repurposed audio go even farther. Repurposed audio takes the copy and makes it *into* the original, the sample *becomes* a piece of the new recording, the recording *becomes* a piece of the live performance. Repurposing undermines the dichotomies and may even render the notion of reciprocity obsolete.

For many musicians and performers the act of making recordings has become more essential than playing live concerts. Perhaps this reflects Barthes's idea that "text's unity lies not in its origin but in its destination,"[27] and for many artists the destination of recordings is considerably broader than that of the live performance. It also reflects Said's observation: "It is appropriate to stress the social abnormality of the concert ritual itself."[28] He describes the concert as "an extreme occasion, something beyond the everyday, something irreducibly and temporally not repeatable, something whose core is precisely what can be experienced only under relatively severe and unyielding conditions."[29] Although it is unlikely that Said intended this reflection on the contemporary concert experience as an argument that favors recording over performing, his assessment may be used as a means of contrasting certain live music experiences with contemporary recording practice. We may now record audio—to the highest contemporary levels of fidelity—in the relaxed atmosphere of our own homes. We can produce music of all types and styles, drawing on instruments and even incorporating performances from all over the world in very elaborate and potentially creative ways. Contrast this with Said's notion that "Above all, the concert occasion itself is the result of a complex historical and social process . . . that can be interpreted as a cultural occasion staked . . . upon the audience's receptivity, subordination, and paying patience."[30] In this context, home recording becomes the more essential, the more integrative experience, and the implication for reproductions made in that environment is that listening to them may be more essential than attending the stilted live performance described by Said.

Said further indicts the evolution of performance in considering the original intention of some of the compositions that are today a part of the classical repertoire. He notes that many of the works by Beethoven and others were written for nonprofessionals. Of these he notes that "executing such a work is no longer an act of affection (*amateur* is a word to be taken first in its literal sense)."[31] Again, to the extent one may value an active amateurism, this exists today in the world of home recording, as evidenced by the proliferation of Ivey and Tepper's "weekend warriors" described above. Of course one may dispute the value of this kind of recreational recording—digital audio applications have enabled unschooled musicians access to complex tools of composition and arranging. Are the results of these capabilities of value? This may depend somewhat on distinguishing between the value of process and the value of product, but that really isn't the question. Were the results of the original amateur performances of Beethoven of value? To the extent one wishes to assign value to forces of egalitarianism one must embrace the advancements in recording technology.

Barthes traces the disappearance of the musical amateur, as they moved from the "province of the idle (aristocratic) class [and the] democracy of the bourgeoisie (the piano, the young lady, the drawing room, the nocturne) [but] then faded out altogether (who plays the piano today?)."[32] Although he mentions that the "practical" music today is embodied in the young generation of guitar and vocal music, he nonetheless asserts that today's performer is the specialist whose whole process is removed from public understanding and who essentially "abolishes in the sphere of music the very notion of *doing*."[33]

> The history of music (as a practice, not as an "art") does indeed parallel that of the Text fairly closely: there was a period when practicing amateurs were numerous (at least within the confines of a certain class) and "playing" and "listening" formed a scarcely differentiated activity; the two roles appeared in succession, first that of the performer, the interpreter to whom the bourgeois public (though still itself able to play a little—the whole history of the piano) delegated its playing, then that of the (passive) amateur, who listens to music without being able to play (the gramophone record takes the place of the piano).[34]

What Barthes fails to anticipate is the rise of the new musical amateur around the technology that first produced the gramophone record, as documented above in the cycling from the iPod to GarageBand. Computers provide the platform for new musical creations, the end result of which is a recording rather than a live performance. The process once again reduces the gap between this new kind of musical "playing" and "listening" and has returned some portion of the population back to the virtual drawing room via mp3's posted on the Internet, podcasted, and burned to CD for friends.

The history of popular music in the twentieth century is rife with examples of how recording created preferred modes of performance. Louis Armstrong came to prefer the studio to live performance during the time of his classic work with the Hot Five: "In the recording studio Armstrong was insulated from both the danger of failure and the lure of easy applause."[35] In 1966 the Beatles ceased performing and declared themselves a studio band. In 1974 the band Steely Dan swore off live performance and proceeded to become an international phenomenon. For these artists production is intended to serve reproduction, and in the hierarchy of original and copy the predilection to privilege the original in the reciprocal relationship is reversed.

While over the latter half of the twentieth century the hierarchy of "live" performance over recordings continued as an idea, in actual practice it had evaporated. And in the realm of popular music, as Toynbee notes, "What seems to have happened by the 1950s was that this need for an authentic moment behind the record, had lost its repressive hegemony. The record had became [*sic*] normalized."[36] The term *live* has become a musical performance qualifier rather than a marker of legitimacy set against the pejorative "canned" that was once used for all recorded music. "Live" is a subset of performance in general, and indeed, a smaller subset of the more frequently experienced musical performances made for recordings.

Recording technology has also transformed live performance. In an early example, the vocal style that came to be called crooning was made possible by the widespread use of amplification. The new technology of the electric microphone allowed the translation of these intimate, softly delivered vocal performances—carrying their sound over loud accompaniment in large public arenas. All of a sudden you didn't have to project to the back of the concert hall. Today, live performances have adopted many recording technologies, including the use of repurposed recordings. Live performances are often simultaneously broadcast (or podcast) to remote audiences, which is to say they are reproductions at the same time that they are live events. Not only has the preference for live music over recordings dissipated, the two have lost a clear distinction to such an extent that even to describe them as reciprocal misses the extent of their comingling.

The emergence of the amateur recordist and the ascendancy in the proliferation of recorded music over live music reflect important new characteristics of music creation and production. They also represent a reversal in the kind of commercialization of music that seemed to condemn music creation to the realm of the professionals. At the same time repurposed audio in the form of identifiable elements from prior recordings may allow for a unique kind of contemporary dialogue between musical histories. The merging and blurring of the relationships between creator, performer, and consumer is characteristic of the broader influence of music participation on cultural structure and function.

Intellectual Property and the Creative Commons

There are two contemporary practices in music that are pervasive and that have received considerable attention from both academic and popular cultural observers. These are sampling and cross-cultural appropriation. Both have implications beyond the scope of my research,[37] but both have a direct connection to the idea of repurposing audio, and it is this relationship that I will explore over the next two sections. This is not intended as comprehensive, but focuses on the ways in which the idea of repurposed audio can bring a new understanding to these sometimes thorny issues.

In the current era of sample usage and repurposed audio, the debates have raged over intellectual property. At the forefront of the debate in this country is the balance between fair usage and copyright. Fair usage argues for a "creative commons"—a cultural heritage that is shared and available to everyone—and copyright seeks to protect creative works so that there is economic protection and stimulation for the act of creation. Internationally there are more generalized issues stemming from essential differences between free and permission cultures. As far back as 1977 Attali foresaw the problems by observing that the capabilities for individual reproduction were falling further outside of the normal economy: "It is conceivable that, at the end of the revolution currently under way, locating the labor of recording will have become so difficult, owing to the multiplicity of the forms it can take, that authors' compensation will no longer be possible except at a fixed rate, on a statistical and anonymous basis independent of the success of the work itself."[38] Attali recognized the requirement of having an economic base for creativity—"people must devote their time to producing the means to buy recordings of other people's time."[39] At the same time he anticipates the new paradigms of audio construction in suggesting that "the destruction of the old codes in the commodity is perhaps the necessary condition for real creativity."[40]

In regard to generalized sampling use (as opposed to cultural appropriation discussed below) Katz asks whether "digital sampling introduced a fundamentally new compositional aesthetic, or is it best understood as an extension of older practices?"[41] He argues that because samples are altered, they bear a relationship to other forms of musical borrowing such as "quoting" from earlier famous pieces (as has long been the case in classical music). By drawing a comparison between digital samples (1s and 0s) and musical notation—both are symbols and thus representations as opposed to actual sound—Katz suggests that while "sampling does not differ from traditional musical borrowing in kind, it certainly differs in degree."[42]

It is appropriate to create a direct link in heritage from these earlier practices, but I think the larger point is the new paradigm of audio construction that has arisen from the use of recorded samples as musical building blocks (as opposed to referencing or quoting musical ideas). Katz certainly acknowledges that this new type of borrowing—which I call "repurposing"—"has led to some astonishingly creative works of modern music,"[43] and he reviews a few interesting pieces of music derived from sampling. What is most important about repurposed audio construction, however, is not its link to these past practices or to specific instances of its creative use, but its participation in the compositional environment in the computer. Repurposed audio lies at the heart of a compositional revolution on the scale that Attali suggests when appealing to the "destruction of the old codes."[44] The practical use of repurposed audio takes us far beyond the idea of musical references to whole new arenas of musical creation through radically different forms of music construction.

Katz recognizes the extent to which sampling "blurs the traditional distinction between ideas and expression."[45] Whose idea is it once a sample (clearly the work of a previous author) has been expressed (repurposed) in a completely new environment? He notes that relative to intellectual property, this confusion between original and repurposed audio created by digital sampling "muddies the distinction almost beyond recognition."[46] This element of the ramifications of sampling brings us back to issues regarding ownership and economics, which have been the source of the white hot debates regarding illegal downloading of music through peer-to-peer file-sharing. At the heart of the debate are complex issues regarding fair usage, copyright, and the history of music creation and ownership that, while beyond the scope of this work, are clearly made increasingly difficult by the technological and communication capabilities in contemporary media culture.

Issues concerning file-sharing also arise on a global level between permission and free cultures. It is not possible to adapt Western principles of intellectual property in all cultures, whether or not it might be deemed to be desirable. There are many oral music traditions that don't even acknowledge the idea of a composer. Cultures may wish to protect the free use of creative materials within their own culture but implement a permission requirement when these materials are used by other cultures. This creates enormous legal and accounting problems. Nonetheless, as we shall see with issues of appropriation as well, it is necessary to tackle these problems and to develop the systems needed to do so wherever possible. While problems surrounding appropriation are most often considered from the perspective of the appropriator the following, from "Gone Digital: Aboriginal Remix and the Cultural Commons" by Kimberly Christen, is indicative of the new attitudes arising within the cultures which have themselves been so frequently appropriated.

> Indigenous knowledge systems are often defined by communal ownership, while Western systems are usually anchored to individual ownership. This individual/communal view often masquerades as the inherent differences between indigenous peoples and the West. But indigenous concerns do not align neatly with any one agenda. In fact, attempts by the U.S. recording industry to define file sharing as "online shoplifting"—especially in the prominent peer-to-peer (p2p) file-sharing debates—resemble the highly visible agendas of some indigenous leaders to protect their cultural heritage from the same types of stealing. The 2003 *Indigenous Position Paper for the World Summit on the Information Society* (WSIS) states for example, that, "Our collective knowledge is not merely a commodity to be traded like any other in the market place. We strongly object to the notion that it constitutes a raw material or commercial resource for the knowledge-based economy of the Information Society." Like some of their corporate counterparts, international indigenous representatives want to limit the circulation of particular ideas, (tech) knowledge, and cultural materials. In fact, they "strongly reject the application of the public domain concept to any aspect related to our cultures and identities" and further "reject the application of IPR (intellectual property rights) regimes to assert patents, copyrights, or trademark monopolies for products, data, or

processes derived or originating from our traditional knowledge or our cultural expressions."[47]

Serious reform of copyright laws and the granting of fair use and public domain rights may be needed, but these would have to be balanced against the global need for some adapted principles of intellectual property. Where this balance lies will be endlessly debated and redefined. "Free" cultures are moving toward protecting their unique cultural expressions. Permission cultures struggle to deal with fairness issues in light of the opportunities created by ease of access. It is critical that in the process we do not lose sight of the benefits at both ends of the spectrum between intellectual property and the creative commons.

Appropriation and Appreciation

There is an oft-repeated quote: "Lesser artists borrow, great artists steal"— attributed with certain variations to Stravinsky, Picasso, and others. While clearly an oversimplification, this statement lends a certain perspective to the issue of musical appropriation. Nonetheless, the creative and communicative power of repurposed audio must be set against questions regarding the appropriation of cultural expressions. Here I will consider economic, ethical, political, and musical issues surrounding the practice of cross-cultural audio repurposing.[48] Ultimately I return to the model of my construction of the African folklore piece "Milee Yookoee." There are no clear or simple answers here. Composers and musicians must struggle with balancing access against fairness, creation against exploitation, and cross-fertilization against empowerment.

Cook dismisses the simply negative view regarding creative encounters with music of cultures other than our own: "the way you become pessimistic is by assuming that music *represents* the world-views of cultures from which we are cut off by time, space, or both."[49] But he wants to provide balance as well: he adds that we must be careful not to take this too far, for "if music can be a means of cross-cultural understanding, it can be a means of cross-cultural misunderstanding, too."[50] Ultimately he describes the potential of cross-cultural music fertilization as a point of connection but not a means of dissolution of cultural differences.[51] This is a nicely balanced position, though it leaves much in the way of specific considerations still to be negotiated.

The most problematic aspects of the use of samples from other cultures have been carefully outlined by Paul Théberge and are summarized in the following three points of view, intended to "deflect ethical, political, or musical criticism of the cultural appropriation that has taken place."[52]

1. Théberge cites a review that raises the typical arguments against appropriation including cultural exploitation, music that is diminished by removal from context, and use of appropriated samples as a "jaded substitute for musicianship," and then seems to dismiss them all through an attitude that suggests that "aesthetic experience—indeed, simple musical pleasure—should take precedence over all ethical or musical concerns."[53] Théberge counters this rather simplistic argument by citing examples of originators of musical samples that do not receive adequate remuneration or credit for their work: "Thus, a basic asymmetry, both in terms of economic gain and artistic acknowledgement, exists between the makers and those who are the objects of the sampling enterprise."[54] Clearly an attitude that disregards some of the concrete problems that are created by sample appropriation, in the name of "simple musical pleasure," cannot stand up to very close scrutiny. This is somewhat reminiscent of the whole covers debate that fueled some of the rhetoric of "authenticity," though recorded cover versions are clearly protected by copyright laws and have legal, statutory payment requirements.

2. "A second discursive strategy trivializes the act of appropriation, depoliticizing it by rendering it banal."[55] Théberge cites the oft-repeated metaphor in which samples are described as a kind of spice—a taste or flavor that a creator uses to enhance their musical creation—making the sampling artist into something of a gourmet as a opposed to an appropriator of someone else's work.[56]

3. Finally, and most significantly, Théberge notes that the music that is sampled is empowered in a way that twists the true hierarchical relationship between the elements "by portraying the recorded subject as active and the sound recordist as passive."[57] Quoting another promo piece that touts certain samples as providing access to (in this case) the heart of African music, he comments: "Here, sampling musicians (descendants of a former conqueror) are not only changed by their encounter with African music but appropriate it fully as a part of their own musical identity: by looking 'within' for true music, one finds not one's own music but 'Africa' in technological forms."[58] Thus the promoter "characterizes appropriation as a form of cultural exchange

among equals and the inevitable byproduct of larger social forces, such as the diffusion of modern communications technologies and increased cultural contact in the 'Global Village.'"[59] Clearly for Théberge such a characterization seeks to subvert the political and economic realities hidden behind such catchall phrases as "Global Village."

Théberge references Stephen Feld, who has done much of the seminal work in the area of pop music's cultural appropriation and the subsequent attempts to hide or ignore economic interests and inequities in order to avoid constraints to the marketplace. And just as appropriation cannot be split from commodification in regard to "the production, marketing, and use of world music samples, questions of musical identity cannot easily be separated from questions of ownership."[60] Yet questions regarding the realistic capabilities of individuals or companies to address these tangled associations remain.

David Hesmondhalgh takes off from this point to address some of these issues surrounding identity and ownership in more detail. In the article "Digital Sampling and Cultural Inequality" Hesmondhalgh acknowledges that "Cultural exchange and cross-fertilisation can be pleasurable, and can suggest the possibilities of communicating across boundaries of social difference. But there may be a darker side to such practices."[61] Through meticulous analysis Hesmondhalgh details the inadequate responses of those who use musical samples from other cultures. He does not suggest that the overall effect of sampling has been negative but he does argue that the response in terms of protection for sampled musicians has been lacking. Ultimately Hesmondhalgh asserts the need for those in positions of power to see that "full and prominent credit . . . be given to the sampled musicians and the musical traditions to which they belong, giving indications of the cultural sources of the music" and for sample users to "make strenuous efforts to establish ways of recompensing musicians, their descendants, or representative organisations."[62]

Taylor affirms the notion that the emphasis on globalization is, at least in part, an obfuscating technique to hide the hegemony of capitalism, which he sees to be exploitative as ever. The term *globalization* itself serves to maintain a distinction between this global marketplace and the notion of local cultures.[63] Taylor adopts the term *glocalization,* which

> emphasizes the extent to which the local and the global are no longer distinct—indeed, never were—but are inextricably intertwined, with one infiltrating and implicating the other. Indeed, it may now be difficult or

impossible to speak of one or the other. Older forms and problems of globalization continue but are increasingly compromised, challenged, and augmented by this newer phenomenon of glocalization.[64]

It is this recognition of the blending of global and local that in part dictates the need to find the distinctions between the good and the dangerous elements of cross-cultural appropriation. Thus Hesmondhalgh begins his critique of the implementation of world samples by acknowledging its benefits. Similarly Théberge acknowledges that the use of other people's music "is at once fragmentary and exceedingly rich."[65] In a case study of a 1998 dance music hit that is laden with samples, Mark Katz notes that the ultimate product is "derivative *and* novel, exploitative *and* respectful, awkward *and* subtle."[66]

We must also factor in some of the cultural shifts that make glocalization a more appropriate term than globalization for contemporary cultural exchange. The fact is that the technological divide is rapidly shrinking—at least as it relates to the creation and production of music: "The ethnographic Other is now fully plugged in, and the ethnomusicologist is no longer the only person in the field with high-tech equipment."[67] The exchange is increasingly two-way with idioms such as Afro-pop and Indian pop sharing extensively in the process of repurposed audio and technologically constructed musical composition. This is not to suggest that all cultures are equivalent, but it is to acknowledge that the notion that musical hybridization is simply a one-way street of Western appropriation of music from indigenous cultures is increasingly inappropriate.

I believe the complexities of so-called appropriation—and I think that as this phenomenon becomes more complex the reduction and connotation of the word *appropriation* become more problematic—go even deeper than this carefully nuanced value system of positive and negative effects. Cook demonstrates that in different cultures the experience of music may be radically different. For example the thumb piano in Africa is thought of as a series of movements, not as sounds; Chinese *qin* music is considered a means of focusing the mind and not thought of as sounds. So "to approach another culture's music from an aesthetic viewpoint is to interpret it in an ethnocentric and therefore partial manner."[68] This not to say that sound doesn't have meaning in those other cultures as well (or that movement, etc., doesn't have musical meaning in our culture)—it's just not what's central to their experience. Cook is saying that when we listen to recordings—or I would add, repurpose them as samples in new compositions—it's not possible to restore their "original social function. . . . To approach music aesthetically—to interpret it in terms of a specific interest in sound and its perceptual experience—is not, then, to transcend Western cultural values, but rather to express them."[69]

So are we really getting a sufficiently complete picture when we label contemporary music's intersection with sampling from other cultures as appropriation? If both the use and experience of music from these other cultures are primarily an expression of one's own culture, then the idea of appropriation would seem to overstate the principle of what such reuse is actually an expression of. Perhaps repurposing is a more accurate and less pejorative term for such reuse. *The term* repurpose *places the emphasis on the audio's new environment, its newly imagined purpose, and not so much on the lifting (or appropriation) of its previous significance, transference of which is not truly possible anyway.*

Another part of the problem with the connotations of the word *appropriation* arises when a relative value judgment is assigned to creative repurposing (as opposed to the judgments regarding credit or remuneration for such usage). Théberge suggests that Bartok's appropriation of Hungarian folk music is "qualitatively different from the fleeting juxtaposition of collage that have become the preferred idiom of contemporary technoculture. . . . With vast decontextualized collections of sampled sound available on CD-ROM, technoculture neither allows for the type of profound encounter experienced by a composer such as Bartok, nor is it required."[70] What constitutes a profound musical encounter? Given the difficulties that one culture might have in truly understanding the musical context of another, how can anyone be sure that such an encounter has taken place? At what point does such decontextualization take place? Isn't such decontextualization an immediate (and even desired) effect of any musical repurposing? Where is the line between intracultural appropriation (from folk music to Bartok's compositions or blues to rock) and intercultural appropriation (from African to Western pop) really drawn?

The piece of African folkloric music that I have constructed is an example of a relatively amateur exploration of music through the newly created capabilities of computer-based audio production.[71] On the surface this may appear to epitomize Théberge's decontextualized encounter with (in this case) African music. But the reality is that I studied African music for many years with a master drummer from Ghana. Yet whatever relationship my work may bear to an original performance of this music by Africans was not the point of this undertaking anyway. This is a satisfying creative endeavor for me. This process provides me with creative access to a form of music that I am not capable of accessing physically (that is, I couldn't play these drum parts as a live performer). It is as much (and as importantly) an encounter with technology as it is with music, and this encounter has enormous context for me, who lives so much of my musical life through my use of the computer for creating and manipulating music. The exercise is intentionally, and for me very positively, a conscious act of decontextualizing.

Similarly whatever relationship this may bear to an original performance of this music by Africans was not the point for whoever may hear this piece. Were Bartok's compositions meant to familiarize or even provide entry to Hungarian music, or were they simply made richer through his personal encounters with that music?[72] When I play my construction of "Milee Yookoee" for friends it provides an experience of some musical concepts and forms that they may never have otherwise had, and this broadening of experience is the point and the value, not its direct African referents (which we can only experience in a very incomplete way anyway because of the cultural differences). So what one critic might characterize as my appropriated (and highly inauthentic) "recording" (which wasn't recorded in any traditional sense of the word) might provide a more interesting and rewarding experience for listeners than what they might have had listening to a recording of the original African piece from which my work was derived. Indeed, were they to have the opportunity to experience an indigenous live performance of this music, they might still prefer my more formalized, recorded version, as it would have more cultural relevance for them. They might identify more strongly with the underlying disco-like beat and the formality of my arrangement. They might also identify with the very act of cross-cultural interpretation, of reaching out from one culture into another, which is so prevalent in contemporary music.

Both Théberge and Hesmondhalgh cite Steven Feld's work,[73] which lambastes some of the early, cavalier attitudes toward sampling of indigenous music, and both are themselves highly critical of such attitudes. However, both wish to go beyond exposing the wrongs of the past. They are attempting to formulate what might constitute right action given the widespread use of indigenous samples. Certainly attempts to better credit and remunerate original artists are worthwhile, but they will become increasingly difficult in the context of glocalization and the massive jumble of worldwide cultural artifacts. Again, this is not to say that all best efforts shouldn't be made, but it is to say that such efforts are ultimately at least partially doomed behind the increasing complexity of our glocalized worldwide culture. I do not wish to minimize the economic hegemony of the West, but cultural expression is playing out on such a broad scale and in such a multiplicity of fragmented contexts as to make both credit and remuneration an increasingly difficult endeavor.

For Frith the current use of samples is a part of the reason that "We certainly do now hear music as a *fragmented* and *unstable* object."[74] As such, it is as much an expression of the urban landscape—urban sprawl, the barrage of media input, and the isolation of automobiles for example—as it is an evolution of recording technology. We might reference contemporary constructed audio projects as expressions of Baudrillard's "*model of the disintegration of functions,* of the indeterminacy of functions, and of the disintegration of the city itself."[75] The difficulties in acknowledgement and credit may become lost in what Baudrillard terms the hypermarket, in which "the objects no longer have a specific reality" and there exists a "deterritorialized function and mode of work."[76] The postmodern forces of complexity and fragmentation will continue to render so-called notions of appropriation more inappropriate to cultural understanding. These forces may undermine certain capabilities of music to reinforce social cohesion, but at the same time they may be providing new forms for music to help us cope with expressions of deterritorialized social functions. Finally, the notion of repurposed audio allows the creative forces the upper hand and rescues many contemporary musical practices from the stigma of appropriation.

Conclusions
Reflections on the Future

To best celebrate music and the efforts of human expression it is necessary to embrace change. While this is not to be done uncritically, it can only be accomplished with an open mind. The meeting of digital tools and audio production is the latest in the never-ending confluence of technology, culture, and the individual. Scholarship is one means of increasing receptivity to new and different ideas and experiences, celebrating human endeavor in all of its complexity and variety. Through its integrative impulses music seeks to provide the potential for cultural understanding and acceptance, and in these ways there are some parallels between the Western tradition of study and the practice of music.[1] At the same time, we "use machines and other technology in the same way as we use music and musical instruments, to interpret the world and give it meaning."[2] Thus it is no accident that the final section (Part III) of this work has focused on an adaptation of an African folklore piece on the one hand and the latest in consumer technology, such as the iPod, on the other. These modes of music participation extend the previous focus on presentation and performance to highlight the positive forces alive in contemporary music creation and reception. While I have worked to maintain a balanced point of view, I have been motivated in large part by a desire to reclaim the joys of music participation in what is sometimes a hostile environment.

Music is bound to a social context. Music is often an essential element in the creation of social meaning, for instance in terms of teenagers' construction of personal and group identity, yet it is often judged on its ability to survive its particular moment, to "stand the test of time" and outlast its historical setting. We must recognize that the meaning of music is dependent on the context in which it is experienced: it is always culturally and historically contingent, whether the music is a creation of the moment or a re-creation (either live or recorded) of the past. Technological reproduction may give us access to music from the past in some form but it does not give us access to the actual experience of that music at the time it was created. There is always a dynamic relationship between the production or reproduction of music and our experience of it.[3] The advent of digital audio technology has heightened our ability to be participants in this dynamic relationship and in that regard moved us closer to the older models of musical integration.

There is currently a changing paradigm of music consumption born of the marriage between digital audio and the Internet. Digital downloading is reversing the model of grouping musical pieces that began with the LP and continued through the CD. Under the new model music is no longer necessarily experienced in preconceived groupings, delivered as sets of pieces to be experienced in a specific order. In a sense this is a return to the multiple discs required to reproduce a single piece of classical music from the days of the shellac 78 rpm recordings, when classical pieces, although sold as sets, may have been listened to out of sequence; or the "singles" culture of the 1950s, when songs were listened to radio style, one artist's song at a time. But the new paradigm broadens both of these long-abandoned models. Via digital downloading and portable mp3 players people are experiencing all kinds of different music, juxtaposed in new and unexpected ways. Vast libraries may be accessed randomly or easily programmed by the consumer, rather than prepackaged for them. Internet sites such as Pandora, TagWorld, and Amazon use either personal or collaborative filtering to recommend music based on the music that you've indicated you like. This cannot be understood as the simple and random movement of technological capabilities to which culture responds. In some way we have dreamed up these new capacities—we have arrived at a desire to integrate divergent musical performances in even more immediate and encompassing ways. We wish to experience a broader palette of musical styles in an even more condensed fashion. This may be understood as a movement toward a widening in the breadth of musical expression as well as a movement to a closer kind of musical integration.

The following rhapsodic evocation of this new technology comes from Alex Ross, and its ultimate assertion of a universal sense of music as simply music is at the heart of my arguments here:

I have seen the future, and it is called Shuffle—the setting on the iPod that skips randomly from one track to another. I've transferred about a thousand songs, works, and sonic events from my CD collection to my computer and on to the MP3 player. There is something thrilling about setting the player on Shuffle and letting it decide what to play next. Sometimes its choices are a touch delirious—I had to veto an attempt to forge a link between György Kurtág and Oasis—but the little machine often goes crashing through barriers of style in ways that change how I listen. For example, it recently made a segue from the furious crescendo of "The Dance of the Earth," ending Part I of "The Rite of Spring," right into the hot jam of Louis Armstrong's "West End Blues." The first became a gigantic upbeat to the other. For a second, I felt that I was at some madly fashionable party at Carl Van Vechten's. On the iPod, music is freed from all fatuous self-definitions and delusions of significance. There are no record jackets depicting bombastic Alpine scenes or celebrity conductors with a family resemblance to Rudolf Hess. Instead, music is music.[4]

So the forces of dislocation that seem so rampant in contemporary culture are not the only forces present, nor are they necessarily aggravated by technology. Together music and technology find new ways to reinforce and expand individual and cultural identity. My own experience as a recordist is bolstered by my pursuit of scholarship, and together they provide me with the enthusiasms of music making and listening. I am more acutely aware than ever of the ways that music in its digital form, from the DAW to the iPod, may inspire community and creativity just as music always has.

When, over seventy years ago, Walter Benjamin considered what was at stake in light of the new technologies of mechanical reproduction, he conceived the withering aura of the original. But perhaps he suffered from his own assessment: "The conventional is uncritically enjoyed, and the truly new is criticized with aversion."[5] It would seem that the new in the technology of music is always seen as a threat, that somehow the new ways of making or hearing music are going to rob music of its mystery. Perhaps Benjamin would agree that now, after over one hundred years of development, the processes that allow for mechanical reproduction may produce art with a different but meaningful aura of its own—that, indeed, the technology of music might help us retain this sense of the mystery of music. *Music, in all of its forms—its creation, its expression, its reproduction and its consumption—remains a window into another, perhaps higher world.* In the words of Jorge Luis Borges: "Music, states of happiness, mythology, faces belabored by time, certain twilights and certain places try to tell us something, or have said something we should not have missed, or are about to say something; this imminence of a revelation which does not occur is, perhaps, the aesthetic phenomenon."[6]

Notes

INTRODUCTION

1. It is appropriate to put the notion of repurposed audio—which is defined and refined over the course of this work—in a broader context of related ideas. Serge Lacasse defines a related concept under the term *transphonography*, and in the process he surveys earlier works that employ the terms *transtextuality, intertextuality*, and others, all of which bear a relationship to the notion of repurposing presented here. See Serge Lacasse, "Towards a Model of Transphonography," in *Incestuous Pop: Intertextuality in Recorded Popular Music,* ed. Serge Lacasse (Quebec: Nota Bene, forthcoming).

2. *Webster's New Collegiate Dictionary* (Springfield, MA: G. & C. Merriam, 1981), 952.

3. The term *repurpose* is hardly new, but I have adapted it here to apply to contemporary audio construction in specific, and I hope, original ways. In Jay David Bolter and Richard Grusing, *Remediation: Understanding New Media* (Cambridge: MIT Press, 1999), 49–50, the authors refer to repurposing as an element in their construction of the word *remediation*. Their notion that "Repurposing as remediation is both what is 'unique to digital worlds' and what denies the possibility of that uniqueness" mirrors the "made new" and "used again" dichotomy that I have introduced here.

4. I do not intend to idealize the listener's position here. The listener's judgment is only one marker of value in the cultural response to music, but it is the one that we each hold as our own.

5. The pun here is intentional and reinforces the notion that the manipulation of recordings is now frequently an essential part of musical play.

6. Brian Eno, interview posted on the Internet from unknown publication and unknown date. http://music.hyperreal.org/artists/brian_eno/interviews/unk-75a.html. Accessed 25 December 2005.

7. Simon Frith, *Performing Rites* (Cambridge: Harvard University Press, 1996), 241.

8. See, for example: Paul Théberge, "'Plugged in': Technology and Popular Music," in *The Cambridge Companion to Pop and Rock,* ed. Simon Frith, Will Straw, and John Street (Cambridge: Cambridge University Press, 2001), 24; Albin Zak III, *The Poetics of Rock* (Berkeley: University of California Press, 2003), 2; Mark Katz, *Capturing Sound: How Technology Has Changed Music* (Berkeley: University of California Press, 2004), 157; Paul D. Greene, "Wired Sound and Sonic Cultures," in *Wired for Sound: Engineering and Technologies in Sonic Cultures,* ed. Paul D. Greene and Thomas Porcello (Middletown, CT: Wesleyan University Press, 2005), 15.

9. Timothy Warner, *Pop Music—Technology and Creativity* (Aldershot, Hants: Ashgate, 2003), 20.

10. Nicholas Cook, *Music: A Very Short Introduction* (Oxford: Oxford University Press, 1998), 99.

11. See Herban Sabbe, "Call for Rectification of Current Musicological Practice," *"Musicæ Scientiæ": The Journal of the European Society for the Cognitive Sciences of Music,* Discussion Forum, 2 (2001): 133; Albin Zak, "Journal of the Art of Record Production," http://www.artofrecordproduction.com/content/view/209/104/.

12. Michael Chanan, *Musica Practica: The Social Practice of Western Music from Gregorian Chant to Postmodernism* (London: Verso, 1994), 27.

13. Ibid., 28.

14. Ibid., 222.

15. Steve Jones, *Rock Formation: Music, Technology, and Mass Communication* (Newbury Park, CA: Sage, 1992), 155.

16. Bonnie Hayes's song "Have A Heart" was written from a sound she happened onto, and the song was a hit for Bonnie Raitt. Ms. Hayes says she has written many songs inspired by synthesizer sound patches, and in casual conversations with other songwriters I have heard similar anecdotes.

17. Chanan, *Musica Practica,* 239.

18. One of the most well known was the denunciation by Matthew Stewart Prichard, assistant director at the Boston Museum, of plaster cast reproductions of sculpture.

> The purpose of art, according to Prichard "is the pleasure derived from a contemplation of the perfect." Casts were worse than merely imperfect, they were subversive; as "data mechanically produced," casts were "the Pianola of the Arts" and no more belonged in an art museum than mechanical music belonged in a symphony hall. Casts were "engines of education and should not be shown near objects of inspirations."

Lawrence Levine, *Highbrow/Lowbrow: The Emergence of Cultural Hierarchy in America* (Cambridge: Harvard University Press, 1988), 152–54.

19. Walter Benjamin, "The Work of Art in the Age of Mechanical Reproduction," in *Illuminations,* ed. Hannah Arendt, trans. Harry Zohn (New York: Schocken, 1968), 220.

20. Ibid., 221.

21. Ibid.

22. Ibid., 224.

23. Ibid.

24. Ibid., 227. "Earlier much futile thought had been devoted to the question of whether photography is an art. The primary question—whether the very invention of photography had not transformed the entire nature of art—was not raised."

25. Ibid., 224.

26. Michael Chanan, *Repeated Takes: A Short History of Recording and its Effects on Music* (London: Verso, 1995), 18.

27. Chanan, *Musica Practica*, 6.

28. Ibid., 31.

29. Benjamin, "Work of Art," 217.

30. Jonathan Sterne, *The Audible Past: Cultural Origins of Sound Reproduction* (Durham, NC: Duke University Press, 2003), 20.

31. Ibid., 21.

32. Sterne, *The Audible Past,* 25, 225, 251, 261–62, 274, 283. Sterne details the history of sound reproduction as a network of people and technologies.

33. Susan Sontag, *On Photography* (New York: Picador, 1977), 147.

34. Ibid., 148.

CHAPTER ONE

1. The "talk-back" is the two-way communication system between those in the control room where the recording is being made and the artist who is performing in the studio.

2. A process whereby a bit of a recording was copied onto a second tape recorder and then painstakingly rerecorded back to the master tape recorder into the correct spot—thereby fixing a rhythmic anomaly or replacing some other problematic piece of audio with an acceptable equivalent.

3. The Eventide Harmonizer is a stand-alone digital device that alters pitch without altering time. This was a forerunner to the current technology that I will be describing for pitch fixing. It was primarily used to "thicken" vocals or instruments by adding slightly retuned and delayed "doubles" of an original performance. It could be used to fix pitch but only in certain fairly rare instances where the problem was a consistent degree of flat or sharp performance, and even then it was very difficult and time consuming to create an effective repair.

4. It is interesting to note that when I inquired at several of the professional studios in the Bay Area, they all said that the 24-track tape recorder was only being used to transfer older material into Pro Tools. Once transferred, these recordings may be remixed or repurposed in any number of ways. Analog tape recorders are rarely used for recording anymore, though they dominated professional recording for close to 30 years.

5. A plug-in is additional software that increases functionality in Pro Tools.

Some plug-ins, such as Beat Detective, come as part of the program, and others, such as Auto-Tune, must be purchased separately.

6. A region is a distinct piece of audio in Pro Tools. Any section of recorded audio in a Pro Tools file can be made into a region, and once it is, it can be edited independently—that is cut, copied, pasted, moved, processed, etc.

7. It should be noted here that it would also have been possible to build in a variety of different kinds of variations from strictly quantized note placement. Notes may be slightly rushed or lagged relative to the ideal beat, or randomly rushed and lagged within user definable parameters available within the "quantize" menu options.

8. *Off-axis* refers to sounds coming to a directional (cardioid) microphone from an area outside its intended pattern of pick-up.

9. For more detail on the capabilities of these plug-ins, you might reference the promotional material from a tuning plug-in called Tune that is a successor to Auto-Tune at http://www.waves.com/content.asp?id=1748. Accessed 4 January 2006.

10. This is a notion that I explore more thoroughly in chapter 6.

11. For Roland Barth see "The Grain of the Voice," in *Image—Music—Text,* trans. Stephen Heath (New York: Hill and Wang, 1997); for Robert Philip see *Early Recordings and Musical Style* (Cambridge: Cambridge University Press, 1992); for David Epstein see the quote from him in Frith, *Performing Rites,* 152.

12. Anthony Gritten, "On Answering Music," *"Musicæ Scientiæ": The Journal of the European Society for the Cognitive Sciences of Music,* Discussion Forum, 2 (2001): 53.

13. See Frith, *Performing Rites,* 237–40.

14. Théberge, "Plugged in," 12.

15. Nicholas Cook, *Music, Imagination and Culture* (Oxford: Oxford University Press, 1990), 93.

16. The contemporary relationship to musical encounters, in regard to technical performance, composition, and cultural encounters, will be taken up more thoroughly in chapters 7–9.

17. This speaks to learning modalities and other education considerations beyond the scope of the current work.

18. In Jacques Attali, *Noise: The Political Economy of Music,* trans. Brian Massumi (Minneapolis: University of Minnesota Press, 1985), ix.

19. Arnold Pacey, *Meaning in Technology* (Cambridge: MIT Press, 2001), 33.

20. Frith, *Performing Rites,* 152.

21. Ibid.

22. Ibid.

23. Leonard B. Meyer, *Emotion and Meaning in Music* (Chicago: University of Chicago Press, 1956), 198.

24. For information on Cholakis's work see Craig Anderton, "Hit Factors: The Link Between Music & Emotional Response," in *Sound on Sound,* May 2002, http://www.soundonsound.com/sos/may02/articles/cholakis.asp. Accessed 25 July 2007.

25. John Goodmanson, "John Goodmanson: ON," *EQ Magazine* 17, no. 1 (2006): 23–24.

26. This point of view is persuasively argued in Robert Philip's *Early Recordings*. Not all researchers agree, however, and I return to a more thorough discussion of this topic in chapter 4.

27. Neal Stephenson, *Snow Crash* (New York: Bantam Spectra, 1993), 134.

28. There may be some debate about the significance of fluctuations that fall below the perceptual threshold. The problem comes in determining what is meant by perceptual. The ability to identify fluctuations (which itself fluctuates widely depending on the relative skill and sensitivity of the musical ear) does not necessarily coincide with the effect such fluctuations may have on the experience of music. I would argue that all fluctuations are perceived on some level and exert some degree of influence over the experience.

29. See Sterne, Eisenberg, Goodall, and many others on the earlier history of audio balancing techniques.

30. For both a conceptual and detailed analytical survey of spatial aspects of mixing see William Moylan, *The Art of Recording: Understanding and Crafting the Mix* (Oxford: Focal Press, 2002), especially 173–219.

31. Cook, *Music, Imagination and Culture,* 188.

32. Ibid., 193.

33. René T. A. Lysloff and Leslie C. Gay Jr., eds., *Music and Technoculture* (Middletown, CT: Wesleyan University Press, 2003), 15.

34. Pacey, *Meaning in Technology,* 30.

CHAPTER TWO

1. I recorded a CD for Freddie in 2005 for Blues Express Records. The vocal tracks were recorded at Laughing Tiger studios in San Rafael, CA, but all of the editing was done at my home studio in San Francisco. Recording, editing, and mixing were all completed using Pro Tools software.

2. For a discussion of these basic audio-processing techniques, see most any introductory recording text such as my book *The Art of Digital Audio Recording* (New York: Oxford University Press, 2011).

3. Théberge, "Plugged in," 5.

4. Much has been written on this subject. For a discussion of the finalizing aspects of CD production see Bob Katz, *Mastering Audio* (Oxford: Focal Press, 2002), especially 128–32.

5. The following is from the developer's promotion for this product at http://www.waves.com/content.asp?id=1748 (accessed 4 January 2006):

> Breathing is something singers seem to insist on doing, even when it spoils a perfectly good take. Now DeBreath lets you not only eliminate those breaths, but also lets you turn them in your favor, using them for new creative effects.

DeBreath is a revolutionary new plug-in that automatically reduces or removes breath sounds on vocal tracks. DeBreath employs a unique template-matching algorithm that detects breath segments and separates them from the main vocal, so breath sounds can be reduced or eliminated without affecting the rest of the signal.

Because DeBreath can be used to separate a vocal track into two elements, one containing only voice and the other only breaths, each can be processed differently, for the emotional effects of breathing to be enhanced with additional processing if desired.

6. Barthes, *Image—Music—Text*, 185.

7. Ibid., 183.

8. Does it matter that in Dylan's time it would not have been possible to "fix" those popped "p's," whereas the Billie Jo's slurred "esses" are intentionally created? What about "fixing" Dylan's "p's" now that it is possible? Is this akin to removing surface noise and pops on old records for reissue? How about colorizing old black-and-white films? This opens a whole other discussion around intentionality, authenticity, and aesthetics too broad to be considered here.

9. Barthes, *Image—Music—Text*, 183.

10. Ibid.

11. Ibid.

12. Ibid., 181.

13. Ibid., 54.

14. Ibid., 61.

15. Nicholas Cook, "Uncanny Moments: Juxtaposition and the Collage Principle in Music," in *Approaches to Meaning in Music,* ed. Byron Almén and Edward Pearsall (Bloomington: Indiana University Press, 2006), 133.

16. Barthes, *Image—Music—Text*, 179.

17. Frith, *Performing Rites*, 215; emphasis added.

18. Ibid.

19. Ibid., 226. Frith is setting "pop" against "folk" and "art" as the three stages of music history "organized around a different technology of musical storage and retrieval" (226).

20. Ibid., 226–27.

21. Barthes, *Image—Music—Text*, 180.

22. Ibid., 180–81.

23. Ibid., 189.

24. Chanan, *Musica Practica,* 193.

25. Barthes, *Image—Music—Text*, 184.

26. Ibid.

27. Ibid., 188.

28. As this book is being written a new piece of software called Throat has been introduced that claims to provide the following powers of vocal processing. "Throat's controls allow you to modify the voice's glottal waveform as well as the

ability to globally stretch, shorten, widen, or constrict the modeled vocal tract. For more detailed control, the graphical Throat Shaping display lets you adjust the position and width of five points in the vocal tract model, from the vocal cords, through the throat, mouth, and out to the lips. Breathiness controls variable frequency noise in the model, resulting in a range of vocal effects from subtle breathiness, to raspiness, to a full whisper." This is especially interesting in light of this discussion, adding more layers of possible interaction between recording techniques and Barthes's idea of "grain."

CHAPTER THREE

1. See also the ethnographic studies in Greene and Porcello, *Wired for Sound.*

2. Ibid., 274.

3. Ibid.

4. Alex Ross, "The Record Effect: How Technology Has Transformed the Sound of Music," *New Yorker,* 6 June 2005.

5. Ibid.

6. Alex Ross, private email communication, 11 July 2005.

7. David Denby, "Big Pictures: Hollywood Looks for a Future," *New Yorker,* 8 January 2007, 56.

8. Ibid., 60.

9. Sterne, *The Audible Past,* 7.

10. Ibid., 26.

11. David Morton, *Off the Record: The Technology and Culture of Sound Recording in America* (New Brunswick: Rutgers University Press, 2000), 177.

12. Jason Toynbee, *Making Popular Music: Musicians, Creativity and Institutions* (London: Arnold, 2000), 91.

13. Ibid., 106.

14. René T. A. Lysloff and Leslie C. Gay Jr., introduction to *Music and Technoculture,* 10.

15. Warner, *Pop Music,* 35.

16. For a more complete description of this process see Sterne, *The Audible Past,* 219–21.

17. Eric W. Rothenbuhler and John Durham Peters, "Defining Phonography: An Experiment in Theory," *Musical Quarterly,* Summer 1997, 246.

18. Andrew Goodwin, "Sample and Hold: Pop Music in the Age of Digital Reproduction," *Critical Quarterly* 30, no. 3 (1988): 25.

19. Ibid., 3.

20. Ibid., 46. Although it is not completely clear here whether Goodwin is referencing the original recording or the original performance, his prior assertions regarding the death of aura imply that he is still referring to the original in terms of the actual performance.

21. Evan Eisenberg, *The Recording Angel: The Experience of Music from Aristotle to Zappa* (New York: Penguin, 1986), 13.

22. Tia Denora, *Music in Everyday Life* (Cambridge: Cambridge University Press, 2000), 30.

23. Ibid.

24. Ibid., 31.

25. Pacey, *Meaning in Technology,* 36.

26. Ibid.

27. Toynbee, *Making Popular Music,* 89.

28. Théberge, "Plugged in," 14.

29. Denora, *Music in Everyday Life,* 30.

30. Slavoj Žižek, *On Belief* (New York: Routledge, 2001). http://josephtate .com/ radiohead/archives/000305.html.

31. David Byrne, posting to his website journal on 5 June 2005. http://www .davidbyrne.com/journal.

32. Howard Goodall, *Big Bangs: The Story of Five Discoveries that Changed Musical History* (London: Vintage, 2001), 190.

33. *Webster's New Collegiate Dictionary* (1981), 75.

34. Ibid.

35. Attali, *Noise,* 87.

36. For other, similar attitudes toward reproduction see Roger Beebe, Denise Fulbrook, and Ben Saunders, introduction to *Rock over the Edge: Transformations in Popular Music Culture,* ed. Roger Beebe, Denise Fulbrook, and Ben Saunders (Durham, NC: Duke University Press, 2002), 6; Katz, *Capturing Sound,* 189; and Allan Moore, *Rock: The Primary Text: Developing a Musicology of Rock* (Burlington, VT: Ashgate, 2001), 7.

37. Oliver Sacks, "The Mind's Eye," *New Yorker,* 28 July 2003, 55.

38. Trevor Pinch and Karin Bijsterveld, "Sound Studies: New Technologies and Music," *Social Studies of Science,* special issue "Sound Studies: New Technologies and Music," 34, no. 5 (2004): 635–48, http://www.jstor.org/stable/4144355. Accessed 9 March 2009.

39. Ibid.

40. Josh Tyrangiel, "Auto-Tune: Why Pop Music Sounds Perfect," *Time,* 5 February 2009, http://www.time.com/time/magazine/article/0,9171,1877372-2,00.html. Accessed 12 March 2009.

41. Sasha Frere-Jones, "The Gerbil's Revenge: Auto-Tune Corrects a Singer's Pitch. It Also Distorts—a Grand Tradition in Pop," *New Yorker,* 9 June 2008, http://www.newyorker.com/arts/critics/musical/2008/06/09/080609crmu_music_frerejones. Accessed 12 March 2009.

42. J. Freedom du Lac, "Motor Mouth: T-Pain Cranks Out Hits Thanks to Auto-Tune Software: Now Everyone Else Wants to Come Along for the Ride," *Washington Post,* 9 November 2008, http://www.washingtonpost.com/wp-dyn/content/article/2008/11/07/AR2008110701033.html. Accessed 12 March 2009.

43. Tyrangiel, "Auto-Tune."

44. Ibid.

45. http://www.idiomag.com/peek/64302/death_cab_for_cutie. Accessed 12 March 2009.

46. Freedom du Lac, "Motor Mouth."

47. Frere-Jones, "The Gerbil's Revenge."

PART TWO

1. Barthes, *Image—Music—Text,* 143.

2. Ibid., 148.

CHAPTER FOUR

1. Brian Eno, *A Year with Swollen Appendices* (London: Faber & Faber, 1996), 396.

2. Théberge, "Plugged in," 11.

3. Denora, *Music in Everyday Life,* 35.

4. Ibid., 40.

5. Steven F. Pond, *Head Hunters: The Making of Jazz's First Platinum Album* (Ann Arbor: University of Michigan Press, 2005), 117.

6. For more on this approach see my contribution to *The Cambridge Companion to Recorded Music,* ed. Nicholas Cook, Eric Clarke, Daniel Leech-Wilkinson, and John Rink (Cambridge: Cambridge University Press, 2009), titled "'It Could Have Happened': The Evolution of Music Construction."

7. A playlist is a new "track" in Pro Tools that occupies the same timeline as an earlier track—usually of the same instrument. Thus I had organized all the piano tracks on alternate playlists across the same timeline. When I would select a new piano playlist I would hear a different piano take, positioned in the same relative position to the overall arrangement as the other piano takes. My composite piano track was a playlist that also played along the same timeline.

8. *Head* is the term in jazz musicians use for the statement of the melody as opposed to the improvised elements. This is typically at the top, or head, of the arrangement. The reference here to "head out" is to the restatement of the melody at the end of the arrangement.

9. Cook, *Music, Imagination and Culture,* 131.

10. Chanan, *Musica Practica,* 11.

11. Ibid., 8.

12. Matthew W. Butterfield, "Jazz Analysis and the Production of Musical Community: A Situational Perspective," Ph.D. diss., University of Pennsylvania, 2000, 4.

13. Ibid.

14. Ibid., 4–5.

15. Ibid., 5.

16. Ibid., 138.

17. Ibid., 291.

18. Nicholas Cook, "Writing on Music or Axes to Grind: Road Rage and Musical Community," *Music Education Research* 5, no. 3 (2003): 251.

19. Ibid.

20. Thomas Porcello, "Tails Out: Social Phenomenology and the Ethnographic Representation of Technology in Music Making," in Lysloff and Gay, *Music and Technoculture,* 276.

21. Ibid.

22. Susan Schmidt Horning, "Engineering the Performance: Recording Engineers, Tacit Knowledge and the Art of Controlling Sound," *Social Studies of Science* 34 (2004): 703–31.

23. Porcello, afterword, in Greene and Porcello, *Wired for Sound,* 277.

24. Ibid., 275.

25. Cook, "Writing on Music," 252.

26. Ibid.

27. This is not to deny the economic challenges for underserved populations that may be exacerbated by music's increasing reliance on technology. This issue is covered more thoroughly in Part III.

28. Ibid., 260.

29. Hans Fantel, "Critic's Notebook; Sinatra's 'Duets' Album: Is It a Music Recording or Technical Wizardry?" *New York Times,* 1 January 1994, http://query.nytimes.com/gst/fullpage.html?res=9905E4DC123EF932A35752C0A962958260. Accessed 4 October 2006.

30. Peter Martin, "Spontaneity and Organization," in *The Cambridge Companion to Jazz,* ed. Mervyn Cooke and David Horn (Cambridge: Cambridge University Press, 2003), 135.

31. Chanan, *Musica Practica,* 285.

CHAPTER FIVE

1. The primary definition for the word *unintentional* according to dictionary.com is "not deliberate." In this case it is the deliberate act of playing for the recorder—playing with the intention of creating a performance that will form a part of the final recording to be made public—that is not a part of Cray's performance and thus unintentional.

2. Benjamin, "Work of Art," 77.

3. For a more complete history of this development see Mary Alice Shaughnessy, *Les Paul: An American Original* (New York: William Morrow, 1993).

4. With the cost of hard drives getting so low, the attendant cost of recording has become remarkably inexpensive. The previous professional analog standard allowed for seventeen minutes of 24-track recording on two-inch tape and cost approximately $200. The equivalent of 24-bit, 44.1 KHz, digital recording currently costs less than $10 in hard drive space.

5. At least the quality of the recording would be suitable. The subjective determination about the performance is, of course, a whole different issue.

6. Bonnie Hayes's credits as a writer include songs for Bonnie Raitt, Bette Midler, Robert Cray, Booker T. and the MG's, and Cher.

7. Pro Tools is the dominant computer-based music recording and editing program.

8. The Bonnie Hayes record that I'm referring to here is *Love in the Ruins* on Bondage Records. It is available through CD Baby, Amazon, and iTunes.

9. From an email correspondence with San Francisco–based drummer John Hanes, 3 February 2004.

10. Greil Marcus, "Corrupting the Absolute," in *On Record: Rock, Pop and the Written Word,* ed. Simon Frith and Andrew Goodwin (New York: Pantheon, 1990), 473.

11. Beebe, Fulbrook, and Saunders, introduction to *Rock over the Edge,* 16.

12. Ibid., 3.

13. Keith Negus and Michael Pickering, "Creativity and Music Experience," in *Popular Music Studies,* ed. David Hesmondhalgh and Keith Negus (London: Arnold, 2002), 184.

14. Marcel Proust quoted in Beebe, Fulbrook, and Saunders, introduction to *Rock over the Edge,* 31.

CHAPTER SIX

1. This is certainly not a universal sentiment, and it has been increasingly undermined over the history of popular music. Certainly virtuosos have long enjoyed the status of artist, from Heifetz to Hendrix. Nonetheless, it is as composers and songwriters that the icons of popular music from Duke Ellington through the Beatles to Radiohead have achieved artistic standing. Many have argued for the elevation of improvisation to the stature of composition, and for the acceptance of musical interpretation on the same level as creation, but the fact that such arguments need to be made speaks to the undercurrent of cultural understanding that has created the separation of artist and artisan that I describe here.

2. Paul F. Berliner, *Thinking in Jazz: The Infinite Art of Improvisation* (Chicago: University of Chicago Press, 1994), 229.

3. Ibid.

4. Ibid., 496.

5. Nicholas Cook, "Making Music Together, or Improvisation and Its Others," in *The Source: Challenging Jazz Criticism* 1 (2004): 18–19.

6. Ibid., 23.

7. Barthes, *Image—Music—Text,* 38–39.

8. Ibid., 39.

9. Ibid., 98, 99.

10. Many jazz critics have commented on the true nature of improvisation,

e.g., Ingrid Monson, "Jazz Improvisation," in Cooke and Horn, *Cambridge Companion to Jazz,* 114. Also, Martin, "Spontaneity and Organization," 134–35.

11. Bruno Nettl, "Introduction: An Art Neglected in Scholarship," in *In the Course of Performance: Studies in the World of Musical Improvisation,* ed. Bruno Nettl with Melinda Russell (Chicago: University of Chicago Press, 1998), 7.

12. Berliner, *Thinking in Jazz,* 496.

13. Nettl, "Introduction: An Art Neglected in Scholarship," 7.

14. Bruce Johnson, "Jazz as Cultural Practice," in Cooke and Horn, *Cambridge Companion to Jazz,* 106.

15. See especially Cook, *Music: A Very Short Introduction* and "Making Music Together."

16. Attali, *Noise,* 147.

17. Ibid.

18. Ibid., 142.

19. Paul Tanner and Marice Gerow, *A Study of Jazz* (Dubuque, Iowa: Wm. C. Brown, 1973), 251.

20. Stephen Blum, "Recognizing Improvisation," in Nettle, *Course of Performance,* 33.

21. Berliner, *Thinking in Jazz,* 263–64, 268, 271, etc.

22. Brian Eno, "PRO SESSION—The Studio as Compositional Tool," 1979, http://music.hyperreal.org/artists/brian_eno/interviews/downbeat79.htm. Accessed 25 December 2005.

23. Ibid.

24. Berliner, *Thinking in Jazz,* 386.

25. Cook, *Music, Imagination and Culture,* 136–37.

26. Stanley Crouch, *Considering Genius: Writings on Jazz* (New York: Basic Civitas Books, 2006), 109.

27. Ibid., 102.

28. Berliner, *Thinking in Jazz,* 241.

29. Ibid., 492.

30. Ibid., 241.

31. Cook, *Music: A Very Short Introduction,* 83.

32. Richard Schechner, *Performance Studies: An Introduction* (London: Routledge, 2002), 22.

33. Crouch defines the high point in jazz improvisation as "that improvised occasion when the entire room—everything on the bandstand and off the bandstand—becomes one force defined by swing. . . . That, for those of you who don't know, is the highest aspect of the performance relationship between the jazz musician and the jazz listener and the jazz place." Crouch, *Considering Genius,* 286. See also Berliner, *Thinking in Jazz,* 497; and Johnson, "Jazz as Cultural Practice," 96.

34. Derek Bailey, *Improvisation: Its Nature and Practice in Music* (Cambridge, MA: Da Capo, 1992), 103.

35. Stephen Travis Pope, "Why is Good Electroacoustic Music So Good? Why is Bad Electroacoustic Music So Bad?" *Computer Music Journal,* Editor's Notes, 24

July 2006, http://mitpress2.mit.edu/e-journals/Computer-Music-Journal/cmjlib/editors-notes/18-3.html. Accessed 9 August 2006.

36. Chanan, *Musica Practica*, 49.

37. Covered extensively in Berliner, *Thinking in Jazz*, under a variety of headings including "Learning Discrete Patterns from Recordings" (101–5) and "Inferring Soloists' Models" (237–42).

38. Berliner, *Thinking in Jazz*, 203.

39. Jed Rasula, "The Media of Memory: The Seductive Menace of Records in Jazz History," in *Jazz Among the Discourses*, ed. Krin Gabbard (Durham, NC: Duke University Press, 1995), 136.

40. Berliner, *Thinking in Jazz*, 106–7.

41. Chanan, *Musica Practica*, 271.

42. Butterfield, "Jazz Analysis," 287.

43. "Too little of improvised music survives recording." Bailey, *Improvisation*, 103.

44. Ibid.

45. Ibid., 104.

46. Dewey, *Art as Experience* (New York: Perigree Trade, 2005), 222.

47. Keith R. Sawyer, "Improvisation and the Creative Process: Dewey, Collingwood, and the Aesthetics of Spontaneity," *Journal of Aesthetics and Art Criticism*, "Improvisation in the Arts," vol. 58, no. 2 (2000): 149.

48. Ibid., 152.

49. Sawyer, "Improvisation and the Creative Process," mistakenly identifies this movie as having been made by Claude Renoir.

50. Crouch, *Considering Genius*, 78.

51. Sawyer, "Improvisation and the Creative Process," 158.

52. Berliner, *Thinking in Jazz*, 246.

53. Chanan, *Musica Practica*, 78.

54. James E. Lewis, "Too Many Notes: Computers, Complexity and Culture in *Voyager*," *Leonardo Music Journal* 10 (2000): 38.

55. Ibid.

56. Leroi Jones, *Blues People: Negro Music in White America* (New York: Quill, 1963), 3, 31.

57. Crouch, *Considering Genius*, 222.

58. This is not to say that improvisations, when transcribed, are equivalent to compositions created originally through notation. Scores made from improvised performances appear to embody a complexity even beyond that of the greatest classical compositions, but the problem in suggesting an equivalency lies in that any such transcription is an abstraction that doesn't take into account the social and musical process. Although it appears to be as concrete as a traditional composition, the improvisation never actually existed as an abstract structure. See Nicholas Cook, "Analyzing Performance, and Performing Analysis," in *Rethinking Music*, ed. Nicholas Cook and Mark Everist (Oxford: Oxford University Press, 1999), 260–61.

59. Lewis, "Too Many Notes," 38.

60. For more on how contemporary composers are stretching the bounds of spontaneity see Justin Davidson, "Measure for Measure: What Conductors Convey to Musicians," *New Yorker,* 21 August 2006, 60–69.

61. Michael H. Zack, "Jazz Improvisation and Organizing: Once More from the Top," *Organization Science* 11, no. 2 (2000): 231.

62. Zack, "Jazz Improvisation and Organizing," 231.

63. This summarizes some of the excellent description and formulation of these issues in Pope, "Good Electroacoustic Music." There is a tremendous amount of activity in this area—most of it well beyond the scope of this research. A good starting point for those interested would be Todd Winkler, *Composing Interactive Music* (Cambridge: MIT Press, 1998).

64. This brief description of "new complexity" was gleaned from a Humanities and Arts Research Center (HARC) Research Training Seminar on Issues in Contemporary Notation delivered by Keith Potter on 2 November 2005. I believe this very cursory discussion is interesting in the context of the larger issues considered here, but it hardly scratches the surface of these musical pursuits, which are well beyond the scope of this research.

65. Lewis, "Too Many Notes," 33.

66. Ibid.

CHAPTER SEVEN

1. The simple explanation for this capability is that, because of the nature of digital audio (using computer language to describe audio through a series of bits and bytes), musical samples can be shortened by eliminating some bytes, or stretched by adding bytes. By using algorithms to make "intelligent" decisions about which bytes to eliminate or add, the resulting music sample may be faster or slower without any shift of pitch and without noticeable audio artifacts.

2. The African bell pattern sets up a fundamental sense of hemiola. It can be described in various ways using notation, but the simplest is to create a phrase in 3/4 time that consists of two quarter-notes, an eighth-note, three more quarter-notes, and a final eighth-note. The same rhythm in 4/4 time would be constructed using eighth-note triplets with the same values (e.g., the first triplet figure would contain one quarter-note and then one eighth-note tied to the first eighth-note of the second triplet in order to create two quarter-note triplets, etc.). The version in 3/4 emphasizes the "three" pulse, while the 4/4 version emphasizes the "four" pulse.

3. John Miller Chernoff, *African Rhythm and African Sensibility* (Chicago: University of Chicago Press, 1979), 30.

4. Kofi Agawu, *Representing African Music: Postcolonial Notes, Queries, Positions* (New York: Routledge, 2003), 64.

5. Christopher Small, *Music of the Common Tongue: Survival and Celebration in African American Music* (Hanover, NH: Wesleyan University Press, 1987), 24.

6. Jones, *Blues People,* 25.

7. Small, *Music of Common Tongue,* 26.

8. Kofi Agawu, *African Rhythm: A Northern Ewe Perspective* (Cambridge: Cambridge University Press, 1995), 183.

9. Paul Gilroy, *The Black Atlantic: Modernity and Double Consciousness* (Cambridge: Harvard University Press, 1993), 74.

10. Small, *Music of Common Tongue,* 23.

11. Ibid.

12. David Brackett, *Interpreting Popular Music* (Berkeley: University of California Press, 1995), 155.

13. Katz, *Capturing Sound,* 153.

14. I have explored this notion in a different musical setting and for a different analytical purpose in chapter 2.

15. Samual A. Floyd Jr., "Ring Shout! Literary Studies, Histories Studies, and Black Music Inquiry," *Black Music Research Journal,* Fall 1991, 267–68.

16. Agawu, *Representing African Music,* 90.

17. Brackett, *Interpreting Popular Music,* 144.

18. Lawrence M. Zbikowski, "Modelling the Groove: Conceptual Structure and Popular Music," *Journal of the Royal Musical Association* 129, no. 2 (2004): 272.

19. Ibid.

20. Ibid.

21. Monson, "Jazz Improvisation," 114; Berliner, *Thinking in Jazz,* 349.

22. Frith, *Performing Rites,* 146.

23. Taylor, *Strange Sounds: Music, Technology & Culture* (London: Routledge, 2001), 4.

24. Cook, *Music: A Very Short Introduction,* 104.

25. Moore, *Rock,* 216.

26. Brackett, *Interpreting Popular Music,* 117.

27. Agawu, *Representing African Music,* 81.

28. Brackett, *Interpreting Popular Music,* 117.

29. James A. Snead, "Repetition as a Figure of Black Culture," in *Black Literature and Literary Theory,* ed. Henry Louis Gates Jr. (London: Routledge, 1984), 69.

30. That this occurred within the context of American slavery cannot be ignored.

31. Goodall, *Big Bangs,* 214–15.

32. Frith, *Performing Rites,* 142.

33. Ibid., 132.

34. This level of fundamental polyrhythmic and contrapuntal expression is found in various schools of jazz and modern classical music, but it is not in widespread use in European or American musical expression.

35. Chernoff, *African Rhythm,* 156.

36. Benjamin, "Work of Art," 221.

37. Sterne, *The Audible Past,* 272.

38. Louis Meintjes, *Sound of Africa! Making Music Zulu in a South African Studio* (Durham, NC: Duke University Press, 2003), 8.

39. Ibid., 11.

40. Sterne, *The Audible Past,* 274, 282.

41. Attali, *Noise,* 120.

42. Ibid.

43. Ibid., 122.

44. This is a distillation and expansion of ideas found in Cook, *Music, Imagination and Culture,* and Cook, *Music: A Very Short Introduction,* and includes some elements that Cook credits to Joanna Hodge.

45. Nicholas Cook, "In Praise of Symbolic Poverty," in *Managing as Designing,* ed. Fred Collopy and Richard Boland (Stanford, CA: Stanford Business Books, 2004), 87.

46. Cook, "Writing on Music," 251.

47. Cook, *Music: A Very Short Introduction,* 80.

48. Butterfield, "Jazz Analysis," 120.

49. Ibid., 288.

50. Taylor, *Strange Sounds,* 20.

51. Jones, *Blues People,* 194.

52. Ibid., 229.

53. Ibid.

54. Ibid., 271.

55. A recent example is the recording of Frank Sinatra's *Duets* CD, where most of his collaborators performed their part of the duet in real time from remote locations—discussed more thoroughly here in chapter 4.

56. A recent example is the offering of all the original multitrack recordings for two complete songs from the record *My Life in the Bush of Ghosts* by David Byrne and Brian Eno. For details see http://bushofghosts.wmg.com/home.php. Accessed 25 June 2006.

57. Clifford Geertz, *Available Light: Anthropological Reflections on Philosophical Topics* (Princeton: Princeton University Press, 2000), 208.

58. Ibid.

59. Pacey, *Meaning in Technology,* 19.

60. Peter Nelson, "Meaning and the Body," *"Musicæ Scientiæ": The Journal of the European Society for the Cognitive Sciences of Music,* Discussion Forum, 2 (1998): 105.

61. Denora, *Music in Everyday Life,* x.

62. Frith, *Performing Rites,* 40.

63. See Frith's conclusions after an evening spent with old friends listening and dancing to music. Ibid., 278.

64. Lysloff and Gay, introduction to *Music and Technoculture,* 10–11.

65. To be thorough one must add the human beatbox (drumming performed by slapping various body parts) as another nontechnologically mediated form of music expression.

CHAPTER EIGHT

1. Benjamin, "Work of Art," 221.

2. Barthes, *Image—Music—Text*, 189.

3. Attali, *Noise*, 106.

4. Said, *The Edward Said Reader*, 319. Said is referencing especially Adorno, "On the Fetish Character in Music and the Regression of Listening," in *The Essential Frankfurt School Reader*, ed. Andrew Arato and Eike Gebhardt (New York: Continuum, 1982), 286–99.

5. Frith, *Performing Rites*, 229.

6. Ross, "The Recording Effect." For the work around which much of this discussion often revolves see Philip, *Early Recordings*.

7. Tia DeNora, Paul Gilroy, Simon Frith, Nicholas Cook, Jonathan Sterne, and others have written extensively on balancing the complex relationships involved.

8. A lot more could be said about the use of the word *currency*, but the economic dynamic that is implicit here is beyond the scope of this research.

9. Frith, *Performing Rites*, 25–26.

10. I don't have statistical data on this, but it does seem this way to me in my contact with many musicians. They may not be fully trained recording engineers (though a surprising number are), but almost all of them do some amount of recording on their own.

11. Cook, *Music: A Very Short Introduction*, 9.

12. At the 1990 Grammy awards the group Milli Vanilli won the Grammy for best new artist. The Grammy was subsequently stripped from the group when it was learned that they did not actually perform the music on the winning recording.

13. Charles Keil and Steven Feld, *Music Grooves: Essays and Dialogues* (Chicago: University of Chicago Press, 1995), 129.

14. Although firmly established in myriad ways today, amazingly, Feuerbach first floated this idea in 1843 (Sontag, *On Photography*, 153).

15. Simon Frith, "Music Industry Research: Where Now? Where Next? Notes from Britain," *Popular Music* 19, no. 3 (2000): 387–93.

16. Chanan, *Musica Practica*, 24.

17. For more on this see "Recording Redefines Improvisation" in chapter 6.

18. Explored broadly in chapter 1.

19. Quoted in Glenn Gould, "The Prospects of Recording," *High Fidelity* 16, no. 4 (1966): 47.

20. Glenn Gould, "The Prospects of Recording," in *Audio Culture: Reading in Modern Music*, ed. Christoph Cox and Daniel Warner (New York: Continuum, 2005), 121.

21. The word *musicking* is taken from Christopher Small's work and is now a widely used word indicating an active participation in the making of music. See Small, *Music of the Common Tongue* and other of his writings.

22. Taylor, *Strange Sounds,* 5.

23. Ibid.

24. Ibid., 5, 6.

25. Ibid., 204.

26. Ibid., 140.

27. Ibid., 205.

28. Lysloff and Gay, introduction to *Music and Technoculture,* 9–10.

29. Ibid., 10.

30. Bill Ivey and Stephen J. Tepper, "Cultural Renaissance or Cultural Divide?" *Chronicle Review,* 19 May 2006, B6, http://www.vanderbilt.edu/curbcenter/culturaldivide.

31. Ibid.

32. Nicholas Cook, personal communication.

33. It should be reiterated here that by musical recordings I include construction of music from previously recorded (repurposed) audio, along with more traditional "recordings" that involve newly recorded audio.

34. http://inventors.about.com/od/wstartinventions/a/Walkman.htm. Accessed 25 April 2009.

35. These earlier manifestations are explored in Serge Lacasse and A. Bennett, "Phonographic Anthologies: Mix Tapes, Memory, and Nostalgia," in Lacasse, *Incestuous Pop.*

36. This borrows from Alex Ross's (2004) ruminations on the iPod in his *New Yorker* piece about a classical music kid that loves pop. The full reference is used in the final chapter of this book.

37. Cook, *Music, Imagination and Culture,* 223.

38. I imagine many on the classical side are still not aware of how "artificially" constructed that music may be, primarily through editing of pieces from multiple performances in order to create the final version.

39. Frith, *Performing Rites,* 225.

40. For reciprocity along the composer/performer/consumer continuum see especially Sterne, *The Audible Past,* 215–86.

41. Cook, *Music, Imagination and Culture,* 85.

42. Because GarageBand is only available for Apple/Mac computers, the depth of its penetration is somewhat limited. However, there are several free recording programs available for the PC such as Audacity and Kristal Audio Engine. These do not have as extensive a feature set as GarageBand but point the way to broader access to these music construction capabilities for all computer owners.

43. Attali, *Noise,* 144.

44. Ibid., 147.

45. Jean Baudrillard, *Simulacra and Simulation,* trans. Sheila Faria Glaser (Ann Arbor: University of Michigan Press, 1994), 31.

46. Chanan, *Musica Practica,* 30.

47. Ibid.

48. Frith, *Performing Rites,* 241.

49. Attali, *Noise,* 147.

50. Théberge, "Plugged in," 23.

51. "For the top thirty-five artists as a whole, income from touring exceeded income from record sales by a ratio of 7.5 to 1." http://www.genericide.net/music_business/. Accessed 10 September 2006.

52. David Byrne, posting to his website journal on 5 June 2005. http://www.davidbyrne.com/journal.

53. Frith, *Performing Rites,* 245.

54. Jonathan Tankel, "The Practice of Recording Music: Remixing as Recording," *Journal of Communication* 40, no. 3 (1990): 44.

55. Frith, *Performing Rites,* 245.

56. Ibid.

57. Ibid.

58. http://discussions.apple.com/category.jspa?categoryID=127. Accessed 14 August 2010.

59. http://www.macidol.com/forum/. Accessed 15 August 2006.

60. http://www.friendster.com/gallery.php?ktype=&kw=1&kword. Accessed 10 February 2006.

61. http://www.soundclick.com. Accessed 14 August 2010.

62. http://www.soundclick.com. Accessed 9 February 2006.

63. http://www.hespos.com/archives/000680.html. Accessed 10 February 2006.

64. http://www.macjams.com/forum/viewtopic.php?forum=1;showtopic=56320. Accessed 9 February 2006.

65. http://www.synthtopia.com/synth_review/AppleGarageBand.html. Accessed 15 August 2006.

66. Ibid.

67. http://people.uwec.edu/KROHNMA/edmt380/garageband.htm. Accessed 9 February 2006.

68. Ivey and Tepper, "Cultural Renaissance or Cultural Divide?" B6.

69. Ibid.

70. Ibid.

71. Greene, "Wired Sound," 3.

72. Ibid.

73. Ibid., 9–10.

74. Ibid., 3.

CHAPTER NINE

1. Benjamin, "Work of Art," 228.

2. Chanan, *Repeated Takes,* 145.

3. Ibid.

4. Ibid., 147.

5. Simon Frith, *Taking Pop Music Seriously* (Aldershot: Ashgate, 2007), 69.

6. Small, *Music of Common Tongue,* 21.

7. Ibid.

8. Chernoff, *African Rhythm,* 16.

9. Ibid., 158.

10. Samuel A. Floyd Jr., *The Power of Black Music: Interpreting its History from Africa to the United States* (New York: Oxford University Press, 1995), 227.

11. Chanan, *Repeated Takes,* 158.

12. Baudrillard, *Simulacra and Simulation,* 9.

13. Nicholas Cook and Eric Clarke, introduction to *Empirical Musicology,* ed. Nicholas Cook and Eric Clarke (Oxford: Oxford University Press, 2004), 5.

14. Review by James Berardinelli. http://www.reelviews.net/php_review_template.php?identifier=27. Accessed 9 April 2009.

15. Review by Roger Ebert. http://rogerebert.suntimes.com/apps/pbcs.dll/article?AID=/20071120/REVIEWS/711200304. Accessed 9 April 2009.

16. Cook and Clark, introduction to *Empirical Musicology,* 5.

17. Ibid., 6.

18. Chanan, *Musica Practica,* 253.

19. Tia DeNora, "Music Practice and Social Structure: A Toolkit," in Cook and Clarke, *Empirical Musicology,* 35–56.

20. Ibid., 36.

21. Cook, *Music: A Very Short Introduction,* 81–82.

22. Théberge, "Plugged in," 15.

23. Katz, *Capturing Sound,* 37.

24. Ibid., 140.

25. Cook, *Music, Imagination and Culture,* 242.

26. Ibid.

27. Barthes summarized by Brackett. *Interpreting Popular Music,* 16.

28. Edward Said, *The Edward Said Reader,* ed. Moustafa Bayoumi and Andrew Rubin (New York: Vintage, 2000), 331.

29. Ibid.

30. Ibid.

31. Ibid., 323.

32. Barthes, *Image—Music—Text,* 149.

33. Ibid., 150.

34. Ibid., 162–63.

35. Eisenberg, *The Recording Angel,* 148.

36. Toynbee, *Making Popular Music,* 87.

37. For interesting contemporary looks at the dangers of expanding intellectual property rights see Lawrence Lessig, *Free Culture: The Nature and Future of Creativity* (New York: Penguin, 2005), and Siva Vaidhyanathan, *Copyrights and Copywrongs: The Rise of Intellectual Property and How It Threatens Creativity* (New York: NYU Press, 2003). For defenders of intellectual property try the resources at the Recording Academy's website, http://www.whatsthedownload.com/.

38. Attali, *Noise,* 100.

39. Ibid., 101.

40. Ibid., 122.

41. Katz, *Capturing Sound,* 138.

42. Ibid., 140.

43. Ibid., 141.

44. Attali, *Noise,* 122.

45. Katz, *Capturing Sound,* 156.

46. Ibid., 157.

47. Kimberly Christen, "Gone Digital: Aboriginal Remix and the Cultural Commons," *International Journal of Cultural Property* 12 (2005): 329.

48. While I am steering clear of analysis of specific examples of popular music that have been tainted with accusations of inappropriate cultural appropriation, I would feel remiss without at least mentioning two of the most prominent examples. Paul Simon's *Graceland* was widely vilified for supposedly improper appropriation of the musical culture of South Africa, while Moby's *Play* was criticized for its supposedly inadequate attributions to the musicians from the Alan Lomax recordings that it used as samples. Both records were enormously popular and considered creative successes by many critics. Both records stirred interest and attention for the music they referenced. Were both records less than perfect in their attribution of credit? Probably. Is the music world a better place for their appearance? One has to make their own judgment, but I would argue that these recordings, despite their flaws, stand as tributes to many of the positive elements of cultural cross-fertilization.

49. Cook, *Music: A Very Short Introduction,* 125.

50. Ibid., 127.

51. Ibid.

52. Paul Théberge, "'Ethnic Sounds': The Economy and Discourse of World Music Sampling," in Lysloff and Gay, *Music and Technoculture,* 102.

53. Ibid., 102–3.

54. Ibid., 102.

55. Ibid., 104.

56. Ibid.

57. Ibid.

58. Ibid.

59. Ibid.

60. Ibid., 105.

61. David Hesmondhalgh, "Digital Sampling and Cultural Inequality," *Social and Legal Studies* 15, no. 1 (2006), http://www.cresc.man.ac.uk/downloads/DHdigital.pdf. Accessed 1 May 2006.

62. Ibid.

63. Timothy D. Taylor, "A Riddle Wrapped in a Mystery: Transnational Music Sampling and Enigma's 'Return to Innocence,'" in Lysloff and Gay, *Music and Technoculture,* 66.

64. Ibid., 67.

65. Théberge, "Ethnic Sounds," 106.

66. Katz, *Capturing Sound*, 151.

67. Lysloff and Gay, introduction to *Music and Technoculture*, 2.

68. Cook, *Music, Imagination and Culture*, 6.

69. Ibid., 7.

70. Théberge, "Ethnic Sounds," 106.

71. Although I was a professional musician, I have not worked as one in many years. I have never composed professionally—my skills are certainly light years away from the likes of Bartók!

72. Bartók may well have had other motivations for borrowing from the Hungarian tradition revolving around both his musical and personal identity. In neither case are these necessary elements in the appreciation of his music.

73. See especially Steven Feld, "Pygmy POP: A Genealogy of Schizophonic Mimesis," *Yearbook for Traditional Music* 28 (1996): 1–35.

74. Frith, *Performing Rites*, 242.

75. Baudrillard, *Simulacra and Simulation*, 78.

76. Ibid. 77.

CONCLUSIONS

1. Chernoff points to this parallel in direct connection to his study of African music, but I think it warrants a broader interpretation. See Chernoff, *African Rhythm*, 21–23.

2. Pacey, *Meaning in Technology*, 17.

3. Both Sterne, *The Audible Past*, 19, and Chernoff, *African Rhythm*, 31, make points similar to this.

4. Alex Ross, "Listen To This: A Classical Kid Learns to Love Pop—and Wonders Why He Has to Make a Choice," *New Yorker*, 16 and 23 February 2004, http://www.newyorker.com/fact/content/?040216fa_fact4.

5. Benjamin, "Work of Art," 234.

6. Jorge Luis Borges, *Labyrinths* (New York: New Directions, 1964), 188.

References

BOOKS, ARTICLES, WEBSITES, AND AUDIO RECORDINGS

Adorno, Theodor W. "On Popular Music." In *On Record: Rock, Pop and the Written Word,* ed. Simon Frith and Andrew Goodwin, 301–14. New York: Pantheon, 1990.

Adorno, Theodor W. "On the Fetish Character in Music and the Regression of Listening." In *The Essential Frankfurt School Reader,* ed. Andrew Arato and Eike Gebhardt, 270–318. New York: Continuum, 1982.

Adorno, Theodor W. *Prisms.* Cambridge: MIT Press, 1967.

Agawu, Kofi. *African Rhythm: A Northern Ewe Perspective.* Cambridge: Cambridge University Press, 1995.

Agawu, Kofi. *Representing African Music: Postcolonial Notes, Queries, Positions.* New York: Routledge, 2003.

Altman, Rick. "The Material Heterogeneity of Recorded Sound." In *Sound Theory, Sound Practice,* ed. Rick Altman, 15–45. New York: Routledge, 1992.

Amos, Tori. "Cruel." *From the Choirgirl Hotel.* Atlantic Records, 1998.

Anderton, Craig. "Hit Factors: The Link Between Music & Emotional Response." *Sound on Sound,* May 2002, http://www.soundonsound.com/sos/may02/articles/cholakis.asp, 25 July 2007.

Arendt, Hannah. Introduction to *Walter Benjamin: Illuminations,* ed. Hannah Arendt, trans. Harry Zohn, 1–55. New York: Schocken, 1968.

Attali, Jacques. *Noise: The Political Economy of Music.* Trans. Brian Massumi. Minneapolis: University of Minnesota Press, 1985.

Bailey, Derek. *Improvisation: Its Nature and Practice in Music.* Cambridge, MA: Da Capo Press, 1992.

Baraka, Amiri. *Blues People.* New York: William Morrow, 1963.

Barthes, Roland. *Image—Music—Text.* Trans. Stephen Heath. New York: Hill and Wang, 1997.

Baudrillard, Jean. *Simulacra and Simulation.* Trans. Sheila Faria Glaser. Ann Arbor: University of Michigan Press, 1994.

Beatles, The. *The Beatles* [*White Album*]. Capitol Records, 1968.

Beatles, The. "A Day in the Life." *Sgt. Pepper's Lonely Heart's Club Band.* Capitol Records, 1967.

Bebey, Francis. Quoted at *African Music: Part I,* http://trumpet.sdsu.edu/M345/African_Music1.html. Accessed 3 March 2006.

Beebe, Roger, Denise Fulbrook, and Ben Saunders, eds. *Rock over the Edge: Transformations in Popular Music Culture.* Durham, NC: Duke University Press, 2002.

Benjamin, Walter. *Walter Benjamin: Illuminations,* ed. Hannah Arendt, trans. Harry Zohn, 217–51. New York: Schocken, 1968.

Berliner, Paul F. *Thinking in Jazz: The Infinite Art of Improvisation.* Chicago: University of Chicago Press, 1994.

Blum, Stephen. "Recognizing Improvisation." In *In the Course of Performance: Studies in the World of Musical Improvisation,* ed. Bruno Nettle with Melinda Russell, 27–45. Chicago: University of Chicago Press, 1998.

Bolter, Jay David, and Richard Grusing. *Remediation: Understanding New Media.* Cambridge: MIT Press, 1999.

Borges, Jorge Luis. *Labyrinths.* New York: New Directions, 1964.

Brackett, David. *Interpreting Popular Music.* Berkeley: University of California Press, 1995.

Browning, Barbara. *Infectious Rhythm: Metaphors of Contagion and the Spread of African Culture.* New York: Routledge, 1998.

Butterfield, Matthew W. "Jazz Analysis and the Production of Musical Community: A Situational Perspective." Ph.D. diss., University of Pennsylvania, 2000.

Byrne, David. Online posting to his website journal, 5 June 2005, http://www.davidbyrne.com/journal. Accessed 1 July 2005.

Byrne, David, and Brian Eno. Audio resources from recordings made available to the public. http://bushofghosts.wmg.com/home.php. Accessed 25 June 2006.

Chanan, Michael. *Musica Practica: The Social Practice of Western Music from Gregorian Chant to Postmodernism.* London: Verso, 1994.

Chanan, Michael. *Repeated Takes: A Short History of Recording and its Effects on Music.* London: Verso, 1995.

Charbeneaue, Travis. "Rehumanize Your Sequence Pt. 5." *Music Technology,* June 1989, 42–46.

Cher. "Believe." *Believe.* Warner Bros. Records, 1998.

Chernoff, John Miller. *African Rhythm and African Sensibility.* Chicago: University of Chicago Press, 1979.

Christen, Kimberly. "Gone Digital: Aboriginal Remix and the Cultural Commons." *International Journal of Cultural Property* 12 (2005): 315–45.

Christo. "A History of African Music: African Music in Social Context." http://www.acslink.aone.net.au/christo/histmain.htm. Accessed 21 March 2001.

Cook, Nicholas. "Analyzing Performance, and Performing Analysis." In *Rethinking Music,* ed. Nicholas Cook and Mark Everist, 239–61. Oxford: Oxford University Press, 1999.

Cook, Nicholas. "Computational and Comparative Musicology." In *Empirical Musicology*, ed. Nicholas Cook and Eric Clarke, 103–26. Oxford: Oxford University Press, 2004.

Cook, Nicholas. "Imagining Things: Mind into Music (and Back Again)." In *Imaginative Minds*, ed. Ilona Roth, 123–46. Oxford: Oxford University Press, 2008.

Cook, Nicholas. "In Praise of Symbolic Poverty." In *Managing as Designing*, ed. Fred Collopy and Richard Boland, 85–89. Stanford, CA: Stanford University Press, 2004.

Cook, Nicholas. "Making Music Together, or Improvisation and its Others." *The Source: Challenging Jazz Criticism* 1 (2004): 5–25.

Cook, Nicholas. *Music: A Very Short Introduction.* Oxford: Oxford University Press, 1998.

Cook, Nicholas. *Music, Imagination and Culture.* Oxford: Oxford University Press, 1990.

Cook, Nicholas. "On Qualifying Relativism." *"Musicæ Scientiæ": The Journal of the European Society for the Cognitive Sciences of Music*, Discussion Forum, 2 (2001): 167–87.

Cook, Nicholas. "Uncanny Moments: Juxtaposition and the Collage Principle in Music." In *Approaches to Meaning in Music*, ed. Byron Almén and Edward Pearsall, 107–34. Bloomington: Indiana University Press, 2006.

Cook, Nicholas. "Writing on Music or Axes to Grind: Road Rage and Musical Community." In *Music Education Research* 5, no. 3 (2003): 249–61.

Cook, Nicholas, and Eric Clark. Introduction to *Empirical Musicology*, ed. Nicholas Cook and Eric Clarke, 3–14. Oxford: Oxford University Press, 2004.

Crouch, Stanley. *Considering Genius: Writings on Jazz.* New York: Basic Civitas Books, 2006.

Davidson, Justin. "Measure for Measure: What Conductors Convey to Musicians." *New Yorker*, 21 August 2006, 60–69.

Day, Timothy. *A Century of Recorded Music.* New Haven: Yale University Press, 2000.

Deadbolt. "The Listener's Participation in the Musical Experience." Posted at everything$_2$ on 6 January 2002 as "(idea) by Deadbolt (4.1 y)." http://everything2.com/index.pl?node_id=1229611. Accessed 8 September 2006.

Denby, David. "Big Pictures: Hollywood Looks for a Future." *New Yorker*, 8 January 2007, 54–63.

Denora, Tia. *Music in Everyday Life.* Cambridge: Cambridge University Press, 2000.

Denora, Tia. "Music Practice and Social Structure: A Toolkit." In *Empirical Musicology*, ed. Nicholas Cook and Eric Clarke, 35–56. Oxford: Oxford University Press, 2004.

Dewey, John. *Art as Experience.* New York: Perigree Trade, 2005.

Dinerstein, Joel. *The Swinging Machine: Modernity, Technology, and African American Culture Between the World Wars.* Amherst: University of Massachusetts Press, 2003.

DJ Danger Mouse. *The Grey Album.* Internet release, 2004.

Dylan, Bob. "Sad-eyed Lady of the Lowlands." *Blonde on Blonde.* Sony Records, 2004. Original release date, 1966.

Eno, Brian. Interview posted on the Internet from unknown publication and unknown date. http://music.hyperreal.org/artists/brian_eno/interviews/unk-75a.html. Accessed 25 December 2005.

Eno, Brian. "PRO SESSION—The Studio As Compositional Tool." 1979. http://music.hyperreal.org/artists/brian_eno/interviews/downbeat79.htm. Accessed 25 December 2005.

Eno, Brian. *A Year with Swollen Appendices: The Diary of Brian Eno.* London: Faber & Faber, 1996.

Eisenberg, Evan. *The Recording Angel: The Experience of Music from Aristotle to Zappa.* New York: Penguin, 1986.

Fantel, Hans. "Critic's Notebook; Sinatra's 'Duets' Album: Is It a Music Recording Or Technical Wizardry?" *New York Times,* 1 January 1994, http://query.nytimes.com/gst/fullpage.html?res=9905E4DC123EF932A35752C0A962958260. Accessed 4 October 2006.

Feld, Steven. "Pygmy POP. A Genealogy of Schizophonic Mimesis." *Yearbook for Traditional Music* 28 (1996): 1–35.

Floyd, Samuel A., Jr. *The Power of Black Music: Interpreting its History from Africa to the United States.* Oxford: Oxford University Press, 1995.

Floyd, Samuel A., Jr. "Ring Shout! Literary Studies, Histories Studies, and Black Music Inquiry." *Black Music Research Journal,* Fall 1991, 267–68.

Foss, Lucas. "Improvisation versus Composition." *Musical Times,* October 1962, 684–85.

Freedom du Lac, J. "Motor Mouth: T-Pain Cranks Out Hits Thanks to Auto-Tune Software. Now Everyone Else Wants to Come Along for the Ride." *Washington Post,* 9 November 2008, http://www.washingtonpost.com/wp-dyn/content/article/2008/11/07/AR2008110701033.html. Accessed 12 March 2009.

Frere-Jones, Sasha. "The Gerbil's Revenge: Auto-Tune Corrects a Singer's Pitch. It Also Distorts—a Grand Tradition in Pop." *New Yorker,* 9 June 2008, http://www.newyorker.com/arts/critics/musical/2008/06/09/080609crmu_music_frerejones. Accessed 12 March 2009.

Frith, Simon. "Music Industry Research: Where Now? Where Next? Notes from Britain." *Popular Music* 19, no. 3 (2000): 387–93.

Frith, Simon. *Performing Rites.* Cambridge: Harvard University Press, 1996.

Frith, Simon. *Taking Pop Music Seriously.* Aldershot: Ashgate, 2007.

Frith, Simon, and Andrew Goodwin, eds. *On Record: Rock, Pop and the Written Word.* New York: Pantheon, 1990.

Gates, Henry Louis, Jr., ed. *Black Literature and Literary Theory.* London: Routledge, 1984.

Gates, Henry Louis, Jr., ed. *The Signifying Monkey: A Theory of African-American Literary Criticism.* New York: Oxford University Press, 1988.

Geertz, Clifford. *Available Light: Anthropological Reflections on Philosophical Topics.* Princeton: Princeton University Press, 2000.

Gendron, Bernard. "'Moldy Figs' and Modernists: Jazz at War (1942–1946)." In *Jazz Among the Discourses,* ed. Krin Gabbard, 31–56. Durham, NC: Duke University Press, 1995.

Gilroy, Paul. *The Black Atlantic: Modernity and Double Consciousness.* Cambridge: Harvard University Press, 1993.

Goebbels, Heiner. Interview by Stathis Gourgouris. "Performance as Composition." *PAJ: A Journal of Performance and Art* 26, no. 3 (2004): 1–16.

Goodall, Howard. *Big Bangs: The Story of Five Discoveries that Changed Musical History.* London: Vintage, 2001.

Goodmanson, John. "John Goodmanson: ON." *EQ Magazine* 17, no. 1 (2006): 12–20.

Goodwin, Andrew. "Sample and Hold: Pop Music in the Age of Digital Reproduction." *Critical Quarterly* 30, no. 3 (1988): 34–49.

Gould, Glenn. "The Prospects of Recording." *High Fidelity* 16, no. 4 (1966): 46–63.

Gould, Glenn. "The Prospects of Recording." In *Audio Culture: Reading in Modern Music,* ed. Christoph Cox and Daniel Warner, 115–27. New York: Continuum, 2005.

Green, Daniel. "A Musical Interlude." *The Reading Experience* weblog, 4 May 2004, http://noggs.typepad.com/the_reading_experience/musicmusic_and _literature/ index.html. Accessed 9 March 2006.

Green Day. "American Idiot." *American Idiot.* Reprise Records, 2004.

Greene, Paul D. "Wired Sound and Sonic Cultures." In *Wired for Sound: Engineering and Technologies in Sonic Cultures,* ed. Paul D. Greene and Thomas Porcello, 1–22. Middletown, CT: Wesleyan University Press, 2005.

Greene, Paul D., and Thomas Porcello, eds. *Wired for Sound: Engineering and Technologies in Sonic Cultures.* Middletown, CT: Wesleyan University Press, 2005.

Gritten, Anthony. "On Answering Music." *"Musicæ Scientiæ": The Journal of the European Society for the Cognitive Sciences of Music,* Discussion Forum, 2 (2001): 51–59.

Grossberg, Lawrence. *Bringing It All Back Home: Essays on Cultural Studies.* Durham, NC: Duke University Press, 1997.

Hayes, Bonnie. *Love in the Ruins.* Bondage Records, 2003.

Hesmondhalgh, David. "Digital Sampling and Cultural Inequality." *Social and Legal Studies* 15, no. 1 (2006), http://www.cresc.man.ac.uk/downloads/ DHdigital.pdf. Accessed 1 May 2006.

Hesmondhalgh, David, and Keith Negus, eds. *Popular Music Studies.* London: Arnold, 2002.

Horning, Susan Schmidt. "Engineering the Performance: Recording Engineers, Tacit Knowledge and the Art of Controlling Sound." *Social Studies of Science* 34 (2004): 703–31.

Hughes, Freddie. *I Know It's Hard But It's Fair.* Blues Express Records, 2008.

Huron, David. "Review of *Music, Imagination, and Culture* by Nicholas Cook." *Music Perception* 12, no. 4 (1995): 473–81, http://www.musiccog.ohio-state.edu/Huron/Publications/huron.cook.review.html. Accessed 8 September 2006.

Huron, David, and Joy Ollen. "Musical Form and the Structure of Repetition: A Cross-Cultural Study." Proceedings of the Eighth International Conference on Music Perception and Cognition, Evanston, IL, 2004, www.music-cog.ohio-state.edu/Huron/Publications/MP040026.PDF. Accessed 9 August 2006.

Huron, David, and Paul Von Hippel. "Why Do Skips Precede Reversals? The Effect of Tessitura on Melodic Structure." *Music Perception* 18, no. 1 (2000): 59–85.

Ivey, Bill, and Stephen J. Tepper. "Cultural Renaissance or Cultural Divide?" *Chronicle Review,* 19 May 2006, B6, http://www.vanderbilt.edu/curbcenter/culturaldivide. Accessed 6 January 2006.

Ivey, Bill, and Stephen J. Tepper. *Engaging Art: The Next Great Transformation of America's Cultural Life.* London: Routledge, 2007.

Jaffe, David. "Ensemble Timing in Computer Music." *Computer Music Journal* 9, no. 4 (1985): 38–48.

Jameson, Frederic. Introduction to *Noise: The Political Economy of Music,* by Jacques Attali, trans. Brian Massumi, vii–xiv. Minneapolis: University of Minnesota Press, 1985.

Jay-Z. *The Black Album.* Roc-A-Fella Records, 2003.

Johnson, Bruce. "Jazz as Cultural Practice." In *The Cambridge Companion to Jazz,* ed. Mervyn Cooke and David Horn, 96–113. Cambridge: Cambridge University Press, 2002.

Jones, Steve. *Rock Formation: Music, Technology, and Mass Communication.* Newbury Park, CA: Sage, 1992.

Katz, Bob. *Mastering Audio: The Art and the Science.* Oxford: Focal Press, 2002.

Katz, Mark. *Capturing Sound: How Technology Has Changed Music.* Berkeley: University of California Press, 2004.

Keil, Charles. "The Theory of Participatory Discrepancies: A Progress Report." *Ethnomusicology* 39 (1995): 73–100.

Keil, Charles. *Urban Blues.* Chicago: University of Chicago Press, 1968.

Keil, Charles, and Steven Feld. *Music Grooves: Essays and Dialogues.* Chicago: University of Chicago Press, 1995.

Lacasse, S. "Towards a Model of Transphonography." In *Incestuous Pop: Intertextuality in Recorded Popular Music,* ed. Serge Lacasse. Quebec: Nota Bene, forthcoming.

Lacasse, S., and A. Bennett. "Phonographic Anthologies: Mix Tapes, Memory, and Nostalgia." In *Incestuous Pop: Intertextuality in Recorded Popular Music,* ed. Serge Lacasse. Quebec: Nota Bene, forthcoming.

Lastra, James. *Sound Technology and American Cinema: Perception, Representation, Modernity.* New York: Columbia University Press, 2000.

Lessig, Lawrence. *Free Culture: The Nature and Future of Creativity.* New York: Penguin, 2005.

Levine, Lawrence. *Highbrow/Lowbrow: The Emergence of Cultural Hierarchy in America.* Cambridge: Harvard University Press, 1988.

Lewis, James E. "Too Many Notes: Computers, Complexity and Culture in *Voyager*." *Leonardo Music Journal* 10 (2000): 33–39.

Lull, James, ed. *Popular Music and Communication.* Newbury Park, CA: Sage, 1992.

Lysloff, René T. A., and Leslie C. Gay Jr., eds. *Music and Technoculture.* Middletown, CT: Wesleyan University Press, 2003.

Marcus, Greil. "Corrupting the Absolute." In *On Record: Rock, Pop and the Written Word,* ed. Simon Frith and Andrew Goodwin, 472–78. New York: Pantheon, 1990.

Martin, Peter. "Spontaneity and Organization." In *The Cambridge Companion to Jazz,* ed. Mervyn Cooke and David Horn, 133–52. Cambridge: Cambridge University Press, 2003.

Maultsby, Portia K. "Africanisms in African-American Music." In *Africanisms in American Culture,* ed. Joseph E. Holloway, 185–210. Bloomington: Indiana University Press, 1990.

McClary, Susan. Afterword to *Noise: The Political Economy of Music,* by Jacques Attali, trans. Brian Massumi, 149–58. Minneapolis: University of Minnesota Press, 1985.

Meintjes, Louise. *Sound of Africa! Making Music Zulu in a South African Studio.* Durham, NC: Duke University Press, 2003.

Menaker, Daniel. "Nashville Postcard: Cash on Tape." *New Yorker,* 24 November 2003, 46.

Meyer, Leonard B. *Emotion and Meaning in Music.* Chicago: University of Chicago Press, 1956.

Monson, Ingrid. "Jazz Improvisation." In *The Cambridge Companion to Jazz,* ed. Mervyn Cooke and David Horn, 114–32. Cambridge: Cambridge University Press, 2002.

Moore, Allan. *Rock: The Primary Text: Developing a Musicology of Rock.* Burlington, VT: Ashgate, 2001.

Morton, David. *Off the Record: The Technology and Culture of Sound Recording in America.* New Brunswick, NJ: Rutgers University Press, 2000.

Moylan, William. *The Art of Recording: Understanding and Crafting the Mix.* Oxford: Focal Press, 2002.

Negus, Keith, and Michael Pickering. "Creativity and Music Experience." In *Popular Music Studies,* ed. David Hesmondhalgh and Keith Negus, 179–90. London: Arnold, 2002.

Nelson, Peter. "Meaning and the Body." *"Musicæ Scientiæ": The Journal of the European Society for the Cognitive Sciences of Music,* Discussion Forum, 2 (1998): 101–9.

Nettl, Bruno. "Introduction: An Art Neglected in Scholarship." In *In the Course of*

Performance: Studies in the World of Musical Improvisation, ed. Bruno Nettl with Melinda Russell, 1–23. Chicago: University of Chicago Press, 1998.

Nketia, J. H. Kwabena. *The Music of Africa.* New York: Norton, 1974.

Pacey, Arnold. *Meaning in Technology.* Cambridge: MIT Press, 2001.

Paul, Les. Interview by Denver Smith. *Jinx/Les Paul.* http://www.jinxmagazine .com/les_paul.html. Accessed 19 March 2004.

Philip, Robert. *Early Recordings and Musical Style.* Cambridge: Cambridge University Press, 1992.

Pinch, Trevor, and Karin Bijsterveld. "Sound Studies: New Technologies and Music." *Social Studies of Science* 34, no. 5, special issue, "Sound Studies: New Technologies and Music," October 2004, 635–48, http://www.jstor.org/sta ble/4144355. Accessed 9 March 2009.

Pond, Steven F. *Head Hunters: The Making of Jazz's First Platinum Album.* Ann Arbor: University of Michigan Press, 2005.

Pope, Stephen Travis. "Why Is Good Electroacoustic Music So Good? Why Is Bad Electroacoustic Music So Bad?" *Computer Music Journal,* Editor's Notes, 24 July 2006, http://mitpress2.mit.edu/e-journals/Computer-Music-Journal/ cmjlib/editors-notes/18-3.html. Accessed 9 August 2006.

Porcello, Thomas. Afterword to *Wired For Sound: Engineering and Technologies in Sonic Cultures,* ed. Paul D. Greene and Thomas Porcello, 269–81. Middletown, CT: Wesleyan University Press, 2005.

Porcello, Thomas. "Tails Out: Social Phenomenology and the Ethnographic Representation of Technology in Music Making." In *Music and Technoculture,* ed. René T. A. Lysloff and Leslie C. Gay Jr., 264–89. Middletown, CT: Wesleyan University Press, 2003.

Radano, Ronald. "Myth Today: The Color of Ken Burns' Jazz." *Black Renaissance Noire* 3, no. 3 (2001): 42–56.

Radano, Ronald. "Soul Texts and the Blackness of Folk." *Modernism/Modernity* 2, no. 1 (1995): 71–95.

Rasula, Jed. "The Media of Memory: The Seductive Menace of Records in Jazz History." In *Jazz Among the Discourses,* ed. Krin Gabbard, 134–62. Durham, NC: Duke University Press, 1995.

Rose, Andrew, and Tricia Rose, eds. *Microphone Fiends: Youth Music and Culture.* New York: Routledge, 1994.

Ross, Alex. "Listen to This: A Classical Kid Learns to Love Pop—and Wonders Why He Has to Make a Choice." *New Yorker,* 16 and 23 February 2004, http://www.newyorker.com/fact/content/?040216fa_fact4. Accessed 20 June 2005.

Ross, Alex. "The Record Effect: How Technology Has Transformed the Sound of Music." *New Yorker,* 6 June 2005, http://www.newyorker.com/critics/at large/articles/050606crat_atlarge. Accessed 20 June 2005.

Rothenbuhler, Eric W., and John Durham Peters. "Defining Phonography: An Experiment in Theory." *Musical Quarterly,* Summer 1997, 246–60.

Sabbe, Herban. "Call for Rectification of Current Musicological Practice." *"Mu-*

sicæ Scientiæ": The Journal of the European Society for the Cognitive Sciences of Music, Discussion Forum, 2 (2001): 131–37.

Sacks, Oliver. "The Mind's Eye." *New Yorker,* 28 July 2003, 48–59.

Said, Edward. *The Edward Said Reader.* Ed. Moustafa Bayoumi and Andrew Rubin. New York: Vintage, 2000.

Savage, Steve. *The Art of Digital Audio Recording.* New York: Oxford University Press, 2011.

Savage, Steve. "'It Could Have Happened': The Evolution of Music Construction." In *The Cambridge Companion to Recorded Music,* 32–35. Cambridge: Cambridge University Press, 2009.

Savage, Steve. "Ignorance is Bliss: Capturing the Unintentional Performance." *Journal of Popular Music Studies* 18, no. 3 (2006): 332–40.

Savage, Steve. *The Rhythm Book.* Emeryville, CA: EM Books, 2000.

Sawyer, R. Keith. "Improvisation and the Creative Process: Dewey, Collingwood, and the Aesthetics of Spontaneity." *Journal of Aesthetics and Art Criticism,* "Improvisation in the Arts," 58, no. 2 (2000): 149–61.

Seabrook, John. *Nobrow: The Culture of Marketing, The Marketing of Culture.* New York: Alfred A. Knopf, 2000.

Schechner, Richard. *Performance Studies: An Introduction.* London: Routledge, 2002.

Shaughnessy, Mary Alice. *Les Paul: An American Original.* New York: William Morrow, 1993.

Small, Christopher. *Music of the Common Tongue: Survival and Celebration in African American Music.* Hanover, NH: Wesleyan University Press, 1987.

Snead, James A. "Repetition as a Figure of Black Culture." In *Black Literature and Literary Theory,* ed. Henry Louis Gates Jr., 59–80. London: Routledge, 1984.

Sontag, Susan. *On Photography.* New York: Picador, 1977.

Spande, Robert. "The Three Regimes: A Theory of Film Music," http://www.franklinmarketplace.com/filmmusic.html. Accessed 5 March 2004.

Stephenson, Neal. *Snow Crash.* New York: Bantam Spectra, 1993.

Sterne, Jonathan. *The Audible Past: Cultural Origins of Sound Reproduction.* Durham, NC: Duke University Press, 2003.

Stewart, Michael. "The Feel Factor: Music with Soul." *Electronic Musician,* October 1987, 57–65.

Talbot, Margaret. "The Baby Lab." *New Yorker,* 4 September 2006, 90–101.

Tankel, Jonathan. "The Practice of Recording Music: Remixing as Recording." *Journal of Communication* 40, no. 3 (1990): 34–46.

Tanner, Paul, and Marice Gerow. *A Study of Jazz.* Dubuque, IA: Wm. C. Brown, 1973.

Taylor, Timothy D. "A Riddle Wrapped in a Mystery: Transnational Music Sampling and Enigma's 'Return to Innocence.'" In *Music and Technoculture,* ed. René T. A. Lysloff and Leslie C. Gay Jr., 64–92. Middletown, CT: Wesleyan University Press, 2003.

Taylor, Timothy D. *Strange Sounds: Music, Technology & Culture.* London: Routledge, 2001.

Théberge, Paul. *Any Sound You Can Imagine: Making Music / Consuming Technology.* Hanover, NH: Wesleyan University Press, 1997.

Théberge, Paul. "'Ethnic Sounds': The Economy and Discourse of World Music Sampling." In *Music and Technoculture,* ed. René T. A. Lysloff and Leslie C. Gay Jr., 93–108. Middletown, CT: Wesleyan University Press, 2003.

Théberge, Paul. "'Plugged in': Technology and Popular Music." In *The Cambridge Companion to Pop and Rock,* ed. Simon Frith, Will Straw, and John Street, 3–25. Cambridge: Cambridge University Press, 2001.

Thompson, Robert Ferris. *African Art in Motion.* Berkeley: University of California Press, 1974.

Toynbee, Jason. *Making Popular Music: Musicians, Creativity and Institutions.* London: Arnold, 2000.

Trow, George W. S. *Within the Context of No Context.* Boston: Little, Brown, 1978.

Tyrangiel, Josh. "Auto-Tune: Why Pop Music Sounds Perfect." *Time,* 5 February 2009, http://www.time.com/time/magazine/article/0,9171,1877372-2,00.html. Accessed 12 March 2009.

Vaidhyanathan, Siva. *Copyrights and Copywrongs: The Rise of Intellectual Property and How It Threatens Creativity.* New York: NYU Press, 2003.

Warner, Timothy. *Pop Music—Technology and Creativity.* Aldershot, Hants: Ashgate, 2003.

Wilson, Olly. "The Significance of the Relationship Between Afro-American Music and West-African Music." *Black Perspective in Music* 2 (Spring 1974): 3–22.

Winkler, Todd. *Composing Interactive Music.* Cambridge: MIT Press, 1998.

Wonder, Stevie. "Signed, Sealed, Delivered (I'm Yours)." *Signed, Sealed and Delivered.* Motown Records, 1992. Original release date, 1970.

Young, La Monte, and Marian Zazeela. "La Monte Young and Marian Zazeela at the Dream House: Improvisation vs. Composition." Interview on 1 October 2003, http://www.newmusicbox.org/page.nmbx?id=54fp02. Accessed 7 August 2006.

Young, Neil. "Digital Is a Huge Rip Off." *Guitar Player,* May 1992, 14.

Zack, Michael H. "Jazz Improvisation and Organizing: Once More from the Top." *Organization Science* 11, no. 2 (2000): 227–34.

Zak, Albin J. "Journal of the Art of Record Production," http://www.artofrecordproduction.com/content/view/209/104/. Accessed 4 August 2010.

Zak, Albin J. *The Poetics of Rock.* Berkeley: University of California Press, 2003.

Zbikowski, Lawrence M. "Modelling the Groove: Conceptual Structure and Popular Music." *Journal of the Royal Musical Association* 129, no. 2 (2004): 272–97.

Žižek, Slavoj. From *On Belief.* New York: Routledge, 2001, http://josephtate.com/radiohead/archives/000305.html. Accessed 2 March 2004.

{ Index

Note: Page numbers followed by "n" plus a number indicate numbered endnotes. Page numbers followed by "q" indicate quotations.